Transforming Images

Contemporary social and cultural life is increasingly organized around a logic of self-transformation, where changing the body is seen as key. *Transforming Images* examines how the future functions within this transformative logic to indicate the potential of a materially better time. The book explores the crucial role that images have in organizing an imperative of transformation and in making possible, or not, the materialization of a better future. Coleman asks the questions: which futures are appealing and to whom? How do images tap into and reproduce wider social and cultural processes of inequality?

Drawing on the recent 'turns' in social and cultural theory to affect and emotion and to understanding life in terms of vitality, intensity and 'liveness', the book develops a framework for understanding images as *felt and lived out*. Analysing different screens across popular culture – the screens of shopping, makeover television programmes, online dieting plans and government health campaigns – it traces how images of self-transformation bring the future into the present and affectively 'draw in' some bodies more than others.

Transforming Images will be of interest to students and scholars working in sociology, media studies, cultural studies and gender studies.

Rebecca Coleman is a lecturer in the Department of Sociology, Lancaster University. Her research is concerned with theoretical and empirical explorations of the relations between bodies and images, with a particular focus on temporality. Publications include *The Becoming of Bodies: Girls, Images, Experience* (2009, Manchester University Press).

International library of sociology
Founded by Karl Mannheim
Editor: John Urry
Lancaster University

Recent publications in this series include:

Risk and Technological Culture
Towards a sociology of virulence
Joost Van Loon

Reconnecting Culture, Technology and Nature
Mike Michael

Advertising Myths
The strange half lives of images and commodities
Anne M. Cronin

Adorno on Popular Culture
Robert R. Witkin

Consuming the Caribbean
From arkwarks to zombies
Mimi Sheller

Between Sex and Power
Family in the world, 1900–2000
Goran Therborn

States of Knowledge
The co-production of social science and social order
Sheila Jasanoff

After Method
Mess in social science research
John Law

Brands
Logos of the global economy
Celia Lury

The Culture of Exception
Sociology facing the camp
*Bülent Diken and
Carsten Bagge Laustsen*

Visual Worlds
*John Hall, Blake Stimson and
Lisa Tamiris Becker*

Time, Innovation and Mobilities
Travel in technological cultures
Peter Frank Peters

Complexity and Social Movements
Multitudes acting at the edge of chaos
Ian Welsh and Graeme Chesters

Qualitative Complexity
Ecology, cognitive processes and the re-emergence of structures in post-humanist social theory
Chris Jenks and John Smith

Theories of the Information Society, 3rd Edition
Frank Webster

Crime and Punishment in Contemporary Culture
Claire Grant

Mediating Nature
Nils Lindahl Elliot

Haunting the Knowledge Economy
Jane Kenway, Elizabeth Bullen, Johannah Fahey and Simon Robb

Global Nomads
Techno and new age as transnational countercultures in Ibiza and Goa
Anthony D'Andrea

The Cinematic Tourist
Explorations in globalization, culture and resistance
Rodanthi Tzanelli

Non-Representational Theory
Space, politics, affect
Nigel Thrift

Urban Fears and Global Terrors
Citizenship, multicultures and belongings after 7/7
Victor J. Seidler

Sociology through the Projector
Bülent Diken and Carsten Bagge Laustsen

Multicultural Horizons
Diversity and the limits of the civil nation
Anne-Marie Fortier

Sound Moves
IPod culture and urban experience
Michael Bull

Jean Baudrillard
Fatal theories
David B. Clarke, Marcus A. Doel, William Merrin and Richard G. Smith

Aeromobilities
Theory and method
Saulo Cwerner, Sven Kesselring and John Urry

Social Transationalism
Steffen Mau

Towards Relational Sociology
Nick Crossley

Mobile Lives
Anthony Elliott and John Urry

Stillness in a Mobile World
David Bissell and Gillian Fuller

Unintended Outcomes of Social Movements
The 1989 Chinese student movement
Fang Deng

Revolt, Revolution, Critique
The paradox of society
Bulent Diken

Travel Connections
Tourism, technology and togetherness in a mobile world
Jennie Germann-Molz

Mobility, Space and Culture
Peter Merriman

China
The cultural logic of contemporary capitalism
Lash Scott, Keith Michael, Arnoldi Jakob and Rooker Tyler

Staging Mobilities
Ole B. Jensen

Transforming Images
Screens, affect, futures
Rebecca Coleman

Forthcoming in the series:

China Constructing Capitalism
Economic life and urban change
*Lash Scott, Keith Michael, Arnoldi
Jakob and Rooker Tyler*

Staging Mobilities
Ole B. Jensen

Transforming Images
Screens, affect, futures

Rebecca Coleman

LONDON AND NEW YORK

First published 2013
by Routledge
2 Park Square, Milton Park, Abingdon, Oxfordshire OX14 4RN

Simultaneously published in the USA and Canada
by Routledge
711 Third Avenue, New York, NY 10017

First issued in paperback 2014

Routledge is an imprint of the Taylor & Francis Group, an informa business

© 2013 Rebecca Coleman

The right of Rebecca Coleman to be identified as author of this work has been asserted by her in accordance with sections 77 and 78 of the Copyright, Designs and Patents Act 1988.

All rights reserved. No part of this book may be reprinted or reproduced or utilized in any form or by any electronic, mechanical, or other means, now known or hereafter invented, including photocopying and recording, or in any information storage or retrieval system, without permission in writing from the publishers.

Trademark notice: Product or corporate names may be trademarks or registered trademarks, and are used only for identification and explanation without intent to infringe.

British Library Cataloguing in Publication Data
A catalogue record for this book is available from the British Library

Library of Congress Cataloging in Publication Data
Coleman, Rebecca.
Transforming images : screens, affect, futures / Rebecca Coleman.
  p. cm. – (International library of sociology)
  Includes bibliographical references and index.
  1. Self-perception. 2. Representation (Philosophy) I. Title.
  BF697.5.S43.C65 2013
  302'.1–dc23   2012022433

ISBN: 978-0-415-67884-1 (hbk)
ISBN: 978-1-138-82060-9 (pbk)

Typeset in Times New Roman
by Wearset Ltd, Boldon, Tyne and Wear

Contents

List of figures viii
Acknowledgements ix

Introduction: transformation, potential, futures   1

1 Screening affect: images, representational thinking and the actualization of the virtual   29

2 Bringing the image to life: interactive mirrors and intensive experience   47

3 Becoming different: makeover television, proximity and immediacy   72

4 Immanent measure: interaction, attractors and the multiple temporalities of online dieting   93

5 Pre-empting the future: obesity, prediction and Change4Life   113

Conclusion: transforming images – sociology, the future and the virtual   133

Notes 147
References 160
Index 169

Figures

2.1	Daniel Rozin (1999) *Wooden Mirror*, Israel Museum	52
2.2	Interactive mirror in Prada store, Manhattan	54
5.1a–b	Images from the Change4Life *What's It All About?* television advert	118

Acknowledgements

There have been numerous people who have, in different ways, been involved in the research and writing of this book, and in shaping the ideas that it explores. Thanks to Debra Ferreday, Anne Cronin and Anne-Marie Fortier for discussing the initial ideas for the book and encouraging me to submit a proposal for it, John Urry for responding so quickly and positively to it, and the anonymous reviewer of the proposal. Drafts of various papers, articles and chapters that make up this book have been read by Anne Cronin, Carolyn Pedwell, Liz Oakley-Brown, Anne-Marie Fortier, Debra Ferreday and Monica Moreno Figueroa and I would like to thank them all for their thoughtful, insightful and generous suggestions. Matt Falla initially got me interested in interactive mirrors (the focus of Chapter 2), Carla Banks has shared a number of different examples of them with me, and conversations with Hettie Malcomson helped me with the Conclusion; thanks to all of them. Thanks too to the other people who have influenced the work for the book or who have offered encouragement, perhaps in ways that they don't recognize: Jen Tarr, Jessica Ringrose, Imogen Robertson, Elaine Swan and, more generally, my colleagues in the Sociology Department at Lancaster.

The ideas for the book were influenced by two series of events: Lancaster University's Institute for Advanced Studies Annual Research Programme on Experimentality (2009–2010) and the ESRC Seminar Series on Researching Affect and Affective Communication (2009–2011), and I would like to thank Bron Szerszynski and Valerie Walkerdine respectively for inviting me to participate in them. Thanks to those at Routledge, and especially Gerhard Boomgaarden, Jennifer Dodd and Emily Briggs for responding to my queries and requests so quickly and good-naturedly. I would also like to thank those who kindly granted permission for me to reproduce their images: Daniel Rozin (Figure 2.1), IDEO (Figure 2.2) and Department of Health (Figures 5.1a and 5.1b).

Every effort has been made to contact copyright holders for their permission to reprint material in this book. The publishers would be grateful to hear from any copyright holder who is not here acknowledged and will undertake to rectify any errors or omissions in future editions of this book.

A version of Chapter 4 has previously been published as (2010) 'Dieting temporalities: interaction, agency and the measure of online weight watching' in *Time and Society*, Special section on Gendered Time, Vol. 19, No. 2, pp. 265–285.

For its focus on transformation and screens, and for lots of other things besides, this book is dedicated to Matt Moran.

Introduction
Transformation, potential, futures

Across a wide range of sources and in a variety of different ways, transformation can be identified as a dominant theme in contemporary Western social and cultural life. At a macro level, social, economic and political life is seen as needing to change and update, and capitalism is thus argued to be an 'unstable and fluid affair which constantly evolves' (Thrift 2005: 1). At a micro level, governments call for citizens to improve not only their economic prospects but also their chances of being healthy and happy; businesses and organizations ask their staff to continually develop their skill-set; television programmes highlight the possibility of moving up the property ladder or becoming thinner, more attractive and/or self-confident. More than a dominant theme, then, this book examines the ways in which transformation is an *organizing feature* of contemporary social and cultural life so that there has become an *imperative of transformation*. This imperative of transformation, I argue, functions both at a socio-cultural level, as a necessity for change and progress, and at a bodily level, as an impulse for *self-*improvement. Thus, the emphasis in this book is on tracing how a transformative logic connects up – and also complicates – the realms of the 'macro', or socio-cultural, and the 'micro', or bodily. It is important to note, then, that my use of the term transformation is intended to signal that my attention is on *both* the socio-cultural *and* bodily.

The argument that is proposed here sees transformation as an *affective* condition of living in present times. Taking up and developing theories of affect and emotion, this book suggests that transformation is a vital, mobile, intense process that is *felt* and *lived out*. It seeks to account for both the affirmative and troubling aspects of transformation – for how some bodies in particular may affectively experience the imperative of transformation. In Britain and the West more widely, transformation can be seen as an everyday aspiration in ideas about upward (class) mobility in the form of home ownership, employment and professionalization, and personal health and happiness. As the chapters in the book explore, these ideas are circulated in and through popular culture; in the spread and intensification of consumer culture (Chapter 2), the popularity of makeover television programmes (Chapter 3) and the emphasis placed on weight and health (Chapters 4 and 5). Such aspirations can be understood in terms of what Lauren Berlant (2011) calls the fantasy of 'the good life', a fantasy that she argues is 'fraying' (2011: 3).[1] This book is interested in the affective pull of the idea(l) or fantasy of the better life that is seemingly promised by transformation. As Berlant suggests, as the possibility of the good life at a social, cultural, economic and political level seems to become more distant, the fantasy as a 'collectively invested form of life' has 'become *more* fantasmatic' (2011: 11).

The specific focus of the book is on the role that *images* play in establishing and reproducing transformation as an organizing principle of daily life. It seeks to understand how images organize transformation through an attention to the *screen*. Drawing on recent work that demonstrates the centrality of screens to everyday life (Manovich 2002; Friedberg 1994, 2006; A. Wood 2007), the case study chapters of the book examine different screens in contemporary popular culture – the screens of shopping, makeover television, online dieting plans, government health campaigns – and attends to the similarities and differences of these screens through exploring the modes of looking, interaction and experience that they arrange and encourage. In particular, I argue that images of transformation function not only or so much as texts 'read' from a distance and capable of being deciphered for their ideological message, but as and through affect; they are felt in, through and as the body. Screens bring particular kinds of bodies to life. The concern of the book is therefore not only what images of transformation are *of*, but also what they *do*. How are images transformative?

The book pays attention to the *temporality* of images of transformation. It suggests that a key means through which the images at stake here are felt and experienced as affect(ive) is through their appeal to the future. That is, transformative images promise the possibility of materializing the body into something better. For example, shop changing-room mirrors indicate a body made better by the purchase of this or that item of clothing, makeover television shows the way to feel better by looking better, online dieting seems to assure a healthier, happier, thinner future and government health campaigns suggest the possibility of a better future via a 'change for life'. Examining these promises further, I develop a notion of the future as *potential* (Adkins 2008, 2009) and am concerned with teasing out how such an emphasis on anticipation or pre-emption of (Massumi 2005; Adams *et al.* 2009) the future works to 'pull in' some bodies rather than, or more than, others. Which futures are seen as desirable or necessary, and to whom? Is the fantasy of the good life 'fraying' for some social groups more than others? Or, conversely, might the need to transform in order to attempt to achieve a better future be intensified for some bodies? In what ways are these futures materialized? How is the future brought into the present through being *felt* as a necessity for transformation? In what ways does the future as potential, involve both changing a difficult present for the better and a temporal orientation around the present as a 'compromised condition [...] of possibility' (Berlant 2006: 21)? What happens to the present when social and cultural life is organized around the future?

These questions are addressed in the case study chapters. The rest of this chapter sets out the theoretical context for asking these questions. It introduces the key themes of the book: the socio-cultural imperative of transformation and a concern with temporality and the future, and sets up ideas that are developed in Chapter 1 on what I consider to be the centrality of affect to these processes. It places these themes in the context of recent sociological work on 'mobilities' (Urry 2007; Elliott and Urry 2010), 'vitality' (Fraser et al. 2005) and 'liveness' and intensity (Lash and Lury 2007), and unpacks the concept of transformation that is developed throughout the book; a logic that both promises potential and which casts some bodies as failing in needing, achieving and maintaining change. In particular, the chapter develops the notion of *potential* in terms of images of transformation and explores this through the relations between potential and *the virtual* and *the future*. The chapter then provides an outline of the rest of the book as a means to demonstrate how this theoretical framework is taken up and developed in the following chapters.

Transforming the body: neo-liberalism, individualization and the experimental life

As the examples outlined at the beginning of the chapter indicate, contemporary life is concerned with and organized around a notion that change and transformation is crucial, at both an individual and socio-cultural level. While this is certainly a feature of current life, the significance of transformation is not a recent phenomenon. Mike Featherstone (2010), for example, discusses how transformation is 'one of the key tenets of Western modernity' (2010: 200), and can be traced to such seemingly different trends and traditions as Christianity, whereby one's life becomes spiritually and materially transformed through serving the world of God,[2] cultural, artistic and aesthetic movements such as Dandyism (which, in the late nineteenth century gave prominence to the notion of self-invention), and the myths of nationhood and national identity as inherently linked to the ideals of meritocracy and self-achievement (as with the American dream for example) (2010: 200–201). In the early to mid twentieth century, Featherstone argues, the expansion of consumer culture further circulated and consolidated the principle of transformation. In particular, the notion of 'the life lived in pursuit of new experiences, sensations and stylized appearance became influential' (2010: 201), and mass media reports of the lives of stars and celebrities from the entertainment, sports, business and political realms became widespread. As such, the cultivation of a fascinating and interesting life became seen as possible and desirable for everyone; '[t]he "look good, feel good" transformational logic of consumer culture is presented as within the reach of all' (2010: 202).

Importantly, for Featherstone the centrality of a transformational logic to consumer culture involves two interconnected trends: first, the new, transient or changing becomes prioritized over the conventional, permanent or enduring. For example, consumer culture is 'preoccupied with the "outgoing" values of "personality" (a charming and engaging appearance), in contrast to "character" (the virtues of consistency and steadfastness)' (2010: 201). Second, an emphasis is placed on *the body* as the locus of transformation. As Featherstone suggests in an earlier, now classic, essay, consumer culture has developed 'a new relationship between the body and the self' (Featherstone 1991: 187) where 'the inner and outer body become conjoined; the prime purpose of the maintenance of the inner body becomes the enhancement of the appearance of the outer body' (1991: 171). While it is now commonplace to state that the body is of prime importance within contemporary (consumer) culture, the relationship between this preoccupation with the body and the importance of change and the new is worth discussing further, not least because a central focus of this book is to examine how images of transformation are felt and lived out through the body.

A number of social and cultural theorists have drawn attention to the increased interest given to the body, and to the ways in which changing the body is perhaps the primary means of transforming the self for the better. Feminist theory in particular has pointed out how this trend involves women's bodies especially. For example, developing Michel Foucault's (1977/1991) concept of the docile body in relation to a 'preoccupation with fat, diet and slenderness', Susan Bordo (1993/2003) argues that, for women, this preoccupation

> may function as one of the most powerful normalizing mechanisms of our century, insuring the production of self-monitoring and self-disciplining 'docile bodies' sensitive to any departure from social norms and habituated to self-improvement and self-transformation in the service of those norms.
>
> (2003: 186)

In a similar Foucauldian vein, Cressida J. Heyes (2007) develops Nikolas Rose's (2001) concept of the 'somatic individual' to explore the normalization of the ways in which 'the self is discovered or developed through transformations of the flesh' (Heyes 2007: 4). '[L]iving up to our inner truth', therefore, 'involves transforming the body to match' (2007: 5), and self-transformation for Heyes is thus a 'contradictory claim': it becomes

> an important aesthetic (in the deeper sense of ethically inflected, as well as appearance-oriented) project for every 'failed' body – that is for every body that does not adequately represent to the world its owner's genuine character, potential, or inner truth.
>
> (2007: 16)[3]

Every body should be able to accurately communicate true selfhood.

Of particular concern in this book are the ways in which the association of the self with the body and the constant requirement for change are processes that involve certain bodies. Some feminist analysers see these trends as symptomatic of 'post-feminist media culture' (Gill 2007; McRobbie 2005, 2008) where, as Sarah Banet-Weiser and Laura Portwood-Stacer (2006) put it, 'a "celebration" of the body, the pleasure of transformation, and individual empowerment function as a justification for a renewed objectification of female bodies' (2006: 257).

As I will go on to explore in the case study chapters, the imperative of transformation necessarily implies that the present is not good enough, and that, through changing the self/body, the future can be better. Such an imperative resonates with those bodies where the present is, in different ways, difficult or unbearable. Tracing how the need to change resonates with specific bodies – bodies that I argue are gendered, classed and raced – is a key aim of this book. It is clear then, that across popular culture 'the positive benefits of bodily transformative work are endlessly extolled' (Featherstone 2010: 200), and that social and cultural differences and inequalities are caught up in and (re)produced through this imperative of transformation. However, to return to the other point that Featherstone makes, what is involved in change and transformation being manifested through the body? Or, to put it another way, what is the relationship between this emphasis on the body and the concurrent emphasis on the new and changing?

While consumer culture is one context through which to understand the transformation of the body, it is also necessary to consider the imperative of transformation as part of the wider logics of capitalism. This is to attend to how, as an economic, social and cultural system, capitalism is itself transformative. One of the primary ways in which social theory has explored the relationship between capitalism and transformation is through the notion of neo-liberalism, a broad and wide-ranging theoretical framework that attempts to account for large-scale changes in the ways in which national and global economies are organized and how power, rule and governance are exercised in advanced liberal democracies. According to David Harvey (2007), neo-liberalism became dominant in the West in the late 1970s and early 1980s with the election of right-wing governments in the United States and the United Kingdom, and involved a large-scale transformation of global economics. For Harvey, neo-liberalism is:

> in the first instance a theory of political economic practices that proposes that human well-being can be best advanced by liberating individual entrepreneurial freedoms and skills within an institutional framework characterized by strong private property rights, free markets, and free trade.
> (2007: 2)

No longer confined to Western countries, Harvey argues that neo-liberal economic practices of privatization and commodification extend beyond the state to permeate many, if not most, aspects of everyday life. As such, neo-liberalism has 'become hegemonic as a mode of discourse. It has pervasive effects on ways of thought to the point where it has become incorporated into the common-sense way many of us interpret, live in and understand the world' (2007: 3).

Of significance here, are the ways in which the relationship between neo-liberalism and power have been theorized. According to Nikolas Rose and Peter Miller (1991/2010) who draw on Foucault's work, neo-liberalism involves power, not so much [as] a matter of imposing constraints upon citizens as of 'making up' citizens capable of bearing a kind of regulated freedom. Personal autonomy is not the antithesis of political power, but a key term in its exercise, the more so because most individuals are not merely the subjects of power but play a part in its operations.

(2010: 272)

In neo-liberal societies, theorists argue, the individual becomes an active participant in bearing responsibility for social and cultural processes. Rose and Miller argue that this is a fundamental re-working of welfarism, where social problems are seen as the responsibility of the government. As indicated, neo-liberalism involves markets replacing regulation, regulation taking the form of economic entrepreneurship and 'active entrepreneurship [coming] to replace the passivity and dependency of responsible solidarity as individuals are encouraged to strive to optimize their own quality of life and that of their families' (2010: 296). Neo-liberalism thus 'entails a reorganization of programmes for the government of personal life' (2010: 298). The realm of personal life is established as autonomous from government, and individuals are seen as 'free' to 'make their own decisions, pursue their preferences and seek to maximize the quality of their lives' (2010: 298). This autonomy and freedom is manifested as 'the energetic pursuit of personal fulfillment and the incessant calculations that are to enable this to be achieved' (2010: 298, references omitted). Transformation is thus a key means through which the 'making up' of citizens works.

A central theme that has been identified within contemporary neo-liberal practices is thus of *individualization*: indeed, Ulrich Beck and Elizabeth Beck-Gernsheim (2002) argue that individualization is *the* decisive feature of the modern world. Individualization for these authors refers to, on the one hand, the 'disintegration of previously existing social forms – for example, the increasing fragility of such categories as class and social status, gender roles, family, neighbourhood etc.'[4] and, on the other hand, the 'new demands, controls and constraints [that] are being imposed on individuals' (2002: 2), such as those pointed out by Rose and Miller. These social changes emerge out of a more general condition of reflexive modernization, in which, as Beck describes elsewhere, 'the more societies are modernized, the more agents (subjects) acquire the ability to reflect on the social conditions of their existence and to change them accordingly' (Beck *et al.* 1994: 174). In reflexive modernization, there is a new relationship between the individual and the social where 'what the social is and does has to be involved with individual decisions' (Beck 1992: 90; cited in Adkins 2002: 15). In this context, individualization is an attempt to account for the form that the relationship between the individual and the social takes in this 'de-traditionalized' reflexive world.

For Beck and Beck-Gernsheim, the emphasis placed on the individual does not mean that he or she is acting outside of social structures and constraints as 'individualization is a social condition which is not arrived at by a free decision of individuals' (Beck and Beck-Gernsheim 2002: 4). Although they do not explicitly draw on Foucault, there are echoes of Rose and Miller's argument in Beck and Beck-Gernsheim's statements that individualization processes 'demand an active contribution by individuals' and that individualization is,

> a compulsion, albeit a paradoxical one, to create, to stage manage, not only one's own biography but the bonds and networks surrounding it and to do this amid changing preferences and at successive stages of life, while constantly adapting to the conditions of the labour market, the education system, the welfare state and so on.
>
> (2002: 4)

Beck and Beck-Gernsheim's interest in the compulsion for individuals to create and manage their own biographies, seeks to account for the prevalence of what they term an 'ethic of individual self-fulfillment and achievement' which 'unfold[s] in accordance with a schematic pattern' (2002: 22). They argue that the 'choosing, deciding, shaping human being who aspires to be the author of his or her own life, the creator of an individual identity, is the central character of our time' (2002: 22–23) and outline how this 'life of one's own' is socially significant in a number of different ways.[5] Of particular interest to the argument being proposed in this book, Beck and Beck-Gernsheim pinpoint how the neo-liberal enforcement of atomization (2002: 24) – which requires individuals to construct experimental and flexible life biographies – functions to mask the standardization of life; if all lives must be created, experimentally and flexibly, then these lives are not 'one's own' but are socially structured and determined. However, neo-liberal policies and practices collapse responsibility of the quality of individuals' lives from the state to the individual – '[y]our own life – your own failure' (2002: 24) – and the notion emerges that '[p]eople are better adapted to the future than are social institutions and their representatives' (2002: 28). Put simply, if an individual's life biography is not successful, it is up to that individual to experiment again, to construct another life, to realize their own potential.

The emphasis placed on the experimental individual in both theory and practice indicates for Elaine Swan (2010) that it is important to consider not only the socio-cultural implications of the dominance of a logic of transformation but also what self-transformation might mean for those who actively participate in it. Drawing on her own experience as a client and practitioner in personal development, Swan's study unpacks the understandings of 'self-work' – 'self-exploration, self-expression, self-reflection, self-improvement and experimentation with appearance, capacities, behaviours, emotions and thinking' (2010: 1) – that personal development workers[6] see as central to their practice. In the context of discussing the notion of the self and its transformation, for example, Swan argues that personal development workers work with different ideas of what the self is and can become, and of what is involved in the transformation of the self: an authentic self where 'transformation is a form of unmasking a self, which has some unity over time' (2010: 141); a 'make-over' model of transformation where 'the gap between the "self that is" and the "self to be", seen to be of great distance, can be instantly closed' through the expertise of the practitioner (2010: 154); a 'quick fix' model where 'some aspect of the self is improved or replaced so that the small transformation sets in motion larger transformations that are needed by the self to move closer to its ideal' (2010: 154–155) and; the experimental transformation where 'changes are seen to be achieved through a series of trail and error whereby the client tries out different therapeutic techniques and practices of the self and evaluates their success' (2010: 155).

There is clearly much more to be taken from the different modes of transformation that Swan identifies, but what is particularly interesting in my focus here is the versions of temporality that they imply. Swan comments on the centrality of temporality to what she and others (for example Rose 1989, 1996; Giddens 1991, 1992) have termed, therapeutic culture and the psychologization of the self. The past, for example, is seen as potentially problematic within therapeutic cultures but is capable of being transformed through techniques which seek to reduce its effect on and the possibility of it 'hanging around in the present' (Swan 2010: 164). For the practitioners in Swan's study, this might involve 'unhooking' the present from the past (2010: 164) and recognizing that the present involves choosing ways in which to interpret the past (by learning from it for instance) (2010: 165). What is of prime significance to the need or desire to transform – and what is in focus in this book – is the possibility of changing the future; the future is that which involves a self different to and better than the self in the past and present. In analysing the notions of the future that personal development practitioners work with, Swan critiques Anthony Gidden's (1991) argument that 'an attempt to shape future selves and future lives through setting up a particular chain of causality located in the self, in which the future unfurls from particular actions in the present' is a 'colonization of the future' (Swan 2010: 161), by suggesting that it rests upon and implies a uni-directional and linear model of time. Instead, Swan argues, for personal development practitioners, the future is not so much detached from the present – that which is yet to be – but is 'innate, contained in the present self' (2010: 168). The future is a 'vantage point' (2010: 168), 'sought out in order to illuminate the present' and 'to offer different perspectives with which to view oneself. The popular notion of the self as the accumulation of the past, and development as a uni-directional linear journey is complicated [...] here in that time can be reversed' (2010: 167). As such, and as I will discuss further below, the future is a kind of *potential* that exists within the present.

The theories of individualization, reflexive modernization and of the construction of an experimental life biography have been influential in social and cultural theory in terms of the attention that they give to large-scale social change and to the increased prominence of the individual within these changes. However, these theories have also been critiqued for over-emphasizing the disintegration of social categories of class and gender, for instance, and the, albeit restricted, agency of the individual to be the author of their life (Swan's research draws on this work). Angela McRobbie (2008), for example, sees theories of individualization feeding directly into post-feminism which 'airbrushe[s] out of existence' the 'enduring inequalities which still mark out the relations between men and women' (2008: 19). Arguing that '[s]elf-help guides, personal advisors, lifestyle coaches and gurus and all sorts of self-improvement TV programmes provide the cultural means by which individualization operates as a social process' (2008: 19), McRobbie points to how (young) women in particular embody the individual who

> must now choose the kind of life they want to live. Girls must have a life-plan. They must become more reflexive in regard to every aspect of their lives, from making the right choice in marriage, to taking responsibility for their own working lives and not being dependent on a job for life or on the stable and reliable operations of a large scale bureaucracy.
>
> (2008: 19)

The choices that young women (must) make then, operate within 'a modality of constraint. The individual is compelled to be the kind of subject who can make the right choices' and such 'choices' 'are productive of new realms of injury and injustice' (2008: 19).

Discussing Beck's individualization thesis, Beverley Skeggs (2004) has also questioned the attribution of class to a traditional, ascriptive identity rather than a modern identity. Drawing on Mike Savage's (2000) point that in understanding class in this way, Beck has fundamentally misconceived the classed relationships between the individual and the social, she argues that what Beck[7] has 'read as the decline of class cultures and the rise of individualization [...] would be better understood as the shift from working-class to middle-class modes of individualization' (Skeggs 2004: 52). Such a shift is especially the case with what Savage has argued is the 'subtle reworking of the relationship between class, masculinity and the individual, enabling the emergence of a new form of self-developmental individualization, premised on particular kinds of middle-class employment relations, defining a new mode of individual identity' (2004: 52). As such, Beck's and Beck and Beck Gernsheim's theory of individualization and the 'free' agent who is able to construct their own experimental life assumes not a neutral individual, as it may seem, but rather a classed individual who has 'access to the resources by which the self can be known, assessed and narrated' (2004: 53). Furthermore, and drawing again on Savage, Skeggs argues that the theory of individualization performs a number of 'rhetorical ploys, designed to convince by claiming plausibility and having more "commonsense" than other accounts; accounts that resonate with middle-class experience' (2004: 53).[8] In Chapters 3 and 5 I pay specific attention to the ways in which experiences which resonate with middle-classness can come to dominate images of transformation and how an understanding of images as felt and lived out through their affective appeal may help to explore the immanent and empirical experience of those bodies that are caught up in the imperative of transformation.

In terms of class and gender then, theories of individualization, reflexive modernization and the experimental life, have been challenged. Indeed, as Lisa Adkins' (2002) detailed and wide-ranging analysis of these theories suggests, they tend to assume an implicit middle-class masculine self/body which has the access and ability to construct and experiment with their life biography. As such, the detraditionalization thesis proposed by writers such as Beck and Beck and Beck-Gernsheim 'fails to register that such mobility and reflexivity is not transgressive, but involves a new arrangement of gender, one which [...] concerns positions of flexibility and immanence in relation to cultural style.' (2002: 80). For example, in the context of work, which is understood by academics and business professionals to be increasingly 'feminized', Adkins points out that the mobility of workers is unequally distributed. That is, while men may take up and perform the aesthetics of femininity, 'women professional workers not only find it difficult to "take on" masculinity, but performances of masculine aesthetics often have negative workplace consequences' (2002: 75). Moreover, as femininity becomes a style that men can be seen to perform,

> rather than a set of workplace skills, strategies or performances, femininity is made immanent for [...] professional women workers. [...] [F]emininity may now be a key aesthetic resource, [...] [b]ut if performances of femininity *by women* at work are not recognized as performances, they will not be recognized as styles which are made up, deployed, and exchangeable as workplace resources. That is, they will not be recognized as concerning the take-up of a reflexive stance towards gender.
>
> (2002: 79)

It is, then, not so much that in neo-liberal societies gender as a category, identity and mode of embodiment is disintegrating in importance, but that gender is *re-organized*; the contemporary emphasis on mobility, flexibility and reflexivity necessarily 'entail[s] new forms of power' (Adkins 2002: 80; see also Swan 2008; Swan and Fox 2009). Indeed, Adkins suggests that 'a politics may well need to be developed around immanent and flexible subject positions' (2002: 80).

I will return to the issue of how gender and class are re-organized in terms of flexibility, mobility, immanence and temporality later in the book through an analysis of the affectivity of images. What these arguments mean for a discussion of the imperative of transformation is that, as Adkins puts it, 'there may be certain embodied and pre-reflexive aspects of identity which are less amenable to self-transformation' (2002: 45). In terms of the creation and management of a reflexive biography then, the experimental life 'needs to be recognized as a technique central to the constitution of gender and sexuality, post social structure or post society. As Ahmed has argued, experimentation reconstitutes differences differently' (2002: 128, references omitted). A key way in which I examine how a bodily and socio-cultural imperative of transformation is involved in the re-organization and re-configuration of difference is through a consideration of how power might be working today. In order to begin to unpack the contemporary workings of power, in the next section I first turn to explore the ways in which other sets of social and cultural theory have sought to understand change.

Theorizing change: mobility, intensity and power

Debates around neo-liberalism, individualization and the experimental life have been a principal way in which recent social and cultural theory have approached and dealt with the dominance of transformation across many areas of contemporary life. Of particular importance for this book is their concern with how power works through the 'making up' of bodies/selves and how this making up is compulsive. Moreover, critiques of theories of individualization draw attention to how the compulsion for transformation is organized differently for some: an issue that is developed further in this book. At the same time, and while not taking transformation as a central focus, social and cultural theory has also drawn attention to the patterns and processes of change, movement and flow in everyday life. What these theories suggest is that social and cultural life is itself transformational, that is, always in process, always moving and changing. These theories are helpful, I suggest, for understanding how contemporary capitalism functions through a logic of change and becoming different and, as discussed in Chapter 1, for thinking through the *affective* dimension of a socio-cultural and bodily imperative of transformation.

The relatively recent emergence of the sociology of mobilities seeks to account for how

> mobilities encompass [...] both the large-scale movement of people, objects, capital and information across the world, as well as the more local processes of daily transportation, movement through public space and the travel of material things within everyday life. Issues of movement, of too little movement or too much or of the wrong sort or at the wrong time, are central to many lives, organizations and governments.
>
> (Hannam *et al.* 2006: 1)

Rather than conceiving the social in terms of the problem of order – for example, how can society be (made to be) more cohesive? – the sociology of mobilities is interested in how the everyday is increasingly characterized by movement and flow, and how these movements create a '"networked" patterning of economic and social life, even for those who have not moved' (2006: 2). Such an approach requires attention be paid, not only to those in the wealthy, privileged north and/or west of the world who are able to move for work and pleasure, but also to those for whom mobility is not an option, or who may be made to move to find work, avoid climate change or escape persecution, for example. It is necessary to 'track [...] the power and politics of discourses and practices of mobility in both creating movement and stasis' (2006: 3–4, references omitted).

12 Introduction

This 'tracking' has involved a wide range of emphases; specific modes of travel (Featherstone et al. 2005; Knowles et al. 2008; Adey 2010), tourism (Sheller and Urry 2004; Burns and Novelli 2008), consumption (Urry 1995; Lury 1997), space and the urban (Graham 2001; Cronin 2008a, 2008b; Cresswell and Merriman 2011) and methodology (Buscher et al. 2010), for example. In *Mobile Lives*, Anthony Elliott and John Urry (2010) discuss mobilities in terms of the relationship between technology and affect/emotion. Taking 'Sandra', 'a composite of two case studies' (2010: 164, n.2), as an example, Elliott and Urry explore the ways in which a 'digital lifestyle of mobile communications' enables a sense of proximity and intimacy across space (2010: 26). Sandra is a 'high-profile advertising executive', married with three young children, and working in London during the week and returning to the family home in Leeds at the weekend (2010: 25). On the move a lot of the time and away from her family, Elliott and Urry discuss how Sandra maintains a feeling of closeness with her children, in particular, through music selected and downloaded on different digital technologies (computer, i-Pod, i-Phone) and through various technologies in her London flat (landline phone, fax, email, Skype) which act as an 'open communication line' to the family in Leeds. Sandra also spends a great deal of time cataloguing thousands of family photographs stored on Google Picasa and editing home-movies on Apple i-Movie.

There is much to be taken from this case study, including the gendered, classed and raced aspects of Sandra's access to a digital lifestyle. However, of interest to the discussion of mobility as a dominant socio-cultural characteristic in contemporary developed capitalism are the ways in which 'mobile lives are fashioned and transformed through various technological forms – virtualities, electronic discourse – in the emotional connections people develop with themselves, others and the wider world' (2010: 28). Digital technologies are integral to making the mobile lives of the privileged successful, not least because they

> facilitate the mobilization of feelings and affect, memories and desires, dreams and anxieties. What is at stake in the deployment of communications technologies in mobile lives […] is not simply an increased digitization of social relationships, but a broad and extensive change in how emotions are contained (stored, deposited, retrieved) and thus a restructuring of identity more generally.
>
> (2010: 28)

For example, as well as feeling that digital communications technologies bring her emotionally closer to her family, Elliott and Urry also discuss how Sandra points to feeling anxious at the amount of time she spends 'immersed' in family photographs and films, which she describes as perhaps 'too obsessive' (Sandra in Elliott and Urry 2010: 36). Elliott and Urry discuss how Sandra reports feeling

> considerable levels of guilt over being away from the family so regularly. She also seems aware of the disquieting scenario of loss more generally. But

Introduction 13

    Sandra's reflexive level of self-awareness also seems to falter in this connection. She feels not on 'solid ground' when it comes to understanding the countless hours she spends organizing their electronic photo library, or editing family videos. Because she does not quite understand the emotional prompts for these activities, she says that she feels worried.

(2010: 36)

What I suggest is significant from this quotation is the connection between mobility, technology, affect and the body. In this case, the technologies that an apparently successful mobile life require, create feelings of guilt, worry and anxiety in the body as well as of family bonds. Mobile technologies are both 'intoxicating' and 'threatening' (2010: 41). The point here, is that tracing the patterns of mobility requires attention to be paid to the body and to the affects that capitalism seems to create. As Nigel Thrift puts it, '[c]apitalism has a kind of crazy vitality. [...] It appeals to gut feelings. It gets involved in all kinds of extravagant symbioses' (Thrift 2005: 1).

    For Thrift, contemporary capitalism has taken on a life of its own. It is not only an overarching, repressive system but is also a performative, perpetually unfinished experiment (2005: 3). Such an understanding of capitalism does not mean that only the 'thrills and spills' (2005: 3) – the new and latest – require attention. As I have discussed above, change and transformation might very well not do away with old differences but organize them differently, and 'the routine, even boring' are key to the performativity of capitalism in establishing its 'stable repetition' (2005: 3). However, an understanding of capitalism as vital, as processual, as unfinished, *does* require an attention to the generative, the inventive and the intensive. For Thrift, who is interested in the 'cultural circuit' of capitalism – 'business schools, management consultants, management gurus and the media' (2005: 6) – capitalism has in part become 'a theoretical enterprise in which *various essentially virtual notions* (network, the knowledge economy, the new economy, community of practice) *are able to take on flesh as, increasingly, the world is made in these notions' likeness*' (2005: 6, my emphasis). One consequence, or, better, an integral part of this circuit, is an emphasis on the body, where '[m]uch of modern capitalism is concerned [...] with producing new kinds of managerial and worker bodies that are *constantly attentive, constantly attuned to the vagaries of the event, through an emphasis on the ludic and affective*' (2005: 6, my emphasis). Capitalism therefore now 'has the power to make its theories and descriptions of the world come alive in new built form, new machines and new bodies' (2005: 11).

    While Thrift's focus is on business and management, the economy and the bodies of workers, his explanation of capitalism here introduces and points to some of the concepts that are pivotal to the ways in which this book tries to account for both the transformative character of images and for how images of transformation are felt and lived out. Two concepts are of particular significance here: vitalism and virtuality. I return to the concept of the virtual below in my discussion of temporality and the future, and develop it further in

14 Introduction

relation to affect in Chapter 1. The notions of *vitality, vitalism* or *vitalization* which Thrift puts to work to refer to the affective 'potency' of contemporary capitalism have been widely developed in recent social and cultural theory to account for how life – social/cultural/artificial and natural/biological – is (now being understood as) increasingly complex, mobile and intertwined. For example, Mariam Fraser *et al.* (2005) argue that vitalism, 'the idea, originating in the 18th and 19th centuries, that life cannot be explained by the principles of mechanism' (2005: 1), encourages a conception of life as both relational and processual: 'Process, in other words, is characterized by a radical relationality: the (social and natural world) is understood in terms of constantly shifting relations between open-ended objects' (2005: 3). As such, life is 'not confined to living organisms, but [is] movement, a radical becoming' (2005: 3).

This conception of vitalism places emphasis on how life involves, and is involved in, *invention*, *difference* and *liveness*. Life is a continual process of change. Life is not only that which can be calculated, regulated and contained, but is also a vital force. For example, Scott Lash and Celia Lury (2007) argue that a key aspect of what they define as contemporary 'global cultural industry', is that things 'come alive, take on a life of their own' (2007: 12). Lash and Lury develop their argument about life/aliveness through the notion of *things*, which they contrast to the commodity, those goods that clutter and are exchanged in the culture industry that Adorno and Horkheimer (see Adorno 1991) describe. Commodities are mechanistic; they are 'atomized and atomizing' (Lash and Lury 2007: 12), externally caused, and involve sameness and instrumentalism. On the other hand, the things of global culture industry are vitalistic, are 'self-transforming and self-energizing' (2007: 12). As I will go on to discuss in relation to images in Chapter 1, things are *experiences*; their life or liveliness mean that their value lies not in exchange but in their ability to create and maintain relations and feelings. Things are therefore not about sameness but are produced through and productive of *difference*. The value of the relations and feelings of things are in their distinctiveness, their difference from each other. Furthermore, when compared with commodities, things are experienced by consumers through this difference.

Lash and Lury's discussion of brands is helpful here. Whereas commodities define consumer industry, in global consumer industry it is brands that have become predominant, brands that have value. Brands are involved in the generation of relations and feelings and, as such, are not so much representational as *intensive*. Brands are virtuals – experiences rather than texts. While actualized in a series of products or objects, brands nevertheless exceed these actuals, they are virtuals. Discussing the brand in relation to the experience of a work of art that Walter Benjamin (1992) describes, Lash and Lury explain that,

> you may perceive the painting, say, as an object, but what you *experience* is non-objectual – that is, colour. This is the experience of an intensity. Brands may embrace a number of extensities, but they themselves are intensities.

Introduction   15

> Brands are in this sense *virtuals*. As virtuals they may be actualized in any number of products. Yet the feeling, the brand experience, is the same.
>
> (2007: 14)

The brand here, as virtual, is an intensive experience or feeling that, while being actualized in different products, exists 'beyond' or 'outside of' them.

In this way, Lash and Lury document a shift in global culture industry, and capitalism more generally, from extensity to *intensity*. Extensity refers to both the historical extension of capitalism across the world and to the way in which power works rationally, from the outside, through equivalence and in the physical (or symbolic) realm (Lash and Lury 2007: 200; Lash 2010: chapter 6). Increasingly, however, power works through intensity; through materiality, the body, affect and feeling, from within. A shift from extensity to intensity might seem to be a move away from a theorization of power and a focus instead on the 'thrills and spills' of the global consumer industry. However, with these theories of vitality, liveness and intensity, is it not that power is neglected or seen as no longer important, but that the way in which power is seen to work has changed. Indeed, for Lash (2010) an appreciation that power is now (at least in part) intensive, indicates a shift to a conception of post-hegemonic society. In a hegemonic society, power works through reproduction and is challenged through practices of resistance. For instance, as the Birmingham School of British cultural studies explored so thoroughly, popular culture has a key role in both reproducing and resisting hegemonic power: the semiotics of everyday style or the ways in which media texts are coded and interpreted are both examples of how this tradition of cultural studies has dealt with the problem of how dominant power relations are maintained over time.

Lash explains hegemonic power as disciplinary power, where 'there is always a discourse (jurisprudence, psychoanalysis, etc.) that lies behind the disciplinary institution it supports' (2010: 131). In the case of the institution of media (one of the core institutions at stake in culture industry), the institution sits between and regulates 'cultural discourse and legitimate power' (2010: 131). Post-hegemonic power, in contrast, 'operates through a cultural logic of invention' (2010: 132). That is, in line with my emphasis so far on power as intensive and affective, Lash argues that contemporary power works through 'chronic production' (2010: 132); in my terms through the imperative of transformation. Lash's argument is developed through three shifts that he sees taking place in how power works. First, he argues that there is a shift from epistemological to *ontological* regimes of power (2010: 132–136). Epistemological regimes involve discourse where 'power works through logical statements or utterances, through propositions that are predications of a subject' (2010: 133). In this sense, power is semiotic and has a *normalizing* function. In ontological regimes of power, which Lash argues now characterize post-hegemonic societies, subjects and objects are predicated not through discourse but through their being, their materiality.

Indeed, the ontological regime of power can be understood in terms of the second shift that Lash identifies, from 'a hegemonic mode of "*power over*" to an intensive notion of *power from within*' (2010: 132). The hegemonic mode of power is what Lash terms *pouvoir* or *potestas*; a form of domination that 'works through external determination, like mechanism' (2010: 136). Discourse can be understood in this way, as that which is external to the subject or object, which works 'over' them in order to regulate them. The post-hegemonic mode of power is instead *potentia* (or *puissance*). It is inventive, 'it works less like mechanism than like "*life*"' (2010: 136) in the way that I have described it above. *Potentia* is 'fully ontological. It is the motive force, the unfolding, the becoming of the thing-itself, whether that thing is human, non-human or some combination thereof' (2010: 136). This intensive or vitalist mode of power highlights my concern in this book on how power works through the compulsive 'making up' of bodies/selves. Moreover, it focuses attention on the *body*, on how power works 'from within' the body, through addressing the body 'directly'. In my terms, through the affectivity of the imperative of transformation. Working 'from within', power is also, according to the third shift Lash identifies, increasingly organized around *facts* rather than norms. For Lash, norms are external to the body whereas the fact is an immediacy, an intensity: 'Instead of facts being a dead abstraction, the factual comes alive' (2010: 142). As I discussed above and explore further in Chapters 4 and 5 especially, this is the way in which abstractions (theories, calculations, descriptions) 'take on flesh as, increasingly, the world is made in these notions' likeness' (Thrift 2005: 6).

It is this conception of power as inventive, immanent and intensive that I take up and put to work in this book for a number of reasons. First, it is intended to make a link with the version of power developed in theories of neo-liberalism that emphasize what Rose and Miller term, the 'making-up' of individuals. This is not to see individuals as being in control of the ways in which this making-up occurs: I am not suggesting that individuals are free to experiment with their life biographies but rather I am drawing on the critiques made of the individualization thesis, discussed above. However, it is to argue that experimentation and transformation have become central to contemporary societies (Lury 1998), and are thus also a central way in which power now operates, a version of power that *invents* bodies rather than being imposed on them/us. Second, and relatedly, as Lash argues, this mode of power works immanently, that is *through the body*. In this sense, power works in the terms that Foucault set out in his concept of bio-power; as *productive*.[9] While Foucault's work has very often been taken up in relation to how power is involved in discipline, docility and governance, in conceiving power as inventive, there is also a way of emphasizing its concern with process and becoming.

The third reason for moving from a conception of power as extensive to intensive is in order to think through what such a move might imply for an understanding of *images*. This is important because, since Adorno and Horkheimer's critical cultural theory and on into the Birmingham School's British cultural studies, an analysis of the ways in which power operates externally has been a linchpin of how images have been approached and critiqued.[10] In Chapter 1 I develop this discussion in terms of a re-thinking of images as representational texts. Here it is worth indicating that, if images are increasingly involving and affecting the body, the implication is that a reading of an image that attends only to what that image means can no longer grasp what it is about the image that makes it so powerful, compelling and appealing. Instead, the focus is on understanding how images work as communications; *self-generative, transformative, relational processes*. They are 'things-in-themselves' (Lash 2010: 150) – *experiences* rather than texts – whose 'true' ideological meaning cannot be uncovered:

> when power enters into us and constitutes us from the inside – not through our normalization but through our difference – [...] it becomes far more difficult to unmask. Indeed, working no longer through a visual paradigm, but through the multiplicity of senses, *un*masking is no longer at issue.
>
> (2010: 138)

What such an argument suggests is that an alternative way of 'getting at' power and of approaching the image is required. What happens to understandings of images when power is conceived as intensive?

Potential: the virtual and the actual

For Lash, an understanding of power as intensive rather than extensive indicates that power is concerned with and involved in the production of *potential*. Power is 'a potentiality [with] an inherent capacity for growth, development or coming into being' (2010: 4). As intensive, power is thus productive; power necessitates change and transformation, and indicates the prospect of other possibilities (methods of thinking, modes of embodiment and ways of living). Working as and through potential, power therefore involves, not only the concrete and material, but also the intangible, experiential, affective; *the virtual*:

> Intensities are virtuals or potentialities. They generate what you encounter. Further, extensities are fixed, while intensities are always in process. They are always in movement. [...] Extensities thus are 'beings' while intensities are 'becomings'.
>
> (2010: 4–5)

While not in itself a new idea (Shields 2002), the concept of the virtual has been recently taken up in different areas of contemporary social and cultural theory in relation to online or 'virtual' worlds (Shields 1996; Adam and Green 2001; Agger 2004); art and film (Bryant and Pollock 2010); Deleuzian theory (Massumi 2002; Coleman 2009); science studies (Mackenzie 2005; Fraser 2006); advertising and consumer culture (Cronin 2010); finance and capital (Carrier and Miller 1998), for example, and arguments from some of these different fields are explored and developed at various points in the book. At this point, however, my main concern is with considering how the concept of the virtual is helpful to understand (one of) the ways in which power currently works through images and, below, for how I think the concept can be developed in relation to the question of time.

In his mapping out of the concept, Rob Shields defines the virtual 'in everyday life as "that which is so in essence but not actually so"' and, '[m]ore philosophically, the virtual captures the nature of activities and objects which exist but are not tangible, not "concrete"' (Shields 2002: 2, reference omitted). While Shields, here, contrasts the virtual with the concrete – the virtual is that which exists but is not concrete – within contemporary social and cultural theory, the virtual is most often 'coupled' (Deleuze 1993/2003) with the actual; the virtual is that which exists but is not actual, is that which might become actual through a process of actualization.[11] The virtual is a potential – process, becoming – which might yet become actualized. This coupling of the actual and virtual enables an understanding of the relationship between intangible experiences or feelings and 'actual' objects. More and more, power as productive, intensive, potential is organized and working not only through the actual but through the virtual, not only through concrete objects but through intangible potentials.

In suggesting that contemporary socio-cultural life involves the virtual, the framework that I am developing here attends to the relationship between intangible potentials and actual ways of living. In this book, I conceive images as virtuals – intensive, intangible potentials. I am interested in exploring how these virtuals are actualized – are felt, experienced and lived out. I argue that images of transformation function as virtuals: as that which exist 'within' the actual and are actualized, but at the same time remain in excess of the actual. Images are virtuals in that while they may be brought to life and lived out as actuals, the feeling or experience that they (help to) create and organize, remains in excess of these actualizations, remains as an intensity. As a key feature of contemporary socio-cultural life, images of transformation can thus never be exhausted: change is ceaseless, necessarily constant and always required. One actualization of a virtual image of transformation is never sufficient. Transformation is required *for life* and across a range of fields: in this book, through shopping, dieting, bodily appearance and health. The way in which I approach the virtuality of images of transformation is to explore the relationship between the virtual as that which is not-yet-so and the future. This is not to suggest that the virtual is always or necessarily a future temporality[12] but rather to argue that what characterizes the different images of transformation discussed here is their emphasis on promising the potential of a better future. In promising the potential of a better future, I argue, that images of transformation are virtuals. This promise, while perhaps in the process of being actualized in and as different and specific modes of embodiment, and/or material forms of life through different processes of self-improvement, is inexhaustible; as virtuals, the *potential* of a better future always exceeds its actualization. What this implies for an understanding of images, then, is that an attention to how power operates in excess of what they are *of* is crucial. Images *do*; they are involved in the production of feelings and experiences and these feelings and experiences are themselves involved in the production of particular ways of life.

Sociology and the future

My interest in how images of transformation organize the potential of the future is in the context of how sociology, and social and cultural theory more generally, have recently turned to explore, in different ways and with different foci, the significance of the future. In Nik Brown and Mike Michael's (2003) terms, this is part of a 'need to shift the analytical emphasis from *looking into* the future to *looking at* the future', that is to 'engage with the future as an analytical object, and not simply a neutral temporal space into which objective expectations can be projected' (2003: 4). For Barbara Adam and Chris Groves (2007), social theory needs to attend to the future because '[i]ndustrial capitalist societies are inescapably wedded to innovation and progress. Change rather than stability is the order of the day' (Adam and Groves 2007: 1). As such, with modernity emerges a condition whereby the future is at once oriented towards – a belief in progress implies that the future will be better, and is itself uncertain – what will the future be if everything is changing? In this book, I am interested in examining the relationship between what is seen to be the increased significance of the future and the emphasis that is currently placed on change, process and transformation in both theory and practice. Drawing through my discussion so far, the focus is on what the future *does*. How do images of transformation organize the future? What does this organization of the future do to the ways in which these images are felt and lived out? What does an examination of the future do to how social and cultural theory might understand the prominence and appeal of transformation?

Adam and Groves trace what they consider to be the different ways in which the future is understood and comes to function in contemporary society, and how the notion of the future has changed with Western industrialization. For example, from being a temporal state 'told' through prophecy and sacred texts, with modernization the future becomes understood as capable of being 'tamed', 'traded', 'transformed' and 'traversed' (2007: Introduction). While these notions of the future imply and involve different relationships to temporality, of particular significance for Adam and Groves is the ways in which industrial capitalism both detaches the future from the past and present – the future is not that which is pre-determined by events in the past – and 'empties' it out; '[t]he future becomes seen as a territory which must be exploited for the sake of delivering ever-greater power to transform reality' (2007: 75). Central to this territorialization of the future is modern capitalism's underpinning by a scientific and social scientific belief in progress, as not only must reality be transformed, but it must be transformed *for the better*, through increased and increasing profits, for example, and through longer, healthier, happier lives. The future is empty, in the sense that it is not pre-determined, but is commodified and colonized by calculation, estimation and trading (2007: 76).

Such practices raise ethical concerns for Adam and Groves, in that a prioritization of the future through a belief in and orientation around progress at the same time as the future is detached from other temporalities results in actions being taken in the present which will affect the future in potentially detrimental ways. An emptying out of the future, then, does not necessarily imply that the future is open. Instead, while the future is conceived as detached from the past and present, it is in practice the time where past and present actions have their effects. John Urry (2010), for example, has discussed the futures that are likely to emerge out of Western capitalism's excessive consumption of the planet. Urry argues that 'the twentieth century has left a bleak legacy for the new century, with a very limited range of possible future scenarios' (2010: 1), including 'a plummeting standard of living, a relocalization of mobility patterns, an increasing emphasis upon local warlords controlling recycled forms of mobility and weaponry, [...] relatively weak imperial or national forms of governance' and 'increasing separation between different regions or "tribes"' (2010: 17).[13] The movement and mobility that characterized capitalism in the twentieth century thus sows the seeds of its own destruction. There is a contradictory logic at work where progress – more travel, more movement, more consumption, etc. – is at once future oriented and organized around the present. In this sense, as I discuss more in Chapter 4, one of the ways in which the future can be understood is in terms of what Helga Nowotny (1994) calls 'the extended present', whereby 'the future mapped out in linear terms draws dangerously close to the present' (1994: 49–50) and 'is increasingly overshadowed by the problems which are opening up in the present' (1994: 50).

As is becoming clear then, one of the central ways in which the future is seen as becoming increasingly important is through its connection with technological changes. Indeed, science and technology studies (STS) is one of the primary ways in which sociology has examined the future – theoretically and empirically – in particular, through a focus on the expectations that emerge out of and are attached to technological innovation (Brown and Michael 2003; Borup *et al.* 2006). In this context, Mads Borup *et al.* (2006) discuss how innovation in contemporary science and technology (including membrane technology, neural computing, gene therapy and pharmacogenomics and nanotechnology) 'is an intensely future-oriented business with an emphasis on the creation of new opportunities and capabilities' (2006: 285). Their interest is in the *expectations* of such technological developments because:

> Expectations are foundational in the coordination of different actor communities and groups (horizontal co-ordination) and also mediate between different scales or levels of organization (micro, meso, and macro – vertical co-ordination). They also change over time in response and adaptation to new conditions or emergent problems (temporal co-ordination). Likewise, expectations link technical and social issues, because expectations and visions refer to images of the future, where technical and social aspects are tightly intertwined.
>
> (2006: 286)

Borup *et al.*'s argument here is that the expectations of science and technology resonate, or are relevant across, different temporalities, different scales or levels of organization and different groups or communities. Moreover, these expectations *organize* or *co-ordinate* these different temporalities, scales and groups. While the focus of Borup *et al.*'s and my interests are clearly distinct, what their argument indicates for this book is that futurity is experienced at the different scales of the bodily *and* socio-cultural level, *and* is involved in the organization of these different levels. Taking this point seriously involves exploring how the images of transformation at stake in this book involve expectations about the future. In what ways do these expectations feed into and map onto how socio-cultural life is organized? How do images of the future co-ordinate bodily potential?

The following case study chapters explore in more detail the specificity of the futures of different images, but I have already suggested that images of transformation in general promise a better future. As well as *expectations*, then, the future also involves *promises*. In the context of the futures of science and technology, for example, Borup *et al.* explain:

> While expectations in their general form can be defined as the state of looking forward (from Latin, *exspectatio*, looking, waiting for), technological expectations can more specifically be described as real-time representations of future technological situations and capabilities. Similar terms, which are commonly used, like technological 'promises' and 'visions' are largely overlapping with 'expectations' but emphasize to a higher degree their enacting and subjectively normative character. They stress that expectations are wishful enactments of a desired future.
>
> (2006: 286)

To begin to connect up the socio-cultural and the bodily, Borup *et al.*'s point, here, indicates that the expectations of (different and specific) futures become enacted as the (different and specific) promises of the future. According to this view, expectations can be understood as *images of the future* and promises can be understood as the *feelings and ways of living out* the image. In this sense, as Borup *et al.* argue, through the wishful enactment of a desired future, expectations 'are made real and [...] expectations can be understood as *performative*' (2006: 286, my emphasis). Indeed, in his study on scientific technologists, Van Lente argues that

> The resulting dynamics of this unstoppable train [of technological progress], and of self-justifying technology in general, is a conversion of promises into requirements. Once technical promises are shared they demand action, and appear as a necessity for technologists to develop, and for others to support them. At the same time, the options that are considered feasible and promising are translated into requirements, guidelines and specifications.
>
> (Van Lente 2000: 57–58)

As such, Van Lente identifies within science and technology discourse and practice a pervasive 'option-promise-requirement-necessity sequence', (2000: 60) whereby 'what starts as an *option* can be labeled as a technical *promise*, and may subsequently function as a *requirement* to be achieved, and a *necessity* for technologists to work on, and for others to support' (2000: 60). Promises are performative in that they become requirements and necessities.

It is not only in science and technology that futures function in terms of promises. Indeed, in relation to the images of transformation examined here, it is interesting to note that Sara Ahmed (2010) argues that *happiness* operates as a promise that 'gives us a specific image of the future' (2010: 29). In this sense, 'the promising nature of happiness suggests happiness lies ahead of us, at least if we do the right thing. To promise after all is to make the future into an object, into something that can be declared in advance of its arrival' (2010: 29). Moreover, for Ahmed, happiness has become an expectation, so that achieving the promise of happiness is understood by individuals as what Van Lente might describe as a requirement or necessity. However, Ahmed argues that happiness is organized according to dominant cultural norms and scripts, thus the promise of happiness prioritizes certain ways of life and is achievable only by those who are willing and able to follow these specific routes and paths. For those who are positioned as Other to the dominant modes of embodiment and subjectivity, the cultural imperative to happiness is rendered unachievable, and the happy future that is expected and demanded is impossible. Ahmed's interest is in how the happy future works normatively, to exclude certain kinds of people. In this book, I am interested in how the image of the better future works to pull in certain kinds of people and, in this way as I have indicated above, is involved in the creation and re-creation of difference. That is, I suggest that working through the promise of a better future, images of transformation appeal to those whose presents are currently difficult. Moreover, as a promise, I suggest that this appeal becomes a requirement; necessitating certain people to transform.

Images, futures, anticipation and affect

Arguing that images of transformation promise a future that is better than the present is not to suggest that the future will necessarily turn out to be better than the present. As is made clear in the discussion so far, the future may very well turn out in various ways to be not as good as the present and past. My focus in this book is thus on understanding the future *as an image of a better life*, and on exploring what happens when the future functions as an image. This is to attend to the ways in which images play a central role in contemporary capitalism in producing and arranging the kinds of expectations, promises and visions that can become material(ized). One of the ways in which I want to address this issue is to return to my discussion above, concerning the virtual and suggest that, *as images*, the futures that transformation are seen to promise operate *as potential*. While there are clearly particular routes and plans that images of transformation propose as the means to achieve the futures they imply – dieting, cosmetic surgery, shopping, healthy eating and exercise – as images the potential of these futures cannot be contained within these routines. As images, the futures of transformation work not only in terms of the actual but also the virtual, not only as materialities but also as immaterialities. In this sense, images can be understood in Lisa Adkins' (2008) terms as 'engaged in the creation of potential' (2008: 194). That is, while depicting particular ways in which a better future body can be planned for and achieved (through wearing clothes in styles that suit a certain body shape, dieting, cosmetic surgery for example), at the same time images of transformation involve the future as *potential*, a future that escapes or exceeds the specifics of planning or its location within an object or a product, a future that involves the not-yet. Images of transformation are thus potentialities in that they function as immaterial possibilities/virtuals that might be actualized.

What is of particular importance to the argument I make in this book is that, as potential, the futures of images of transformation are pervasive, appealing and powerful because they are *affective*. The promises made by images of transformation are affective in that they address hopes and dreams of a better future, and engage the body through the intensity of feeling. Images of transformation contain something that is 'waiting to happen'; 'This future, while it has not yet happened, is held in anticipation by the image' (Lury 1998: 103). While anticipation has been theorized in relation to the image, according to Vincanne Adams *et al.* (2009), it is also more generally a 'defining quality of our current moment' (2009: 247). For these authors, whose focus is on the implication of young girls in contemporary biomedical practices, 'anticipation now names a particularly self-evident "futurism" in which our "presents" are necessarily understood as contingent upon an ever-changing astral future that may or may not be known for certain, but still must be acted on' (2009: 247). Moreover – and crucially for my argument here – anticipation defined as such is an '*affective state*':

> Anticipation is the palpable effect of the speculative future on the present. [...] *As an affective state, anticipation is not just a reaction, but a way of actively orienting oneself temporally.* Anticipation is a regime of being in time, in which one inhabits time out of place as the future.
>
> (2009: 247)

While the specificities of the biomedical practices at stake for Adams *et al.* and images of transformation of interest in this book are clearly different, what is of significance in the identification of anticipation as a 'defining quality' of contemporary social and cultural life is that it is an affective state that requires a temporal orientation to the future. Adams *et al.* describe this as a temporal orientation to the future 'as if the future is what matters most. Anticipatory modes enable the production of possible futures that are *lived* and *felt* as inevitable in the present' (2009: 248). As an affective state, anticipation can be understood as the future being affectively felt and oriented around – seemingly inevitably – in the present.

Adams *et al.*'s point that the future has become the dominant temporality is also made by Brian Massumi (2005) who focuses on, what he calls neo-conservative capitalism.[14] Discussing the form that economic projections take on following 9/11 – an argument I return to and explicate further in Chapter 5 – Massumi explains a shift from sovereign power and biopolitical power to neo-liberal power. Neo-liberal power is characterized by a rationality or logic that works, not through 'a conformal truth deducible from first principles (as were the foundational truths of sovereign power)', nor through 'a normative law arrived at by induction (as in the liberal-disciplinary regime of biopolitical power)' (2005: 3). Rather, neo-liberal power is *affective*: organized around fear and what is seen as its corrective correlate, (consumer) confidence; consumers must be encouraged to have confidence in the financial system so as to stave off the uncertainty at its heart. For example, in the case of 9/11, '[t]he most immediately articulable response, amid the horror of first impact, was the fear that the attack would lower public confidence to the point that a recession would trigger' (2005: 5), hence, the 'exhortations to the public from government officials to *keep shopping*' (2005: 3). Fear is a threat, an affective anticipation of what might yet happen that must be acted on in the present: 'Threat triggers fear. The fear is of disruption. The fear *is* disruption' (2005: 8). Perhaps the most fundamental disruption that fear triggers is to the linear progression of time. The anticipation of fear, Massumi argues, functions as a threat, 'an indefinite future tense: what may yet come' (2005: 3). Therefore, it is the future that that becomes the focus of attention. Discussing the example of the need to maintain consumer confidence in the United States immediately following 9/11, Massumi argues,

> The hope that confidence will be restored, and the fear that it won't, shifts the centre of gravity of economic reasoning from the past-present axis describing trends whose arc will continue more or less predictably into the future, onto a present-future axis wobbling with uncertainty, trembling in anticipation of fear.
>
> (2005: 3)

Thus, to be effective, to take uncertainty into account and to negate it with confidence, the political axis must shift 'to *act on the future*' (2005: 3).[15] Furthermore, '[i]n agreeing to act on the future, government is agreeing to *act on time*' (2005: 5). The shift from the dominance of the past-present axis to the present-future axis is what Adkins has called 'a material reworking of time itself' (Adkins 2009: 335). Massumi argues that '[t]o act on the future, the first thing that must be done is to sidestep or suspend this blurry present' (Massumi 2005: 5). He discusses President – or 'commander-in-chief'[16] – George W. Bush's dislike of deliberation, which became linked to a reliance on the factual and depicted as waffling or 'verbosity lead[ing] to unclear, inarticulate things' (Bush quoted in Massumi 2005: 5).[17] In contrast to decision-making that relied on facts, the neo-conservatist government preferred the 'directly affective' (2005: 5). This is a distinctive form of 'command power' that sidesteps or suspends the uncertainty of a present that demands deliberation and moves instead straight to the future.[18] As such, for Bush's government,

A trustable decision is not made in any dangerously deliberative way. A confident decision strikes like lightening. It *happens*.

(2005: 5)[19]

This happening of decision-making eliminates the present; this is instead an affective temporality whereby the future is *pre-empted*. This pre-emption 'overlays' the before and after of decision-making so that '[t]he before-after seizes the moment. The future-past colonizes the present' (2005: 6). The present is wiped out, felt only as an affective anticipation of what might come.

I return to the issues of anticipation and pre-emption in Chapter 5 and the Conclusion. Here though, it is worth highlighting how the mode of power that Massumi describes can be understood in Lash's terms of potential and intensity. That is, it is a mode of power that engages the body 'directly'; through affect.[20] In particular, here potential indicates a temporal disruption or re-working of linear time. My argument is that this kind of temporality is affective and that a key way in which this mode of power as affective potential works is through images. Images are affective potential. They contain within them the virtual future, and they co-ordinate the ways in which this future is oriented around. As such, the relationship between the futures promised by images of transformation and the ways in which those futures are felt and lived out in the present can be understood, I suggest, through affect. Put another way, in order to trace the actualization of the virtual, it is necessary to consider how the potential of the future is intensively felt in and as the present. In the rest of the book, the materialization of the immaterial is explored through the modes of looking, interaction, action and experience that different images of transformation arrange and encourage. As I have suggested above, such a project is concerned to connect up the bodily and the socio-cultural; to focus on the affectivity of images is not to concentrate only on transformation as an individualized project, but rather to consider the ways in which an impulse for *self*-transformation is entangled with a wider socio-cultural imperative of transformation which itself is integral to contemporary capitalism.

As will become clear, the book is interested in examining often quite mundane transformative processes. This is intended to focus attention on how a transformative logic, which emphasizes movement, change, becoming and is organized around a promise for a better future, is deeply embedded within contemporary culture. As I have argued above, the vital and experimental processes of transformation operate through 'the routine, even boring' (Thrift 2005: 3). Indeed, as Berlant (2008) argues, 'tender fantasies of a better good life' (2008: 1) permeate popular culture and are powerful, precisely through their entrenchment within conventionality and normalcy. Thus, the 'good intention' required to believe in the fantasy of the better good life 'produces an orientation toward agency that is focused on ongoing adaptation, adjustment, improvisation, and developing wiles for surviving, thriving, and transcending the world as it presents itself' (2008: 2). I return to Berlant's work in the Conclusion, but I want to point out here that to explore the organization of everyday feelings is to take seriously the appeal of the conventional. This is not to be 'on the side' of conventionality but to examine how aspirations towards a normal life are felt through everyday images and processes of transformation. This is a particularly important project for an understanding of how contemporary socio-cultural differences are a process that takes place on and through the body.

Overview of the book

The rest of the book is structured around a chapter that further develops the theoretical framework of the book and a series of case study chapters, each of which take up a different screen through which images of transformation are organized. These are the interfaces of interactive mirrors (Chapter 2), makeover television screens (Chapter 3), the computer screens of internet dieting (Chapter 4) and the various advertising screens and surfaces through which the public health campaign in England, Change4Life, operates (Chapter 5). It is worth pointing out here that the book covers a range of different images of transformation, in part, because of my interest in tracking how the imperative of transformation circulates via a wide range of different sites. As such, while the case study chapters each build on the Introduction and Chapter 1 in order to attend, in more detail, to the specific kinds of bodies to which the imperative of transformation affectively appeal, they can also function as (almost) stand-alone case studies. The case study chapters therefore do not need to be read linearly to make sense. Each of the chapters concludes with an issue that is returned to in the Conclusion: the idea of indeterminacy or being open to suggestion (Chapter 2); a re-thinking of what critique might involve if power is intensive (Chapter 3); the version of measure that is at work if power is inventive (Chapter 4); and the way in which social differences are being made and remade through temporality (Chapter 5).

Drawing on the discussion of transformation in the Introduction, Chapter 1 focuses on how affect has been theorized in relation to images. It frames this discussion through three specific concerns that the affective turn has raised: (1) that affect is central to how social and cultural life operate; (2) that affect requires a re-thinking of the body (Blackman and Venn 2010) and; (3) that theories of affect problematize representational thinking (Thrift 2007; Blackman and Venn 2010; Coleman 2009). Working with these concerns, the chapter argues that a problematization of representational thinking has significant consequences for the way in which images have tended to be approached through a model of the politics of representation, where they are analysed in terms of their representational practices and deciphered for their ideological message. Shifting to a concern with not so much what an image is *of*, as what images *do*, requires, in turn, a shift in how to conceive bodies. The chapter introduces the screen as one of the organizing themes of the book and discusses how a focus on the screen raises questions about the ways in which the affectivity of images is framed, arranged and engaged with; how is affect screened and in what ways are screens affective? The chapter argues that, far from containing the image, *screens bring the image to life* through the ways in which they are looked at and interacted with. Thus, affective images are felt and lived out and images of transformation, which indicate a materially different and better future, function as virtuals that are (seen as) capable of being actualized. The chapter then moves to outline the way in which this actualization of the virtual is addressed in the book through an attention to materialization, or, put simply, to how images are brought to life as specific kinds of bodies – specific ways of living.

Indeed, the actualization of virtual images is one of the key themes of the case study chapters, in which I argue that different screens arrange or co-ordinate intensive experiences differently. At stake in the chapters is how images of transformation are actualized through the *experience* of shopping (Chapter 2), the modes of *looking* that makeover television encourages for some viewers (Chapter 3), the *interaction* with online dieting plans (Chapter 4) and the *action or activity* that is impelled for some bodies through the Change4Life campaign (Chapter 5). These different processes of actualization are not intended to suggest that virtual images are made concrete once and for all. Actualization is not a one-off or finished project. Rather, as I have discussed in this chapter, my conception of images as virtuals, as affective potentials, draws attention to how images are always excessive. If actualization is never fully complete, never fully concrete, this implies also that materialization is itself a continual process of change and transformation. I discuss this in Chapter 1, but here it should be noted that the intensive experiences, modes of looking and interaction, and the activity that I suggest images of transformation work through are also processual, unfinished. The kinds of bodies that they bring to life are thus themselves always in the process of change. This is especially important to note in relation to images of transformation: transformation is an ongoing process.

While being a stand-alone case study chapter, Chapter 2 also acts as a bridge between the more theoretically focused and example-led chapters in taking up the idea that images function not (only) as representations but in terms of aliveness, affect and intensity. Its focus is on interactive mirrors, and in particular those designed to be part of a 'revitalized' in-store shopping experience. This attention to shopping highlights how consumer culture is, as Featherstone argues, both saturated with images and a key means through which transformation is organized. The chapter explores the popular assumption that mirrors are an unmediated technology which simply 'reflect' the body in front of them and instead considers the mirror as a screen; an interface that both appears and disappears, is transparent and reflective, making the consumer aware of its presence at some points and unaware at others (Bolter and Gromala 2005). Taking up predictions that screens and 'the virtual' will be an increasingly significant aspect of shopping, the chapter considers the ways in which the interactive mirrors bring the virtual into the actual and, in doing so, help to create an intensive experience. It concludes by thinking through the ways in which power is working through intensity.

Chapter 2 sets up ideas on the role of the screen in organizing the gendering and classing of intensive experiences. These are taken up in Chapter 3, which focuses on makeover television as a prevalent way in which ideas about the

28 Introduction

transformation of the body are circulated. The chapter considers the affectivity of such images, and argues that the television screen 'disappears' for certain viewers. Drawing on recent theoretical, textual and empirical research on makeover and reality television, the chapter argues that makeover programmes resonate with the bodies of working-class women so that what is seen 'on screen' is not distanced from these viewers but is immanently felt and experienced as both pleasurable and problematic. As such, I argue that taking seriously the immanent experience of makeover television requires a re-thinking of critique in order to understand and intervene in contemporary power relations.

Chapters 4 and 5 are both concerned with how the imperative of transformation is experienced through a problematization of weight. Chapter 4 examines the screen of Weight Watchers online dieting websites and plans. It argues that, while the screen of makeover television disappears, in order to analyse the affectivity of the images of the better future that these websites produce, it is necessary to attend to the screen itself. Taking up the conception of power as inventive, outlined above, this chapter explores the way in which dieting has often been framed in terms of discipline and repression and proposes instead an attention to dieting as productive and enabling. This is not to suggest that dieting is 'empowering' but rather to attend to the ways in which dieting is organized around the suggestion that transformation extends agency (Heyes 2006) through prioritizing a better (slimmer) future. It is to be concerned with dieting as productive and inventive. This is particularly the case with *online* dieting, where dieters *interact with* the screen and can be described as constructing their own 'route through' (A. Wood 2007) the temporalities of dieting. The chapter explores the ways in which these routes are co-ordinated by 'attractors' (A. Wood 2007; de Landa 2002) and considers the forms of measure that emerge from this interaction; measures that are not so much set externally, but that emanate from the relationship established between the dieter and the online dieting plan.

Chapter 5 develops the argument that dieting emphasizes the future as potential through an analysis of the British government's Change4Life campaign. In particular, it explores the temporalities of the campaign which aim to prevent – or pre-empt – future bad health by bringing the future into the present and requiring this future to be acted on now. It argues that through the affective anticipation of future concerns in the present, the images of the campaign 'move from' billboards, television and computer screens to become embodied experiences, felt and lived out in and as the present. The chapter analyses how it is that certain bodies more than others are caught up in the imperative to change for life, and concludes by considering how, in requiring these bodies to live out a pre-emptive politics, time itself has become an organizing principle of difference. The Conclusion takes up the challenge to linear time that the Change4Life campaign implies and discusses recent arguments in cultural, feminist and queer theory about the relationship between and status of the present and future. It returns to the question of the virtual and actual, and argues that an examination of the actualization of the virtual is a helpful project for sociology to extend.

1 Screening affect

Images, representational thinking and the actualization of the virtual

In the Introduction, I proposed that images of transformation be understood not only in terms of what they are of but also as potential, that is in terms of what they *do*. This potential, while taking the form of certain practices, also exists in excess of them, and thus is processual in that it is not exhausted or completed. In this way, images as potential function as virtuals; they are intensive and transformative intangibles. This book conceives images as potential and explores both the appeal of the image as potential and some of the ways in which this potential is actualized, is felt and lived out. In beginning to discuss how the image functions as potential, in the previous chapter I identified the centrality of futurity. Images of transformation, I suggest, involve *the future* as potential, in that the future is seen to be (capable of being made to be) materially better. As I have discussed, much has – quite rightly – been written on the neo-liberal and regulatory underpinnings of the imperative of transformation; at a socio-cultural level, transformation is tied up with a capitalist logic of progress, and at an individualized embodied level, transformation is part of a process in which individuals are forced to take on increased responsibility for their own success and failure. The future, according to this perspective, is that which is understood to unfold in a linear manner from the present.

While these theories are adept at accounting for the regimes that images of (self-)transformation put in place, they can miss or overlook their popularity and appeal; their affectivity. As such, I want to explore further the ways in which transformation is such a prevalent and attractive idea. In this book, I examine the ways in which interactive mirrors, makeover television, online dieting and government health campaigns involve an image of a better future that also operates outside or in excess of the ways in which that future might be seen as the result of a linear plan. This is to see the future of images of transformation as open, as alive, as potential. It is in these ways that I want to suggest that the future is affective.

The previous chapter introduced some of the theories of intensity, potential, the virtual and temporality that I will take up and develop in the book. Drawing on these theories, in this chapter I discuss what has been called the 'affective turn' in social and cultural theory, and focus on how affect has been, and can be, conceived in relation to images. This includes a re-thinking of the dominance of a model of representational thinking about images in sociology. In particular, I suggest, theories of affect require a shift from representation(alism) to 'the surface'. With this in mind, I examine how images might then be theorized, and introduce the screen as a key theme of the book. The screen, I argue, is a surface or a line that frames and organizes the affectivity of images through how ways of seeing, modes of interaction and experience are made possible, or not. The relationship between the imperative of transformation, the future as potential and the feeling and living out of the image is then considered; I return to the idea of the actualization of the virtual and discuss this in terms of the process of materialization. The aim of this and the previous chapter is therefore to set out the theoretical framework that is taken up in relation to the following case studies.

The 'affective turn'

It is not coincidental that I am thinking affect and images of transformation together. While there is a long history of exploring the affective and emotional, not least in work that takes a feminist approach, theories of affect have recently come to occupy a more prominent position in social and cultural theory. In terms of the case studies in this book, in the context of research on consumer culture, for example, the relationship between emotions, imagination and consumption has been considered by Eva Illouz (2009), who argues that more than other concepts such as desire, emotion is able to account for both the socio-cultural system of consumer capitalism and the more specific and embodied responses to particular 'images, pictures and concepts of consumer products (as in advertising)' (2009: 383). As such, '[c]onsumer culture is [...] saturated with affects because the signifying capacity of goods is their main attraction' (2009: 383), and an attention to emotion enables a consideration of 'the relationship of the self to its environment' (2009: 383). With a specific focus on the branding of spaces, Liz Moor (2003) has argued that contemporary marketing seeks to 'forg[e] durable affective connections between consumer and brand across time and space' (2003: 47). The branding of spaces creates an 'experience', and it is these affective and emotional experiences that become central to the relationship between consumer and brand, between the body/self and the wider environment (see Chapters 2 and 5). In research on makeover television, the relationship between affect and images of transformation has also been highlighted. For example, Tania Lewis (2008) argues that makeover programmes have links with popular television genres including melodrama, sit-coms and dramas because of their emphasis on emotion (Lewis 2008: 442; see also Gorton 2009), and Skeggs (2009) links 'self-transformational television' with a classed affect where the audience 'see affect-in-action, people out of and in control, relationships visualized, broken-down and opened-out, amplified in intimate detail' (2009: 234, see Chapter 3). It is clear, then, that the imperative to transform, which is distributed across different media and socio-cultural sites, has an affective dimension.

The concerns and foci of the affective turn in social and cultural theory are wide-ranging and have been well documented (for overviews see, for example, such collections as Blackman and Venn 2010; Gregg and Seigworth 2010; Clough with Halley 2007). While it is not my intention to rehearse these overviews, it is worth mapping out the field in a little more detail. Of importance here, is that one of the key routes of emergence of a revived interest in affect comes from work over the last three decades on the body. Indeed, Gregory J. Seigworth and Melissa Gregg (2010) argue that, since 1995 when two influential essays on affect were published, there have been two dominant, though not all-encompassing,[1] trends in theorizing affect that emerge from thinking about and through the body. The first angle follows from the work of psychologist Silvan Tomkins, whose ideas were reinvigorated by Eve Kosofsky Sedgwick and Adam Frank's (1995) essay, 'Shame in the cybernetic fold' (and later by Sedgwick's book *Touching Feeling: Affect, Pedagogy, Performativity*, 2003). Tomkins differentiated a range of eight different affects: interest-excitement; enjoyment-joy; surprise-startle; distress-anguish; anger-rage; fear-terror; dissmell (or revulsion at a bad smell) and disgust. These affects are, for Tomkins; neurological, biological and physiological, and his theory thus 'follows a quasi-Darwinian "innate-ist" bent towards matters of evolutionary hardwiring' (Seigworth and Gregg 2010: 5). Affects for Tomkins are located 'within' the body and can be identified as discrete reactions and responses to 'outside' influences.

Taking as its starting point this 'innate-ist bent', where 'the body' is broadly conceived as universal, cultural theory has begun to develop Tomkins' work to include attention towards the influence of social and cultural relations. For example, Anna Gibbs (2010) takes up Tomkins' work because of its ability to 'chart with […] some precision' (2010: 195) the translation of affects between different bodies and subjects. Discussing the engagement between mother and baby, Gibbs argues that this translation helps to 'order' experience into 'affective scripts' that provide a sense of on-goingness and continuity to the bodies and subjects involved: mother and baby recognize each other and their relation to each other. In this sense, 'affect *organizes*, both intra- and inter-corporeally, though it does so in very different ways in different cultures' (2010: 196). Similarly, in her work on shame, Elspeth Probyn (2005) explains her position as beginning from the point that 'shame is biologically innate – we are all born with the capacity for shame' as a means to consider our 'human similarities' (2005: xiii). She goes on to argue that:

> This is not to say that we all experience shame in the same way or that some will not be more vulnerable to shame. I experience shame differently from an Aboriginal man. But surely that does not annul our shared capacity for feeling it. […] When we deny shame or ignore it, we lose a crucial opportunity to reflect on what makes us different and the same.
>
> (2005: xiv)

In these accounts of affect, working from the inside-out becomes a way of tracing processes that move from the biological to the socio-cultural and, in so doing, provides a means of probing the boundaries between nature/culture and examining further cultural similarities and difference.

If this first tradition of affect works from the inside-out, the second trend in affect theory can be understood as working from the outside-in.[2] This second approach, which derives largely from a Deleuzian tradition (and which includes Spinozian and Bergsonian ideas), has been taken up by social and cultural theory following Brian Massumi's (1995) essay 'The autonomy of affect' (and later his book *Parables for the Virtual: Movement, Affect, Sensation*, 2002). Seigworth and Gregg define this perspective as 'locat[ing] affect in the midst of things and relations (in immanence) and, then, in the complex assemblages that come to compose bodies and worlds simultaneously' (2010: 6). In this account, affect is relational; 'in the midst of things'. Moreover, affect is also constitutive. That is, in contrast to the inside-out model of affect, where affects are innate and *then* come to shape relations between different bodies and subjects, this Deleuzian account of affect argues that it is *through* the affective relations between things that these things come to take shape, come into being/becoming. As Deleuze says, drawing on Spinoza, a body can be defined in terms of its capacities to 'affect [...] other bodies, or [be] affected by other bodies' (1992: 625); it is through these affective relations that bodies are constituted.

Massumi (2002) argues that this latter account of affect shifts the emphasis of empirical inquiry away from a focus on things themselves and towards an attention to how things are produced, created and invented through their relations with other things (see also Coleman 2009). This approach therefore connects with the ways in which I have so far discussed my approach to images of transformation as linking up a socio-cultural emphasis on transformation with a bodily feeling that transformation is necessary and desirable. Drawing on contemporary social and cultural theory, my argument is that capitalism functions as intensive change and process and that this intensive change and process is felt in and co-produced by bodies. Bodies and the world are thus in these affective relations, and co-produce each other. In this sense, as I suggested in the Introduction, it is not so much a case of an individual's agency being constrained or liberated by social structures as it is that the individual and the social are in affective relations with each other: are affected by each other, are invented through each other. It is this idea that is examined further in this book.

Affect, relationality, process

While it is clear that the 'affective turn' traverses a range of issues relevant both to the body and contemporary socio-cultural life, three specific inter-linked assertions made by this approach to theorizing affect are of significance to my argument in this book: (1) an emphasis on relationality and process; (2) a related concern with the body (or materiality) as process and (3) a re-working of representational thinking. The first takes up the emphasis on relationality and process outlined in the 'outside-in' approach to affect discussed above, in its understanding of contemporary social and cultural life as characterized by 'aliveness and vitality' (Clough 2007: 2), as 'changed and changing' and as 'exceed[ing] all efforts to contain it' (2007: 28). In terms of my focus here then, images of transformation can be understood as affective not only through how they might be felt but also because they are themselves concerned with change and transformation; they are affective in their 'aliveness' and emphasis on process. Indeed, as Banet-Weiser and Portwood-Stacer (2006) argue, in makeover television programmes there is a shift from 'the visual presentation of the *result* of a female liberal subjectivity' to the 'physical evidence of transformation' (2006: 265): '[T]he *process* has become the product' (2006: 265, my emphasis). Affect is thus inherent to the way in which I discussed my approach to images of transformation in the Introduction, where I suggested that the contemporary logic of transformation be understood in terms of process and intensity.

A second and related emphasis of the affective turn that is of significance here is on what Lisa Blackman and Couze Venn (2010) call a re-thinking of 'what [...] we mean when we invoke, examine and enact the *body* in *body*-studies' (2010: 8). Blackman and Venn identify a theoretical shift in the affective turn to understand 'bodies as processes (rather than fixed unchanging objects or entities)' (2010: 9). This consideration of the body as process is part of the wider move in social and cultural theory that I have outlined so far, where research questions examine, not so much what something 'is' as what things 'can do'. In the Introduction, I discussed how asking not what an image is but what it can do is key to the exploration carried out in this book, and I return to that question below. Blackman and Venn discuss how asking 'what can a body do?'

> shifts our focus to consider how bodies are always thoroughly entangled processes, and importantly defined by their capacities to affect and be affected. These capacities are mediated and afforded by practices and technologies which modulate and augment the body's potential for mediation.
>
> (2010: 9)

Indeed, one of the ways in which this theorization of affect has been deemed necessary is in relation to what Patricia Ticineto Clough (2007) terms 'a new configuration of bodies, technology, and matter' (2007: 2) produced by

> changing global processes of accumulating capital and employing labour power through the deployment of technoscience to reach beyond the limitations of the human in experimentation with the structure and organization of the human body, or what is called 'life itself'.
>
> (2007: 3)

In earlier work, Clough (2000) has theorized the relationship between bodies, technology and the social through a focus on television, where television is 'the machine central to the technology defining postmodernity' (2000: 10). While Clough's work is extensive in its attention to postmodern and poststructuralist cultural theory, one specific aspect of it is significant to the argument developed in this book, and to the ways in which virtual images are actualized: are made material. This concerns the prevalence of Marxist arguments about culture in the 1970s and 1980s and the implications this tradition had on defining images as texts to be understood in terms of their ideological effects. This Marxist approach is important given that I have set out as one of the tasks of this book, an attempt to conceive images as affects rather than as texts to be read. In particular, Clough discusses Fredrick Jameson's (1984) essay on the cultural logics of postmodernity which took television as one of its foci. Clough argues that,

> [n]o matter what was argued in this debate, culture seemed to flatten out into a barrage of meaningless texts. Jameson, along with other Marxist cultural critics, all but sealed the fate of the concept of textuality. They both linked textuality to the superficial and connected it to the development of technology, which, however, was reduced to the capitalist organization of production.
>
> (Clough 2000: 9)[3]

For example, in Jameson's essay, postmodern culture is seen as a series of inter-related and self-referential texts; in comparing Andy Warhol's *Diamond Dust Shoes* with Vincent Van Gogh's painting, *A Pair of Boots*, for instance, Jameson sees the latter as bringing into being a whole world associated with the peasant's life – in particular, nature and the peasant's seemingly intimate relationship with the earth – while the world of Warhol's art has 'lost its depth and threatens to become a glossy skin, a stereoscopic illusion, a rush of filmic images without density' (Jameson 1984: 76–77).[4] As such, for Jameson, Warhol's art posits the world not in terms of content but instead as 'a set of texts or simulacra' (1984: 60). Implicit in Jameson's argument, then, is a conception of culture as 'really' or 'authentically' deep and meaningful, a density that postmodernity has flattened out and therefore distorted or denigrated. As Clough points out, this superficiality of postmodern texts is linked with the development of technology; the mechanical way in which Warhol's art is produced and reproduced – screen-printing, found objects rather than the artist's brushstrokes on canvas – means the artwork is detached from the world it depicts and from the artist's labour and is instead connected to systems of economic exchange. Technology, then, is in binary opposition to nature and to authentic art, and, moreover, *distorts* nature.

While this relationship between nature and culture is interesting in and of itself, Clough argues it has specific consequences for cultural theory, and for cultural theories of television in particular. Discussing the Birmingham school's approach to television, which emerged prior to but was nevertheless later influenced by, Jameson's argument, Clough suggests that television is understood primarily in terms of ideology. For example, Stuart Hall's emphasis on encoding/decoding prioritizes the audience's reading and interpretation (decoding) of the ideological messages encoded within television texts. 'Without addressing the specificity of television as a medium', Clough argues that Hall,

> treated the television text as a discrete cultural production that, for him, raised the question of how the circulated text is consumed, that is how it is read. For Hall, however, the question of how a text is read was a question about ideology. Abandoning the idea of class-specific ideologies, Hall preferred instead to focus on the political action of hegemony. He therefore assumed that television texts carry 'the dominant hegemonic discourse' and are aimed to win 'active consent' for a symbolic order or the belief in the way things are. The television text is therefore to be treated in terms of the larger ideological struggle between 'the people' and the dominant discourse of a symbolic order.
>
> (2000: 72)

In the previous chapter I indicated the problem for this book in treating images in terms of hegemony and ideology and drawing on recent social theory, I suggested that power no longer or not only works in terms of ideology and hegemony but instead or as well engages the body affectively. Below, I develop a conception of images that seeks to account for the affectivity of the image, that is for how the image is in excess of a representational text.[5] At stake in Clough's argument though, is a desire to re-work the focus on television as ideological texts and to conceive television as a technology that is not opposed to 'authentic' culture or the body, but is constitutive of bodies, and of the very ways in which cultural theory is able to think the body.

For Clough then, television is 'not primarily about texts' (2000: 75) but is rather a machine, a circuit, communication; an 'autoaffective', social unconscious. Television is not involved in making a distinction between production and reception but is, especially in its contemporary connection with computers, 'beyond a broadcast model' (2000: 96); 'Transmitting both entertainment and information, television will always be on' (2000: 96). As a circuit or machine that is 'always on', television as a technology is not separate to nature or the body; it is not a set of texts, for example, that work on or inscribe a body through its dominant ideological messages. As such,

> nature and technology, body and machine, the virtual and the real, and the living and the inert might be understood in terms of *differential* relationships rather than oppositionals or even dialectical ones. [...] the body and the machine, the virtual and the real, and nature and technology are inextricably implicated, always already interlaced.
>
> (2000: 11)

Clough suggests that television and the viewer cannot be conceived in terms of a

> 'subject-system', that is, a technological system understood to be perfecting the human being, serving as an extension of the human body, while maintaining

the intentional knowing subject at its centre and as its agency. Instead, television makes the subject only one element in a 'network imagination' of teletechnology.

(2000: 99, references omitted)

Displacing the human from the centre of analysis, the relations between technologies and bodies are conceived as a system, or assemblage, where what is at stake is not oppositions but rather *difference*. The system that attaches television and the viewer is forged through continuous and affective communication:

> [t]elevision aims primarily to capture attention and modulate affect through a logic of exposure, over- and underexposure; television works [...] in attaching the screen/image and the body. To borrow from Beller's description, television is able 'to burrow into the flesh'.
>
> (2000: 99, reference omitted)

The body, as conceived by Clough, is therefore actively constituted through its affective relations with technology, with the screen/image. The body is thus always in process, is the actualization of the virtuality of the social unconscious that technologies such as television produce. In this sense, as Blackman and Venn put it, in conceiving the body, 'affect is invoked to gesture towards something that perhaps escapes or remains in excess of the practices of the "speaking subject"' (2010: 9). For Clough, what escapes or remains in excess of the 'speaking subject' is the affective relations between bodies and television (and media more widely): the system that connects the body to technology. These relations between bodies and technology cannot be contained within the textual approach theorized by early cultural studies. Clough's argument can be understood in light of Lash's argument about 'post-hegemonic' power that I discussed in the Introduction, as both suggest that discourse and hegemony are now only part of the way in which power works today. In the highly mediated worlds that they describe, images address the body directly, intensively and affectively. Media are materials/materialized: they 'burrow into the flesh' as Clough refers to, or work through the body, inventing the body as Lash puts it. In terms of the case studies discussed in this book, I suggest that images of transformation work in this way. Images of transformation engage the body. They work not (only) as texts, but (also) as affects that become materialized. For Blackman and Venn, the affective turn involves a re-working of the problem of what Blackman and Venn term 'representational thinking'. This problematization of representational thinking constitutes the third means by which the affective turn is taken up and concerns a reconceptualization of images.

Affect and representational thinking

Representational thinking is a mode of thought that has ontologically and epistemologically organized sociology and other social science disciplines. For

John Law and Kevin Hetherington (1998), representational thinking 'images or performs a distinction between a pre-existing real world to be described, and its description' (1998: 2).[6] Recently, social and cultural theorists have challenged representationalism by arguing that descriptions of the world are involved in the constitution of those worlds; descriptions are not separate from the 'real world' but performative of it. For example, Thrift's (2005) argument, discussed in the Introduction, is one account of what he terms 'non-representational theory'. Thrift argues that calculations and predictions come to take on flesh; they exist not as abstract descriptions but as that which are made real (see also Cronin 2008b, 2010). For non-representational theory, the emphasis is on the affective, both in terms of the processual and relational (in the sense that Clough's work emphasizes), and of intensity and sensation (as I have discussed in relation to Lash's and Lash and Lury's work). Indeed, Blackman and Venn contrast affect theory with representational thinking, which they characterize as a mode of analysis that has tended to focus on discourse and ideology, and that 'assumes that [...] producing a discursive representation of our research object(s), is enough to illustrate the mediated nature of matter, or what we might also call the "matter of mediation"' (Blackman and Venn 2010: 9). What is of concern in the affective turn then, is how to conceive that of the body that cannot be contained or captured within representationalist thinking.[7]

For my focus in the book, it is necessary to consider bodies and images as processual, relational and non-discursive. That is, a challenge to representational thinking seems especially noteworthy in relation to the ways in which images have predominantly been conceived, approached and analysed according to an interest in the politics of representation. This approach can be traced, at least in part, to the emergence of British cultural studies, where, as I discussed above, images are read and deciphered for their ideological content. As Clough points out, this model has been and still is exceedingly important, not least in its aim to point out and intervene in the ways in which the kinds of bodies that are represented in popular media and culture come to (re)produce certain meanings that are attached and attributed to certain bodies. For example, in Stuart Hall's (2003) words, representations need to be understood in terms of the 'work' they do in 'regulat[ing] and organiz[ing] our conduct and practices – they help set the rules, norms and conventions by which social life is ordered and governed' (2003: 4). As such, images are analysed in terms of their politics; who or what is represented and how? Those working in the areas of gender, sexuality, race and ethnicity, and disability have been especially interested in the relationship between representations and 'real' social life. Thus, in her discussion of the relationship between representation and difference, Kathryn Woodward (1997) argues that representations are the 'signifying practices and symbolic systems through which meanings are produced' and which come to structure 'how we can make sense of our experience and of who we are' (1997: 14). Representations – including images and language – therefore 'involve relations of power' where processes of inequality, subordination and domination are constructed (1997: 15).

In analysing images as texts that can be deciphered for their underlying ideological message, what is focused on, I suggest, is the *content* of the image and its role in the discursive inscription on or construction of bodies. Furthermore, bodies and images are conceived as separate from each other. If what is focused on is the content of the image, the image can be understood as a description, in Law and Hetherington's terms, of a 'real world', a 'real body'. In these senses, analysing the politics of representation can be understood as part of the model of representational thinking which 'illustrate[s] the mediated nature of matter'. While such approaches remain necessary, what also requires attention is what images of transformation *do*.[8] In other words, if power is working through intensity, in order to understand how images are connected to patterns of inequality in contemporary culture, images need to be seen not only as representations but also in terms of their affects. Images are not separate from bodies but are in constitutive relations with them. As Clough argues in relation to television, images are materials/materialized. Indeed, in drawing together a number of arguments made in theories of images as affects, Featherstone (2010) explains that images 'move us' in ways that might not be immediately apparent according to representational thinking:

> bodies and the images of bodies in the media and consumer culture may literally move us, make us feel moved, by affecting our bodies in inchoate ways that cannot easily be articulated or assimilated to conceptual thought. Here we think of the shiver down the spine or the gut feeling. Affect points to the experience of intensities, to the way in which media images are felt through bodies.
>
> (2010: 195)

Here, Featherstone points to affect as 'the experience of intensity': the 'burrowing' of images into our flesh; the 'shiver down the spine or the gut feelings'. An attention to intensity is, as discussed in the Introduction, a move to exploring how power works now, at least in part, through affect and the body. In the case of images, this involves understanding the power of images – where power refers both to their prominence and appeal *and* to the ideas that they circulate – not so much in terms of reading and deciphering as *feeling or experiencing*.

What a non-representationalist understanding of images suggests is that an objective, external reading of what the image *is of* cannot capture the intensive experience of it. Contemporary socio-cultural life involves,

> subjects encounter[ing] not a signifying structure, or even the materiality of the signified, but the signified or sense itself as it is materialized. This is communication. This is information. The media environment, or mediascape, is a forest of extended intensities, of material signifieds around which subjects find their way. [...] [T]oday's global culture industry has the intensity of a mediascape, is a scape of flows.
>
> (Lash and Lury 2007: 14, reference omitted)

Lash and Lury's view here of the intensive, moving and changing mediascape problematizes an approach to images which treats them as representations. Images exist not (only) as texts but as things, material, or better, *as materializations*. In addition, while images as representations function primarily on the level of meaning, '[w]hen media become things, we enter a world of operationality, a world not of interpretation but of navigation. We do not "read" them so much as "do" them ("Just Do It"), or do with them' (2007: 8).

The 'doing' of or with images is central to the argument I make in this book. My interest is not so much in analysing images of transformation in terms of the politics of representation – what images represent about transformation – as in examining *how* images make transformation seem an appealing and achievable thing *to do*. The images of transformation at stake here, I suggest, work not only through what they depict (the better future) but also through how they are felt in, through and as the body (as a series of feelings, anticipations, inclinations towards living out this better future). Images are therefore involved in the creation and organization of experience.

Exploring these issues through a focus on the affectivity of images – intensity, feeling and experience – rather than through more well-established concepts – politics, representation and ideology – is an emerging project.[9] A focus on affect requires, as Blackman and Venn put it, different methodologies of '"noticing" and attending within our research endeavours' (2010: 9). One of the things that I aim to 'notice' in this book is the *distribution* of the affectivity of images; *which* bodies in particular feel and live out images of transformation? At the same time, to say that a focus on affect is an emerging project is also to pull through the emphasis on process and invention: what images do is always in the process of change, becoming or emergence. For example, Alan Latham and Derek McCormack (2009) argue that the question of 'what images do' becomes especially significant 'if we don't understand their function to be solely or primarily a matter of representation' (2009: 253). Latham and McCormack's focus is on everyday urban life, and they put to work a range of what they term 'non-representational' methodologies to explore this field.[10] Beginning from the position that images 'make sense not just because we take time to figure out what they signify, but also because their pre-signifying affective materiality is *felt* in bodies', Latham and McCormack identify how taking seriously the question of what images do requires an openness to where that question might lead, what the answers might be. '[W]orking to hold open this potential (another word for which is the virtual)', they argue, 'does not mean that images can do everything, but that within a given set of constraints they always have the potential to surprise us, however gently' (Latham and McCormack 2002: 260, see also Coleman 2009).[11] If images are not (only) representations, how, then, does one think through their potential?

Screens: surfaces, windows, life

Given the focus of this book on screens, to begin to answer this question it is helpful, as Lisa Adkins and Celia Lury (2009) put it, to 'turn to the surface'

(2009: 18). That is, if attention shifts from uncovering the ideological meanings underpinning images to understanding images in terms of potential, intensity and excess, it is necessary to think of images not only in terms of depth but also in terms of flatness, networks and relationality: *surfaces*. For Adkins and Lury, a turn to the surface is part of this move to 'non-representational' thinking. It

> forces Sociology to break with representational models of the empirical (and with this, to make a move from why to how) and requires the discipline to confront a new co-ordinated reality, one that is open, processual, non-linear and constantly on the move. This co-ordination does not take place in relation to an externally fixed space, that is a space in which epistemology is 'above', 'behind' or 'beyond' ontology, but in relation to a surface in which the co-ordinating axes or categories of knowing are implanted, producing a space of possible states.
>
> (2009: 18)

Here, the surface is 'no longer defined in contradistinction to depth, causal or explanatory models' but is 'a space in itself' (2009: 16). Importantly, this space itself is 'open, processual, non-linear and constantly on the move'. It is a space that is vital, alive and intensive: 'This surface is the topological space of all the possible states that a system can have' (2009: 16). The surface is virtual.

How, then, to *research* the surface? I would suggest that the screen is an exemplary instance of a surface that is 'a space in itself'; as I will explore further below and in following chapters, screens are surfaces that both offer a 'window' onto another world, and an interface that demands attention in and of themselves. Screens are a surface through which the potentiality of images is co-ordinated. As potential, images and the lives that they promise are 'open, processual, non-linear and constantly on the move'. My attention in this book is thus on screens as 'a surface in which the co-ordinating axes or categories of knowing are implanted' rather than as a space that has an ' "above", "behind" or "beyond" ' – an ideological message underpinning the image, for example – that should 'really' be the focus of attention.

Of course, screens have long been theorized in disciplines such as film studies, where screen theory (or 'screen theorizing') seeks to understand what 'are the moving image screen or screens, what is displayed on those screens, and the nature of our encounter with them' (Kuhn 2009: 5). In taking up the notion that the screen is a surface, in this book my focus is on how screens have become a central part of everyday life. I examine four different screens via which images of transformation are accessed and experienced. In this way, while I draw on various theories of the screen in different chapters (including interactive design, television studies, film and animation studies, and visual culture theory more generally), my main concern is with thinking about screens as an empirical problem; how screens co-ordinate the relations between bodies and images so that images are materialized.

The dominance of the screen today is pointed to by Lev Manovich (2002) in his now classic work, where he argues that we live in 'a society of the screen'

(2002: 94): 'Today, coupled with the computer, the screen is rapidly becoming the main means of accessing any kind of information, be it still images, moving images, or text.' (2002: 94). While different kinds of computer screen may dominate contemporary Western cultures, what is remarkable, Manovich suggests, is that if conceived as a 'frame that separates two absolutely different spaces that somehow coexist' (2002: 95), screens can be seen as having a much longer history:

> The visual culture of the modern period, from painting to cinema, is characterized by an intriguing phenomenon – the existence of *another* virtual space, another three-dimensional world enclosed by a frame and situated inside our normal space.
>
> (2002: 95)

In drawing attention to the screen, Manovich is interested in examining the ways in which the virtual – the other 'three dimensional world' – is brought into the actual – is 'situated inside our normal space'. In order to trace the historical development of how the screen frames this relationship between the virtual and actual, Manovich conducts what he calls 'a genealogy of the screen' and identifies three types of screen: the 'classical', the 'dynamic' and the 'computer' screen.

The classical screen, Manovich argues, is

> a flat, rectangular surface. It is intended for frontal viewing – as opposed to a panorama for instance. It exists in our normal space, the space of our body, and acts as a window into another space. This other space, the space of representation, typically has a scale different from the scale of our normal space.
>
> (2002: 95)

This type of screen may have emerged with the Renaissance painting, but it also endures today, with both the television and the computer screen being of similar dimensions and requiring frontal viewing. While the classical screen remains today, with the technological developments associated with cinema (and later with television and video), another type of screen, the 'dynamic screen' also becomes prevalent. The dynamic screen 'retains all the properties of a classical screen while adding something new: It can display an image changing over time' (2002: 96). Manovich argues that with the dynamic screen, the viewing regime 'already implicit in the classical screen [...] fully surfaces':

> A screen's image strives for complete illusion, and visual plenitude, while the viewer is asked to suspend disbelief and to identify with the image. Although the screen in reality is only a window of limited dimensions positioned inside the physical space of the viewer, the viewer is expected to concentrate completely on what she sees in this window, focusing her attention on the representation and disregarding the physical space outside.
>
> (2002: 96)

42 Screening affect

In this sense, the moving image that characterizes the dynamic screen demands attention: the viewer is required to focus on the image and 'disregard' the context in which the image is located.[12] The screen is thus far from being a 'neutral medium presenting information' and instead is 'aggressive. It functions to filter, to *screen out*, to take over, render nonexistent whatever is outside its frame' (2002: 96).

This 'visual plentitude' of the dynamic screen is carried through in one of the trends that Manovich identifies as occurring in the shift to the third type of screen; the computer screen. From the late twentieth century onwards, when computers became ubiquitous in certain workplaces and homes, it is this type of screen that dominates. Writing about the relatively new technology of virtual reality (VR) at this time, Manovich argues that

> VR typically uses a head-mounted display whose images completely fill the viewer's visual field. No longer is the viewer looking at a rectangular, flat surface from a certain distance, a window into another space. Now she is fully situated within this other space. Or, more precisely, we can say that the two spaces – the real, physical space and the virtual, simulated space – coincide. The virtual space, previously confined to a painting or a movie screen, now completely encompasses the real space. Frontality, rectangular surface, difference in scale are all gone. The screen has vanished.
>
> (2002: 97)

I will return to the notion of the virtual below; here what is of significance is that 'the screen disappears altogether' (2002: 97). The screen – *the surface* – of the image has disappeared and the viewer is fully immersed in the world that she sees. Moreover, the visual field requires action, or doing (with). The image displayed in VR is not a one-dimensional picture which needs to be consumed 'from a certain distance' but is a space where the viewer enters, moves, engages and interacts. It is through this movement and interaction that the image makes sense, is brought to life. The disappearance of the screen through the coexistence of 'real, physical space' and 'virtual, simulated space' suggests a new space, a virtual space, rather than a representational space underpinned by – and more or less accurately depicting – a 'real' world.

While the disappearance of the screen is one of the trends that occurs with the computer, on the other hand, Manovich argues, the screen becomes increasingly apparent, no longer seeking a 'complete takeover of the visual field' (2002: 98) but rather requiring attention towards multiple and perhaps competing 'windows':

> rather than showing a single image, a computer screen typically displays a number of coexisting windows. Indeed, the coexistence of a number of overlapping windows is a fundamental principle of the modern GUI [graphical user interface]. No single window completely dominates the viewer's attention. In this sense, the possibility of simultaneously observing a few

images that coexist within one screen can be compared with the phenomenon of zapping – the quick switching of television channels that allows the viewer to follow more than one programme. In both instances, the viewer no longer concentrates on a single image.

(2002: 97)

Anne Friedberg (2006) also discusses the phenomenon of 'windows' on computer screens and outlines the development of windows by computer software companies. A computer operating system where the interface was visual and pictorial rather than text-based was originally developed by Apple in the 1980s but was later adopted by Microsoft, who called their software Windows (2006: 231). As Manovich describes, a Windows interface displays different content, image and text – moving and still – networked and located on the hard drive. The screen here is not transparent, requiring the viewer to 'enter into' the image seemingly directly, but its content is 'mediated to a high degree through its proprietary or trademarked "software"; and its representational logic is highly iconic' (Friedberg 2006: 231). The 'Windows' screen involves and requires multiplicity of action – 'Multiple "windows" made computer "multitasking" possible' (2006: 233) – and implies that one's subjectivity and identity is fragmented, distributed and manifold (Friedberg 2006: 135; Turkle 1995).

The fragmentation of screens and the distribution of images across the screen is an issue that I discuss in more detail in Chapter 4 in relation to internet dieting, while Chapter 3 focuses on the disappearing screen in the context of makeover television. I also return to the two concurrent trends of the screen as transparent and apparent that Manovich and Friedberg identify in Chapter 2, which explores further the relationship between the window and the screen in the context of interactive mirrors and the in-store shopping experience. Here, though, it is worth flagging up one of the central issues that the relationship between the window and screen poses, which concerns not only *what* one sees but also *how* one sees. Indeed, Friedberg notes that a window is '*a membrane where surface meets depth, where transparency meets its barriers. The window is also a frame, a proscenium: its edges hold a view in place*' (2006: 1). Conceived as such, the window transforms three-dimensional materiality into '*a two-dimensional surface; the window becomes a screen. Like the window, the screen is at once a surface and a frame – a reflective plane onto which an image is cast and a frame that limits its view*' (2006: 1). Taking up Friedberg's argument then, *what* we are able to see is always framed in certain ways. 'As we spend more of our time staring into the frames of movies, television, computers, hand-held devices – "windows" full of moving images, text, icons and 3-D graphics', Friedberg argues, 'how the world is framed may be as important as what is contained within that frame' (2006: 1). As Manovich argues, the screen is 'aggressive'. Paying attention to the ways in which images are framed is perhaps particularly important when, as I have argued, images operate through affect, where there is a – deliberate or not – attempt to bypass interpretation and to make the body feel, to engage 'sense itself' (Lash and Lury 2007: 14). For example, if contemporary consumer culture involves marketing and branding as *affective experience*, it becomes important not only to think about what that experience *is* but also how it has been arranged and organized to engage and move bodies, seemingly 'directly'.[13] How, then, are screens involved in the framing and arrangement of how images make bodies feel? How is it *as a surface* that screens organize affect? And what is the relationship between the surface, transformation and affect?

Materialization and the actualization of the virtual

One of the issues that is apparent in Manovich's and Friedberg's theorizing of the screen is the importance of vision. Different screens produce different viewing regimes and it is therefore necessary to attend to how vision is framed and arranged. Looking is key to how I explore the relationship between bodies and images in this book. I argue that looking is one way in which images are materialized, the virtual actualized. In this sense I am drawing on the idea that is prevalent in studies of visual culture, that ways of seeing are ways of life; that is, as Donna Haraway argues (1991), in framing the ways in which we know and understand the world, in Western cultures vision plays a central role in shaping the kinds of life that it is possible to live. The understanding of vision that is developed by Haraway and others indicates that looking is more than only sight, that vision is embodied and multi-sensory. For example, film theorist Vivian Sobchack (2004) argues that 'vision is not isolated from our other senses' (2004: 64), and that it is important to understand how images are *experienced*:

> Experiencing a movie, not ever merely 'seeing' it, my lived body [...] subverts the very notion of *on-screen* and *off-screen* as mutually exclusive sites or 'subject positions'. Indeed, much of the 'pleasure of the text' emerges from this carnal subversion of fixed subject positions, from the body as a 'third' term that both exceeds and yet is within representation; thus 'it would be wrong ... to imagine a rigid distinction between the body inside and the body outside the text, because the subversive force of the body is partly in its capacity to function both figuratively and literally'.
>
> (2004: 66–67, references omitted)

As I have argued so far in this chapter then, images are not separate from bodies but rather are experienced through bodies. There is no 'rigid distinction' between the body on one side and the other of the screen.

I look at multi-sensory experience most explicitly in Chapter 3 in relation to makeover television, where I argue that for working-class women viewers, makeover television images are experienced as 'real life'. However, the argument that images are increasingly interacted with, that I have discussed here also makes clear the ways in which images are in excess of texts; are lived out. The interaction with images is a topic developed in Chapter 2 in relation to interactive mirrors. While mirrors have always involved images that are engaged with and done with – mirror images are made to move and change through the doing of them – interactive mirrors make this process clear and in doing so, I suggest they indicate some of the problems of representational thinking about images. Interaction is also the subject of Chapter 4 on online dieting where I examine the computer screen as an interface that encourages the 'viewer' to concentrate on the screen, to produce temporal 'routes through' dieting via the ways in which they engage with the screen. In Chapter 5 the focus is on how action (rather than interaction) becomes the required way in which images of the better future from the Change4Life campaign are to be lived out. Images 'move off' screens and become embodied as the need to move more and eat better; indeed, the campaign literature sees screens as an inappropriate means of communicating with those who need to make changes in their life.

The inter-related concepts of looking, interaction and action are all means of exploring the specific ways in which screens organize how images are felt and experienced. My attention is therefore on how images are lived out. In this book, images are conceived as virtuals, and ways of feeling and living out the image are conceived as actuals. Drawing on the discussion of affect theory in this chapter, throughout the book I stress the *processual* nature of the actualization of the virtual. The actualization of the virtual is not complete(d) and actualization is not a finished product but rather is always in movement and change. Thus, when I refer to 'the actual' or 'actuals', this is intended to account for the open-ended ongoing-ness of the actual. This is particularly important to note in relation to my focus on *images of transformation*, which emphasize process, and indicate that actualization is incomplete. Images of transformation function, I have suggested, as and through potential in that they indicate that a better life in the future is possible and desirable and are part of wider socio-cultural trends that organize change and transformation as an imperative. Furthermore, this potential is *affective*; for example, it requires bodies to be oriented towards the future as if the future is the only temporality that matters (Adams *et al.* 2009, see Introduction). The feelings of the imperative of transformation – the orientation around the future that Adams *et al.* describe – imply that there is always 'more' that might, potentially, be made real.

Taking up the affective turn to examine images of transformation involves this focus on process then. It also involves a concern with *the body*. Images of transformation function as potentials that engage some bodies affectively; they are not so much texts, separate from and different to bodies, but instead are felt as and through bodies (the gut feeling, the shiver down the spine, etc.). In this sense, images are made real or actual; images are *materialized*. The virtual future is thus always in the process of being actualized as and through the materiality of the body. What this suggests is that images of transformation are not representations; they are not independent, bounded units that mediate between other independent, bounded units (bodies), but are in *constitutive* relations with matter and with what comes to be materialized. While there are many different theories of materialization, and the concept has recently taken hold in feminist, cultural and social theory (see, as just a few examples, Butler 1993; Barad 2007; Alaimo and Hekman 2008; Coole and Frost 2010), my understanding of materialization is developed in relation to the actualization of the virtual. Throughout the book I therefore refer to the materialization of images in order to draw attention to how the actualization of the virtual is about the making real of certain feelings, orientations, inclinations and ways of life.

In order to explore these processes of materialization, the case study chapters explore how screens organize the ways in which the virtual is actualized. I argue that the screen is the surface through which the co-ordinating, arranging and organizing the actualization of the virtual takes place. As I have discussed so far, this is not an understanding of the screen as a solid, static demarcation between one space or time and another (the 3D 'real' world and the 2D representation, the present and the future). Rather, it is an understanding of the screen as *mediating* between different contexts. Mediation here refers to something quite specific, in Anne Cronin's (2010) terms, 'not in the sense generally deployed in studies of the media which see social institutions such as radio or television shaping, reflecting or relaying certain ideals, discourses or ideologies' (2010: 144). Rather, this is 'a form of mediation that is fully embodied, that confounds conventional distinctions between the material and immaterial' (2010: 120). The screen can be understood as organizing interaction between the virtual and actual, the immaterial and material.

Indeed, in the previous chapter I discussed the relationship between the material and immaterial, the present and the not-yet, in terms of the 'coupling' of the actual and the virtual. The virtual in this sense is that which exists but is not (yet) concrete. The virtual is a 'realm' of intensive potential that, through movement, process and change, might be actualized. The virtual is thus not detached from the actual – it is not a realm of unlimited potential – but rather the virtual, in ways that cannot always be known in advance (see Conclusion), unfolds into and as the actual. A productive task for contemporary sociology, then, is to examine the actualization of the virtual, that is to examine the ways in which intensive potential is actualized into concrete ways of living. The modes of materialization that I examine in the case study chapters are one of the means through which it is possible to track how virtual images are actualized. Moreover, my focus on these different modes of materialization stress how the virtual image is actualized in ways that are not necessarily open, but organized and inclined to certain patterns or paths. The imperative of transformation both appeals to and addresses some bodies more than others, and works to produce certain kinds of bodies and ways of life. That is, the future as potential is actualized in particular ways. The book now turns to examine these issues in more detail.

2 Bringing the image to life
Interactive mirrors and intensive experience

In the previous chapter I outlined the idea that the screen is a prevalent way in which images are organized. Screens, I argued, bring images to life; they organize the ways in which the virtual potential of images may be actualized. In this sense, I began to examine one of the central ways in which sociology and associated disciplines such as media and cultural studies, and film studies have tended to approach images through the issue of representation, and to introduce an alternative understanding of images through the concepts of interactivity (or 'doing with'), intensity and the virtual. My aim in this chapter is to explore interactive mirrors as a particular kind of screen, and to argue that they produce images that problematize the notion of representation by focusing attention on the screen. Interactive mirrors vary in terms of the purposes for which they are designed (artistic and/or commercial), the sites in which they are located (galleries, shops, homes, etc.) and the applications they include (some record and play back images, others enable the user to draw on the screen, others connect up to social networking sites and facilitate textual conversations). My discussion is centred on the production of images by different interactive mirrors; one a piece of artwork and the others intended to be part of what is described by designers and retailers as an attempt to revitalize the shopping experience.[1] I thus primarily focus on interactive mirrors that are, or are intended to be, located in high-end shops and/or department stores.

The focus on shopping is intended to draw attention to how consumer culture works through a transformative logic whereby, as I discuss in the Introduction, transformation is seen as in reach of everyone and is enacted on and through the body (see Featherstone 1991, 2010). Developing my argument concerning how the image functions as potential, in this chapter I see 'going shopping' (Bowlby 2000) as the folding of the future as potential into particular objects and experiences.[2] Successful or effective shopping experiences and the products that customers may try on and purchase indicate a better future that may be actualized. In this sense, as Lury (2011) puts it, 'consumption must be understood as transformation rather than use' (2011: 192). Going shopping is increasingly designed to be an interactive environment. These interactive environments are deemed necessary in part as a response to online worlds; stores must both draw on the online shopping experiences that more customers are becoming familiar with, and must (re)create themselves in contrast to online shopping so that they offer something distinctive. I concentrate on how interactive mirrors are seen by designers and retailers as one of the ways in which these in-store shopping experiences are to be created and, towards the end of the chapter, make connections between the kinds of experiences that the 'revitalization of in-store shopping' produce and those described by historians of the emergence of department stores in the nineteenth century and of window-shopping.

This chapter acts as a bridge between the previous theoretical chapters and the following three case study chapters. My concern here is with understanding how interactive mirrors function as an interface, a screen that requires interaction, and I examine especially the kind of *experience* that such interaction is understood by the mirrors' designers and users to create; an experience that is embodied, 'alive', *intensive*. I argue that interactive mirrors organize images through the screen and encourage particular modes of experiencing the image that operate through intensity and the body. In this sense, interactive mirror images are not so much representational texts to be read and deciphered, but are virtuals that are felt and lived out. I argue that if representation is no longer the only way in which images can be understood, it is helpful to continue to develop other ways of thinking about the power of images, both in terms of the pervasiveness of images in contemporary society and the ways in which power works through images, or more specifically, through the virtuality of images. More specifically, the chapter introduces ideas about the screen as a reflective surface and transparent window, ideas which are returned to later in the book. To conclude the chapter, I return to the issues of power, affect and intensity in order to track how the imperative of transformation takes place through the gendering (and racing, classing and aging) of shopping. I explore how shopping can be understood as an indeterminate process (Bowlby 2000) where certain bodies are susceptible to suggestion (Blackman 2007); those susceptible to suggestion through being associated with emotion and affect rather than rationality and reason. In this sense I set up ideas about the unequal distribution of affects co-ordinated by images of transformation that I develop in later chapters.

Mirrors: transformation, the self and the body

Mirrors are an imaging technology that is thoroughly embedded in everyday life. Despite this, mirrors have received little academic attention outside of Lacanian psychoanalysis where the mirror-stage signifies the child's recognition of itself as an autonomous being and hence its entry into the symbolic (see Lacan 1977). My approach in this chapter is instead to explore the ways in which mirrors – both reflective glass and interactive – are involved in the imaging of bodies. As a technology that images bodies across a whole range of public and private spaces – bedrooms, bathrooms, hallways, bars, restaurants and shops – mirrors are commonly understood to be simply a reflective surface, a piece of glass that reflects back what is placed in front of it. While the processes through which bodies are imaged and come to be understood through reflective glass mirrors are more complex than this assumption suggests (see for example de Beauvior 1949/1997; Melchoir-Bonnet 2001; Coleman 2009), with interactive mirrors the practices through which bodies are imaged and made sense of are explicitly highlighted. In so doing I suggest that they pose a particular relationship between the actual and virtual, and the present and future. As I have discussed in previous chapters, I am interested in the imperative of transformation in terms of these kinds of temporal relationships and, as a technology that images the body, mirrors have long been associated with the possibility of transformation. In order to explore the connection between mirrors and transformation, and the ways in which this connection works through *images*, Sabine Melchoir-Bonnet's (2001) careful tracing of changing historical understandings and cultural myths of the mirror is helpful to consider.

For Melchoir-Bonnet, mirrors – both real and metaphorical – come to be part of the Christian tradition of regulating moral and spiritual behaviour in the medieval and Middle Ages.[3] Discussing the belief expressed in Genesis that God created man 'in his image and his likeness', Melchoir-Bonnet indicates that the image has had a central role in establishing appropriate Christian behaviour; if man is made in God's image, then man must do his best to live up to this image. Mirrors became a means through which man could reflect on his own capacity to successfully live as a Christian. Thus, the Bible is seen as the 'true mirror in which man should contemplate himself' (2001: 110) and moreover, 'the medieval mirror offered man a model for governing his outward behaviour as well: it showed him what he was and what he ought to be' (2001: 114).[4] As such, if used correctly as 'a tool by which to "know thyself"', mirrors 'invited man to *not* mistake himself for God, to avoid pride by knowing his limits, and to **improve himself**'. As an imaging technology, mirrors are not so much associated with passive imitation – with 'simply' emulating an appropriately moral and spiritual lifestyle – but are instead concerned with '**active [...] transformation**' (2001: 106, bold my emphasis).

While the Christian tradition of thinking through the mirror continued, with the Renaissance and scientific revolution in Europe in the seventeenth century, 'the disturbing mystery of the mirror' was explained with new understandings of vision, optics and processes of reflection and refraction (2001: 129). Alongside these scientific developments, self-consciousness – the notion that 'I' am an individual, autonomous and separate from other individuals – began to become more significant. Melchoir-Bonnet describes the emergence of self-consciousness as 'coincid[ing] first of all with the consciousness of one's reflection, with one's outward representation and visage – I am seen, therefore I am' (2001: 134). As technologies for producing them were honed, mirrors became more affordable and accessible and they began to be located, not only in the homes of the very wealthy but also, gradually, in those of the working classes. Through the integration of mirrors into daily life – used daily for grooming, for example – Melchoir-Bonnet argues that there is a shift in its role from managing *moral* behaviour to organizing *social* behaviour: the mirror 'was not consulted in order to scrutinize one's features in a self-hating way, but rather to realize an image others were expecting' (2001: 142). Mirrors become consulted to ensure that social codes were met, and that the body would be transformed in light of these social expectations.

As the importance of self-consciousness as a means to understand the self became more significant, so too did the body take on increased importance; the body 'was not a mute thickness, a mechanistic construction' but 'was the vessel of each person's singularity, which fashion, with its new aesthetic example, expressed in its own way' (2001: 175). The convergence of the importance of appearance, the body and the mirror can be seen in the example of the dandy of the late eighteenth and early nineteenth century, who spent hours in front of the mirror, grooming and perfecting each element of his appearance. The mirror here 'defended an art of living that was delicate and free from the contingencies of work' (2001: 178) and moreover,

> offers each person an image of his own creativity, [...] according to which the subject says not 'I like myself as I am', but 'I am or I should be as I love myself ... I want to appear this way, so I must better my appearance'.
> (2001: 178)

As with the Christian tradition, here the mirror is an impulse for transformation, showing the dandy what he could and should try to become.

Examining the role of the mirror in organizing moral and then social behaviour highlights the historical emergence of a new way of understanding, or becoming conscious of, the self through the body. The invention and gradual dissemination of the mirror as a glass that reflected who one *was* and who one *could be* helps to establish what Featherstone (2010) calls the transformative logic of Western consumer cultures, whether that be in religious or aesthetic modes. This transformative logic ties together new ways of seeing, new knowledges of the self and new kinds of behaviour; seeing and reflecting on one's image in the mirror became bound up with both one's own understandings of one's self and with one's 'outward behaviour'. Moreover, as Featherstone also points out, it is through the appearance of the body that transformation is seen to take place: the spiritual or moral transformation that the mirror initially made evident is replaced by an emphasis on transformation as a physical process.[5] What is also produced, and what I explore in more detail below, is a collapse of a version of linear time into an *intensive time*, whereby '[t]he mirror of introspection shines light on the past, the present and the future *all at once*' (Melchoir-Bonnet 2001: 107, my emphasis). What one has done and been, what is and what one could and should be, are all at once reflected in the body of the mirror. The mirror shows multiple temporalities simultaneously, or, in the terms developed in the book so far, the mirror image is *both* the virtual and actual *at once*. The temporalities of the mirror are key to the argument developed in this chapter and to the ways in which I argue that mirrors problematize an understanding of images as representations. The intensive temporality of mirrors is, I suggest, created through the mirror as a *surface or screen*.

Mirrors as screens: reflection and interaction

The relationship between the image, the body and the self that Melchoir-Bonnet examines occurs through the reflective glass mirror. Here, reflection takes on two meanings; it refers to the technology of imaging itself, where the silver or aluminium applied to a plane of glass reflects back to its viewer their image in real time, and it refers to the process of reflecting or speculating on the image that is produced (that is, the self-consciousness mentioned above). In the previous chapter I discussed recent work that attends to images 'outside' a model of representation. In requiring a consideration of processes of reflection – what reflection refers to and involves – mirrors are a helpful example through which to examine how images might function other than as representation. Indeed, understood as reflections, mirror images trouble the notion of representation in different but inter-related ways. First, while popular understandings of photographs and films are that they have captured a body in the past, mirror images are seen as created in and as the present. They are created by, and valued for, their ability to reflect the movement of the body/self in front of them at that time (Coleman 2009). It is thus difficult to capture and convert the movement of mirror images into a 'text' that can then be read and deciphered. Second, existing only ephemerally, mirror images are created and seen by the body/ies in front of the mirror. In this way, mirror images are commonly understood to be images that emanate from the body itself rather than as created through relatively complicated and complex technologies.[6] Third, in being seen as created in the present by the body in front of them, mirrors blur the boundary between representation and reality; mirror images are seen to depict reality as it is/as it is happening. Indeed, as Simone de Beauvoir among others has pointed out, mirror images are seen to provide the most accurate or 'real' image possible; 'woman [...] believes she really sees *herself* in the glass' (de Beauvoir 1949/1997: 643; Coleman 2009). In these ways, while other technologies of and techniques for imaging bodies – portraiture, photography, film and video, and medical scanning, for example – are understood in terms of representational practices involving processes of selection, framing, mediation and perhaps manipulation, mirror images are seen to escape such procedures.[7]

The challenge to the notion of images as representations that reflective glass mirrors establish is both drawn on and extended by the interactive mirrors that I discuss here. The interactive mirrors, I argue, carry through the assumption that mirrors 'reflect' the body directly and immediately and at the same time draw attention to the processes through which the body is imaged. What I am particularly interested in exploring in this chapter is how the mirror as a reflective surface is replaced with the mirror as a computer interface, a screen that requires interaction. More specifically, in what ways does the emphasis that interactive mirrors place on the screen trouble representational understandings of images?

One example of an interactive mirror is artist Daniel Rozin's *Wooden Mirror* (1999), (see Figure 2.1), an installation of polished wooden tiles 2m tall by 1.5m wide[8]:

52 *Bringing the image to life*

> Move in front of it, and its surface of wooden tiles comes alive. The tiles tilt up and down, and the resulting pattern of light and shade creates an image of whatever is before the mirror. Movement is reflected instantly by the tiles in ripples of motion, accompanied by a rustling sound reminiscent of a stiff breeze in a forest.
>
> (Rozin 2001: 1)

The artwork films movement with a small concealed video camera, which is connected to a computer that analyses the differences between the image captured by the camera and the previous arrangement of tiles, and sends commands to those tiles that need to alter. Thus, as Jay David Bolter and Diane Gromala (2005) put it, '[w]hen you stop, the tiles stop too, and you realize that they have formed a coarse image of you' (2005: 32). Rozin (no date) describes the 'minimal' reflection that *Wooden Mirror* shows as,

> the least amount of information required to convey a picture (less than an icon on a computer and with no colour). It is amazing how little information this is for a computer, and yet how much character it can have.

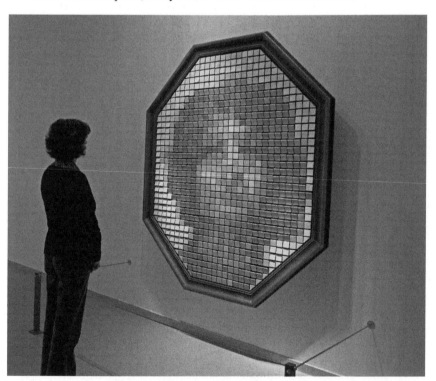

Figure 2.1 Daniel Rozin (1999) *Wooden Mirror*, Israel Museum. Image available at: www.smoothware.com/danny/. Permission for use of image kindly granted by Daniel Rozin.

Working through the medium of wood rather than glass, *Wooden Mirror* raises interesting questions regarding how mirrors create images that reflect the body in front of them. For example, although the artwork is a digital installation, Rozin argues that the wood 'conceals' 'the power of digital computation' and operates instead through a material and physicality 'more in touch with the human condition' (Rozin 2001: 2). In this sense, the artwork encourages the spectator to consider 'the line between analog and physical vs. digital and computational' (2001: 2). Indeed, Bolter and Gromala suggest that, while

> [w]e are used to seeing our image captured by video cameras and displayed on monitors, and this mirror should seem low tech in comparison to a conventional video, [...] the blend of digital technology and wooden material is so unusual that it seems less 'natural' and at the same time more engaging than a video display.
>
> (2005: 32–33)

Wooden Mirror engages the viewer because it 'is a paradox. It is a mirror made of the unlikely material of wood. It is opaque, and yet it reflects' (2005: 34).

Other examples of interactive mirrors can be found in high-end shops. One of the first interactive mirrors to be located in-store were those made by design company IDEO and sited in the interactive changing-rooms in the Rem Koolhaas/Office for Metropolitan Architecture (OMA) designed Prada 'Epicenter' store in Manhattan, New York (2001) (see Figure 2.2).[9] The store opened in December 2001, to what Daniel Huppatz (2009), writing on the architecture of the store, describes as 'predictable media hype', in particular about 'the staggering cost, upwards of $40 million, [which] was repeated in newspaper and journals'. The store was an explicit attempt to create an intensive shopping experience. Indeed, the synopsis of the design of the store on the OMA's website explains how commercialization has meant that 'museums, libraries, airports, hospitals, and schools become increasingly indistinguishable from shopping centres', resulting in 'a deadening loss of variety. What were once distinct activities no longer retain the uniqueness that gave them richness'. The Prada store was created with 'the equation [...] reversed [...]. What if the shopping experience were not one of impoverishment, but of enrichment?'[10] I will discuss below the ways in which the various materials help to achieve this 'rich' atmosphere, but here it is worth noting the importance of technology. Huppatz argues that:

> Technological innovation featured high on the Prada store's priorities, not only visibly in the store, but with IT innovations such as a global customer database, RFID tags for inventory control or protection from theft, and digital customer loyalty cards that might create a personal 'virtual closet'.

The technological innovation and its cost attracted attention, with Gregg Lindsay (2004) noting that three years later '[m]ost of the flashy technology today sits idle' and 'many gadgets, such as automated dressing-room doors and touchscreens, are

54 *Bringing the image to life*

either malfunctioning or ignored'. An OMA architect described the failing technology in terms of the design company being 'too anticipatory with our custom elements' (cited in Lindsay 2004).

The interactive changing-rooms, in which the interactive mirrors of interest in this chapter were located, were one of the technologies that did not work as planned. The changing-rooms are described by the OMA as an attempt to 'augment the experience of trying on clothes for the customer and enhance [...] the relationship between the sales assistant and the customer'. The changing-room is

> presented as a simple eight-foot-square glass booth. One wall forms the door, which the customer can make opaque for privacy during changing or clear to show off a garment to someone outside the booth. Another wall incorporates a 'magic mirror', a camera and display that adds a four-second delay so the customer can spin around and view all sides of the garment. The opposite wall has two interactive closets, one for hanging clothes and one with shelves. Sensors in the closets detect the electronic tags on store items and trigger a touch screen that displays the item and its related information, from availability to permutations of color, fabric, and size.
>
> (IDEO, designers of the changing rooms, www.ideo.com/work/
> staff-devices-dressing-rooms/)

Lindsay's report lists a number of problems with the changing-rooms, including customers who 'derobed in full view, thinking the door had turned opaque', the doors getting stuck and the touchscreen being either 'blank or broadcasting random video loops'. Lindsay quotes a branding consultant, Peter Dixon, as

Figure 2.2 Interactive mirror in Prada store, Manhattan. Image available at: www.ideo.com/work/staff-devices-dressing-rooms/. Permission for use of image kindly granted by IDEO.

saying that the changing-rooms were 'too delicate' for the 'high traffic' that the store generated (visitors as well as customers), and that only the 'magic mirror' was 'tough enough'. Although the interactive changing-rooms are no longer in use, they nevertheless constitute an interesting example of the design of a shopping experience. Moreover, as I will go on to discuss, the interactive mirrors have more recently been superceded by other kinds of interactive mirrors designed for other kinds of stores: the interactivity of mirrors is a 'tough' idea that is beginning to permeate the experience of 'going shopping'.

To return to my earlier discussion of *Wooden Mirror*, the changing-room mirrors also raise productive ways of thinking about the issue of reflection. While *Wooden Mirror* challenges assumptions about reflection through the opacity of its material, this interactive mirror seeks to carry through ideas about the reflective qualities of mirrors, by making the interactive mirror look and act like a reflective glass mirror, for example, and by placing it within a familiar setting of a changing-room booth. However, the time-delay play-back function, its ability to show the customer parts of her or his body that they would not be able to see in a reflective glass mirror, and its connection with other objects that emphasize interaction (the door, the closets), highlight the ways in which this mirror is not a commonplace (reflective glass) mirror, but is instead a 'magic mirror'.

While both *Wooden Mirror* and the changing-room mirrors reflect what is in front of them, through the opaque materiality of the former and the time-delay of the latter, the mirrors highlight their surface; the screen on which the image is shown is brought into focus. For Bolter and Gromala, this emphasis on the surface troubles the way in which mirrors are usually understood in terms of transparency, as providing 'an experience of looking at and looking through at the same time' (Bolter and Gromala 2005: 34). While mirror images are always virtual rather than real, and we are always 'really looking at the surface' of the mirror rather than through the mirror, *interactive mirrors are* 'a playful reminder that a mirror is a surface and not a window onto a different world' (2005: 34).

Bolter and Gromala's interest in questions of windows and surfaces, transparency and reflection, is developed in relation to the theory and practice of interaction design. They argue that designing digital interactive products, environments or experiences focuses attention on the screen where decisions are made regarding how far and when the surface is made apparent to the user and how far and when it disappears, or is transparent. They argue that interaction design makes explicit 'the myth of transparency', located in the longer history of painting and design, where the ideal interface through which images and data are organized and made available is understood to be transparent. For example, discussing the influence of Leon Battista Alberti's fifteenth-century work on painting and perspective, Anne Friedberg (2006) argues that Alberti thinks through the window in order to explain how painting is a process of framing a view. Alberti describes painting as a practice whereby 'on the surface on which I am going to paint, I draw a rectangle of whatever size I want, which I regard as an open window through which the subject to be painted is seen' (quoted in

56 *Bringing the image to life*

Friedberg 2006: 27). The window is a metaphor for Alberti to explain the process of successfully rendering a view of the three dimensional world as a realistic two-dimensional image. Moreover, the window is further described by Alberti in terms of another device, the veil (*velo*), 'a grid-like netting stretched on a frame'and 'set [...] between the eye and the object to be represented, so that the visual pyramid passes through the loose weave of the veil' (Alberti quoted in Friedberg 2006: 38). The veil allows the real world, through the window, to be depicted accurately on the canvas. Painting is thus understood to be an exercise of representing the world as precisely and authentically as possible.

Alberti's notion of the veil raises interesting questions regarding framing – what is included and excluded? – and of positioning – the artist located inside, looking out at the real world which is placed at a distance.[11] Importantly for my discussion here though, is the understanding of the window as *transparent*, as that which we look through.[12] Friedberg suggests the centrality of windows in art and design has extended from painting into material and digital culture, citing the Microsoft Windows operating system as a contemporary example. As with Manovich's interest in the relationship between screens and vision in his genealogy of the screen (see Chapter 1), Friedberg's concern is with how the Windows computer screen involves 'the collapse of the single viewpoint', in that

> the 'interface' of Windows extends screen space by overlapping screens of various sizes; each 'window' can run a different application; the user can scroll through a text within a 'window', arrange 'windows' on the screen in stacked or overlapping formations, decorate 'windows' (with wallpapers, textured patterns), and conduct new forms of 'window shopping'.
>
> (2006: 229)

Interestingly, she argues that the Windows interface disrupts the association between windows and transparency and instead *'relies on the model of a window that we don't see through, windows that instead overlap and obscure, are resizable and movable'* (2006: 229, my emphasis).

Friedberg's point that computer screens disturb the conception of windows as transparent is also made by Bolter and Gromala. On the one hand, they argue, it is not coincidental that 'we have spent the past twenty years opening, staring at, resizing, minimizing, and closing "windows"' (Bolter and Gromala 2005: 42) on our computers, as the close relationship between windows and transparency 'help[s] us to forget the interface and concentrate on the text or data inside' (2005: 42). The prevalence of this myth of transparency means that '[t]he user is not supposed to notice the interface' but instead 'should look through' it (2005: 35). However, this version of the interface is challenged by digital media, where, for interaction designers, the ideal interface should

> disappear for the user at least some of the time, but not completely and not irrevocably. At some subliminal level, the user must be aware of the interface

at all times. She must know she is using a computer and not actually writing on a piece of paper on the desktop. In VR, she must know that she is looking at a virtual world, or she is likely to run into a wall in the physical world.

(2005: 53)

The goal of interaction design is thus to establish 'an appropriate rhythm between being transparent and reflective' (2005: 6). In this sense, for Bolter and Gromala, the computer screen is *both* a window, offering a 'world of information' so that, '[c]oncentrating on the text or images, the user forgets about the interface (menus, icons, cursor) and the interface becomes transparent' *and* a mirror, 'reflecting the user and her relationship to the computer. The interface is saying in effect, "I am a computer application, and you are the user of that application"' (2005: 26).

Both of the mirrors I have discussed so far involve 'rhythms' of transparency and reflection. They both make explicit the fact that they are an interface, 'reflecting' what is before them only through specific practices of framing and mediation. For example, the idea of transparency is contested by interactive media through the ways in which the screen does not only disappear to provide seemingly unmediated access to the world it depicts, but becomes more apparent in that it requires engagement and interaction. What this suggests, as Manovich argues, is that not only is the screen a 'window onto another world', seeking a 'complete takeover of the visual field' (Manovich 2002: 98), but is also an interface, requiring attention in and of itself (see also Chapter 4 and A. Wood 2007). In attempting to 'augment the experience of trying on clothes for the customer and enhance [...] the relationship between the sales assistant and the customer', the interactive changing-room mirror both highlights its surface in turning from a mirror into a screen that plays back a film and acts as a 'window onto a different world' in showing the customer who and what s/he is now, and who and what s/he might become with the purchase of these garments, an issue that I return to below. The changing-room mirrors thus 'play' with notions of transparency and surface, pulling through the idea that mirrors provide accurate reflections of the body and self and at the same time making explicit the processes through which such images are produced.

Thus, while both of the mirrors draw through the assumption that mirrors reflect, seemingly unmediated, the body in front of them, they also complicate the notions of reflection, representation and mediation by making explicit the fact that they are an *interface*, 'reflecting' what is before them only through specific practices of framing, filming and play back. Furthermore, the *interactivity* with the surface through which the image is created is also made explicit. With *Wooden Mirror* people move to create an image for the hidden video camera to capture and reflect, a process that Bolter and Gromala describe as encouraging people to 'experiment playfully to see how their actions will affect the image. Two women discover that if they stand very still and then blink their eyes, a few of the tiles mirror their blinking' (2005: 33–34). With the changing-room mirrors, customers move for the camera, turning around in order for the mirror to film and play back a view of the entire garment, learning more about the garment via the information on the touchscreens and making the glass doors transparent or opaque. Through this interactivity with different interfaces, I suggest that the images produced by these mirrors are not so much texts, to be read and decoded from an external position, nor representations that are separate from the real world. Rather, interactive mirror images are *intensive experiences*; images created and lived out immanently, through the body.

Bringing the image to life

Both *Wooden Mirror* and the IDEO interactive mirrors in the Prada store have been designed specifically to create and be part of an intensive experience. The changing-room mirrors are part of an attempt to shift a store from being a 'deadening' commercial space to a 'unique' space that engages the customer through appealing to their distinctiveness or difference. This 'rich' shopping experience is created via imagination, sense and the body:

> Experimental technology, intriguing materials, and innovative display methods are utilized everywhere to enrich and transcend the shopping experience: customers touch a button to make the glass doors of the changing rooms opaque, and see their new clothes from various angles on video projections; a circular glass elevator serves as a display area for accessories as well as a means of transport to the basement; unfinished gypsum board walls on one side of the store contrast with a translucent polycarbonate wall overlaying the original brick structure on the other; movable large metal cages hang from the ceiling for the display of clothes; an all-white 'clinic' area contains VIP rooms and tailoring and catering facilities.

Although designed for and located in a different location, *Wooden Mirror* also engages viewers through sense and the body. Discussing how the artwork contests the opposition between digital media technology and the natural/humanness, Rozin explains that in drawing attention to its surface through its 'natural' material, *Wooden Mirror* is an attempt to appeal seemingly directly to the body by making the technological computer interface disappear; an interface 'means putting some sort of membrane between you and the experience. With [*Wooden Mirror*], you understand immediately that it's a mirror, you know to operate it, and no interface is involved' (Rozin 2001: 2).

In the case of both of these mirrors then, images are produced through and as part of an interactive intensive experience and engage the body through affect and sense. The interactive mirrors indicate, as I suggested in Chapter 1, that we 'enter a world of operationality, a world not of interpretation but of navigation' (Lash and Lury 2007: 8). In other words, we *interact* with the mirror images, '[w]e do not "read" them so much as "do" them [...], or do with them' (2007: 8). The mirror image is perhaps an exemplary case through which to think about this doing of or with the image. For instance, reflective glass mirrors depict the movement of the body in front of them, reflecting movement as it happens in the present. Both *Wooden Mirror* and the shop changing-room mirrors also work through 'reflecting' movement 'on' the screen, requiring the 'viewer' to interact with the screen to create their reflection. As a *reflection*, the image is animated through the movement of the body that 'operates' (in front of) the mirror. The mirror image is, quite literally, produced through doing (with) it and, importantly, this immediacy is made explicit. Moreover, and as I have suggested, this doing with images is organized through the screen. The screens of the interactive mirrors are interfaces that are interacted with. In this sense, the screen is a *surface* that animates, that *brings images to life*.

The conception that I am proposing here then, is that the screen is not a defined or solid line between one space or time and another. The screen does not demarcate a 'real world' and a virtual image. Instead, the screen can be understood as mediation, in Cronin's (2010) terms (see Chapter 1), that troubles the distinction between the material and immaterial. Indeed, the screen is a form of mediation that encompasses both the material and immaterial/not yet material, that 'confounds' the distinctions between the body and the image, the real or actual and the virtual. Through the interactive screen, the image is done (with), the body is doing (with) the image. The screen is that which therefore works between and troubles – rather than establishes and bounds – the material and immaterial, the actual and the virtual. As I have discussed in previous chapters, the concept of the virtual that I am developing refers to the intangible, immaterial or 'not-yet' aspects of actual, real or concrete everyday life. The virtual can thus be understood as images – and I argue as images of the future. The images created by the interactive mirrors (as well as images more generally) can therefore be understood in terms of the virtual. Images are that which exist but are not actual. The interactive mirrors work through the virtual in that the image on screen exists but is not (yet) material (see Chapter 1 for a discussion of materialization).

Indeed, discussing the seeming 'reality' of the image of reflective glass mirrors, Bolter and Gromala suggest that,

> the image offered by a mirror is what optics calls "virtual" not "real". The rays of light only appear to come from beyond the glass. We are really looking at the *surface* of the mirror, and what we are seeing is a reflection of ourselves and the world around us.
>
> (2005: 34, my emphasis)

It is in this way that *Wooden Mirror* is a paradox; drawing attention to how we are looking at a 'reflection' on a surface of wood. The interactive mirrors in the Prada store may also be understood in terms of the virtual image. First, the interactive mirror's play-back device requires the customer's movement to create a virtual image. The image is created through movement and it is this movement that animates or gives life to the image. Second, the interactive mirror's playback device is designed to show customers 'all sides of the garment'. The image is virtual in that it exists but is not concrete; it exists as an image in the past (it is a *film* rather than reflection) and in excess of what the customer is able to see in 'reality', without the assistance of the time-delayed film. Third, the mirror can also be understood in terms of the virtual through the ways in which it draws on and puts to work notions of transformation that are central to consumer culture. Here, the virtual image exists not only in the past but also signals future potential, a future that is indicated by the intensive experience of shopping and a future that might yet become concrete (perhaps with the purchase of this particular item). Fourth, as it is designed to be part of an intensive experience, the mirror works through the body, requiring the image of the body to not only be viewed but also to be interacted with, to be 'done with' and lived out.

In all of these ways, the changing-room mirror draws attention to the screen that shows the virtual image, as well as to the 'reflection' itself. It mediates, in the terms set out above, between the actual body in the store and the virtual image 'on screen'. The screen is not only transparent, drawing the viewer into a window of another world, but is also apparent; requiring interaction, attention and reflection. In this sense, it is the screen that organizes the virtual; that is, it is the screen that organizes that which exists but is 'not actually so'. Furthermore, to draw on my discussion in Chapter 1 on how interaction with images is one of the ways in which the virtual is actualized or materialized, the reflection of a garment that the customer tries on is a virtuality that becomes actualized. In reflecting the customer trying on (and then potentially purchasing) the garment, the mirror actualizes the virtual. In the remainder of the chapter, I develop the role of interactive mirrors in this co-ordination and materialization of the virtual. Taking up the analysis of the IDEO interactive mirrors in the Prada store so far, I broaden this discussion to consider further examples of interactive mirrors that have been designed for and located in other shops. This focus is intended to account for the ways in which the virtual is seen by the designers and promoters of these mirrors as an increasingly significant aspect of the 'actual' world, and to return to the ways in which mirrors are an imaging technology through which the imperative of transformation is circulated. In discussing these mirrors, what emerges as particularly important are the ways in which the interaction with the virtual that the mirrors encourage, creates an intensive experience. As I have suggested that power is increasingly working intensively, I conclude the chapter by exploring some of the implications that a focus on intensive experience indicates for understanding contemporary power.

Shopping (with) the virtual

I have argued that the IDEO interactive mirrors located in the Prada store work through and are involved in creating virtual images. These images are virtual in that, in different ways, they are immaterialities. These virtuals are brought into the actual through interaction with the screens of the mirrors. These mirrors were situated in the store in 2001 as an early case of the importance of interaction, screens and the virtual to 'enriching' the shopping experience. Although now defunct, the kind of experience that these mirrors sought to create have recently been discussed and taken up more broadly in retail and consumer culture.

For example, the global trend firm, trendwatching.com, published a briefing in 2011 on the 'twelve consumer trends for 2012'[13] predicting that 'screens will be (even more) **ubiquitous/mobile/cheap/always on**; **interactive and intuitive** (via touchscreens, tablets and so on); an **interface to everything and anything that lies beyond the screen**'. For retailers in particular, these screens are argued to be part of a 'retail renaissance',[14] where the 'offline' world of retailing must 'adapt' to customer's growing familiarity and comfort with screens and the online world. The briefing suggests on the one hand that shops are increasing incorporating screen-based experiences into their physical stores. As just one example:

> UK supermarket chain Sainsbury's, in a partnership with television provider Sky, is allowing shoppers to watch key sports events while they shop using in-cart iPad docks and speakers. The Sky Go trolley comes complete with a tilting iPad holder, speakers and an onboard battery with self-charging solar panel. All sports-minded shoppers need to do is download the Sky Go streaming app onto their tablet and then load it into the shopping cart's dock.

On the other hand, the *in-store* retail renaissance is a response to the increase in online shopping, where the UK Office of National Statistics reported that in 2011 online sales accounted for 9.6 per cent of sales, up from 3 per cent in 2007. Moreover, trendwatching.com's Retail Renaissance report suggests that '8 out of 10 consumers research purchases online. While 42% research online and then buy online, 51% research online and then buy in-store'. This, it argues, is a significant trend in that '[e]-commerce conversion rates have been hovering around 2–3.5% while **brick-and-mortar conversion rates** for fashion retailers have been around **20–25%**'. In addition, '[m]ulti-channel consumers who receive information from more than one source (store, online, mobile, or catalogue) prior to purchase, **spend 82% more per transaction** than a customer who only shops in store'. Encouraging customers into stores through multi-channel information, as I will go on to discuss, is thus important to convert research and browsing into sales.

That screens are more ubiquitous, mobile, cheap and always on means for customers that 'the online world is now completely accessible even when "offline"'. 'For retailers', the trend briefing continues,

> this means a world where not only have **consumer expectations been set by a decade of shopping online**, but one where consumers can **access all the things they love about e-commerce** – convenience, the ability to hear other consumers' experiences, total price transparency, and virtually endless choice – out in the 'real world' too.[15]

In these ways, 'the virtual' is understood here in terms of the 'everything or anything that lies beyond the screen'. This 'beyond the screen' is conceived in the world of retail as e-commerce or online shopping, that which customers are keen to access 'out there in the "real world" too'.[16] As I have suggested above then, the screen here becomes a way of mediating between the virtual and actual, or of bringing the virtual to life in the actual.

More recent examples of interactive mirrors that have been designed by Five Faces (2011), IconNicholson (2007) and Cisco Internet Business Solutions Group (2011) to be located in shops support the issues that are identified in the trend briefings. For example, Five Faces explain their mirror, called SocialEyes, as such:

> Individuals or groups take photos of themselves in a reflective digital mirror, and customers can easily post the image to your stores [sic] Facebook page (or other social media/websites). All images are branded to your store, allowing friends of the customer to see exactly where they have shopped, and your brand, instantly!
>
> Customers can then share their photo with friends to receive live feedback, which in turn drives them to your Facebook page, and this interactivity creates a virtual experience for the customer, while they are in-store.
>
> With the average Facebook user having 130 friends and growing, the viral nature of this allows your brand to be delivered further and faster, in real time.[17]

In their promotional material aimed at the store (rather than the customer), they describe SocialEyes as one 'node' in a circuit between physical stores, customers, social networking sites and virtual and 'real' friends. It is an interactive mirror that 'integrates seamlessly with Facebook, Twitter, YouTube, Flickr and any other web medium. SocialEyes will keep a consistent online and in-store message, engage your customer and keep them engaged in-store and back at home'.

Other examples include an interactive mirror, designed by IconNicholson, that was trialed in 2007 by fashion designer Nanette Lepore in the Manhattan Bloomingdale's department store.[18] This mirror connects up to the internet and involves a customer standing in front of the mirror trying on 'virtual' clothes. Then, as a *New York Times* article on the trial of the mirror puts it:

> a camera relayed live video images of [the customer] to an Internet site where online participants could view her outfit. When Web viewers responded by sending her comments, their instant messages popped up on the left side of the mirror for [the customer] to read. They also selected clothes for her to try on, casting virtual images of the clothing to appear before her in the middle of the mirror, like life-size holograms.

This prototype was expected to be developed to connect up to customer's social networks, such as Facebook, YouTube, Friendster and MySpace, rather than the specially established internet site used in the trial.

A similar mirror, called StyleMe™, has been developed by Cisco (2011)[19] and is explained in terms of what the company call '*mashops*—solutions that bring together the virtual and physical worlds in the store environment' (2011: 1). StyleMe™

> consists of a life-sized mirror that overlays the customer's image with pictures of clothing they select using gesture- and touch-based interfaces. It enables shoppers to quickly create outfits by mixing and matching a wide range of garments from the retailer's in-store and online inventory.
>
> (2011: 1)

The images created by the mirror can then be saved to a 'digital wardrobe', and sent to social networking sites or texted or emailed to friends. The mirror has been trialed in eight different retailers in the UK, including the national department store John Lewis, and is described by Cisco to 'add value by providing customers with expert fashion advice and allowing them to receive feedback about their choices through social media and messaging', a capacity that is seen as especially valuable for women in their teens and early twenties, for whom 'shopping is all about having fun':

> This group of consumers also enjoys shopping with friends. In tests, younger women spent a significant amount of time using Cisco StyleMe™ because it gave them a different way to shop with their friends. The newness of Cisco StyleMe™ also resonated with this group because it was fresh, exciting, and enhanced their shopping experience.

Indeed, as one woman in this age bracket who tested StyleMe™ is quoted as saying, '"I could spend hours using StyleMe™. It was great that I could share the outfits I liked with my friends. I can't wait until this is in all of my favorite stores"'.

All of these recently designed mirrors connect with social networks and thus make links from the physical space of the store to the virtuality of the internet. They are explained in terms that emphasize making connections with friends; SocialEyes in terms of the '130 friends and growing' that the average Facebook user has, and the IconNicholson and StyleMe™ mirrors in terms of shopping with (virtual) friends. Customers shopping in the Nanette Lepore concession in Bloomingdale's were 'invited to use their cellphones to call or text friends and ask them to log onto a Web site where they could see a live video of the outfits being tried on'. Lepore explained her interest in trialing the mirrors in terms of 'see[ing] how the idea of the companion critic could extend to a client's online community':

> 'We're all asking each other: "Do I look fat? How does it look from the back? Can I wear this with jeans?"' Ms. Lepore said, 'If you want the truth, you need to shop with a critic whose opinion you trust'.

64 *Bringing the image to life*

While Lepore and IconNicholson emphasize the potential experience of the mirror from the customer's point of view, a customer interviewed by the *New York Times* argued that the mirror is 'really more for the stores and the brands, to take advantage of people's networks and connect the in-store activity with what's happening outside the store'. Five Faces also explain the benefits to the retailer:

> Interactive and positive purchasing outcomes in Retail can be influenced by friends (Facebook friends) or the user to provide 'how do I look' feedback which is unbiased and not influenced by sales staff.
> The result is to engage the customer and influence purchasing decisions without leaving the store and coming back a second time, and perhaps most importantly, giving the customer a fantastic in-store experience.

The way in which the 'fantastic in-store experience' is conceived, in different ways, by promotional materials and journalistic articles on these mirrors is through connecting up the customer with their friends and 'what's happening outside the store'. In the previous sections, I have argued that interactive mirrors bring together the virtual image of a customer with the actuality of that customer. In these more recent examples, the interactive mirrors bring together the actual and virtual of the customer with the virtualities of the customer's friends. These virtual friends offer 'unbiased', 'truthful' opinions to customers which are likely to 'influence purchase decisions' and result in the customer trying on a garment and then purchasing it. Indeed, the head of multichannel sales at John Lewis, Simon Russell, says of the StyleMe™ mirror,

> Our goal is to be a leader in the multichannel world. With Cisco StyleMe™, our customers can see our entire assortment, try on many different outfits, and get the sizes and colors they want. And because they can use social media to share and get advice, they'll be inspired to shop and buy even more.
>
> (2011: 7)

StyleMe™, SocialEyes and the IconNicholson interactive mirror bring the virtual (friends) into the actual (the physical store). At a time when shopping is moving online,[20] the interactive mirrors become 'a powerful new weapon in the battle to innovate and reinvigorate the in-store experience', as Cisco put it (2011: 8); 'executives should position their stores at the centre of the shopping experience rather than letting them become simply showrooms for online sales' (2011: 8). Indeed, the Retail Renaissance Trend Briefing from trendwatching.com suggests that '[s]hopping moments are now ubiquitous: offline (in the real world, nearly *everything* now has a retail component!) *and* online […] over the last years, smart retailers have looked hard at what would make them unique and forever desirable'. Part of the way in which this 'unique' shopping moment is created is, as the briefing goes on, that ' **"going shopping" is a leisure activity:**

a way of relaxing, a source of entertainment or a chance to meet up with friends and share experiences'. As such, 'when consumers go shopping in person, they increasingly **expect to feel or experience something that they can't get online**: a compelling spectacle, exclusive products, the ability to test and feel things, or learning to use products'. The 'in-store experience' is thus (re-created) by 'smart retailers' as exciting and innovative – an experience – as a key way to 'inspire' customers 'to shop and buy even more', 'without leaving the store and coming back a second time'. In the following section, I explore this shopping *experience* in terms of the concepts of transformation, intensity and temporality that I have introduced above and in previous chapters. In particular, to set up ideas developed further in following chapters, I consider to which bodies specifically shopping experiences are designed (perhaps implicitly) to appeal.

Transformation and the intensive shopping experience

An important impetus for the location of interactive mirrors, and screens more generally, within actual stores is the need for a revitalization, enrichment or renaissance of shopping. For example, one of the reasons provided for the integration of the interactive changing-rooms into the re-design of the Prada store was to 'enrich' the shopping experience; shops and shopping were understood by the architects and designers as increasingly synonymous with other leisure activities so that the experience of shopping was no longer 'unique' or 'distinctive' but instead, 'deadening'. The 'deadening' of shopping as a leisure activity is relatively recent, and as I have discussed, is described by the literature on the mirrors as a consequence of online shopping and the extension of commercialism to other spheres of life. The compelling experience of shopping that the literature on the different interactive mirrors discussed here indicates that shopping needs to be (re)created as the kind of sensory, exciting and inspiring experience that historians and theorists of consumer culture in modernity have described.

Mica Nava (1997) for example, has argued that the opening of department stores across Europe, Scandinavia and America in the nineteenth century was a key new experience of modernity and that such stores are good examples of 'the complexity and danger, as well as the richness and excitement, of everyday life in the modern city' (1997: 56). Nava's focus is on the ways in which department stores were part of a 'rapid expansion of what counted as respectable, or at least acceptable, public space for unaccompanied women' (1997: 61), which included not only these new spaces for shopping, but also, in a list of spaces that echoes the OMA's (discussed above), 'great exhibitions, galleries, libraries, restaurants, tearooms, [and] hotels' (1997: 61). While already established for the upper classes, department stores 'democratized' shopping for middle-class women (1997: 64), and can be seen as part of the more general expansion of consumer culture that Featherstone discusses, where identity, the body and appearance became solidified around a transformative logic (see Introduction),[21] and where women were 'confirmed as the arbiters of taste and interpreters of the new – the modern' (1997: 66). The transformative logic of the nineteenth century that I am arguing is converted into the contemporary imperative of transformation is therefore gendered[22]; indeed, as the StyleMe™ trials suggest, there is a particularly strong resonance between the interactive mirrors and young women.

In order to think about the gendering of the shopping experience, my interest here is in tracing how shops and shopping are exciting and dangerous, rich and complex and, more especially, on how windows and mirrors contribute to such experiences. Again it is helpful to make links between the contemporary revitalization of shopping and the modern shopping spaces. Nava describes the luxurious designs of early department stores, many of which 'had grand open staircases and galleries, ornate iron work, huge areas of glass in domed roofs and display windows, mirrored and marble walls, parquet floors covered with eastern carpets, and furniture upholstered in silk and leather' (1997: 66). Department stores were 'more than just places where merchandise was bought and sold' then; they were 'visited [...] as tourist attractions – as monuments to modernity – for the interest and pleasure they afforded in themselves' (1997: 66). Discussing an early twentieth-century department store, EPA, which opened its first store in Sweden in 1930, Cecilia Fredriksson (1997) explores the embodied, sensory experience that they create, in part through transparent and reflective glass and other materials: 'Glass, stainless steel and mirrors attracted, reflected, and multiplied the range of goods. The mirrors could be deceptive: people sometimes waved to themselves in them' (1997: 119). The mirrors here function to create a multi-sensory and slightly perplexing environment that people might lose themselves within. Indeed, Fredriksson describes this in temporal terms, contending that '[t]ime was an important factor in the new department stores. There were no limits to how long you could spend on the premises. The interior was vast and diverse enough to swallow all the visitors' (1997: 119). In these ways, the modern(ist) department store *experience* can be understood to be *intensive*.

While the specific techniques and technologies of the department stores of the nineteenth and early twentieth centuries are clearly different to those made use of in the stores in which the interactive mirrors are intended for, what occurs in both is the creation of a distinctive, embodied, affective experience. These similarities are established in part through the materialities of the stores, from the luxury of the early department stores to the '[e]xperimental technology, intriguing materials, and innovative display methods' of the Prada store. More specifically, while the mirrors in modern department stores help to create a 'timeless' intensive experience, the interactive mirrors function as part of the intensive shopping experience through encouraging customers to make purchases immediately. That is, by bringing virtual friends in-store, customers will be able to make a decision on purchasing the garment(s) they are trying on without leaving the store. In this sense, the intensity of the shopping experience works through a sense of *immediacy*; both spatially and temporally, what is distant is made proximate.

The intensive, immediate shopping experience that the mirrors are seen to create is interesting in terms of my argument in this book, that the imperative of transformation affectively brings the potential of the future into the present. As I have discussed above and in the Introduction, the centrality of transformation in Western culture developed alongside and as part of the expansion of consumer culture. As Nava points out, the department store 'offered a language to imagine a different and better future: one in which the injuries and wants of everyday existence could be soothed and family lives enhanced' (Nava 1997: 72). Shopping is a leisure activity through which the 'different and better future' that transformation can bring can be imagined and made real, as customers try on and purchase what they could become. Shopping is therefore in itself a process through which the virtual might be actualized, a process that is made explicit by the interactive mirrors considered here. The stores become spaces and times where the virtual or future, and actual or present coincide, where customers make decisions about and through the virtual without needing space and time to think.

In bringing the virtual future into the actual present, a 'fantastic' shopping experience creates a sense of timelessness, or of no time. The department stores are spaces and times in which customers could lose themselves, in part through the slight disorientation that the mirrors and other reflective surfaces produce. It is helpful to focus on these surfaces in more detail in order to consider the relationship between intensity, time/timelessness and transformation further. Indeed, to return to my earlier discussion of reflection and transparency, Rachel Bowlby (2000) explores how the shop window functions at different levels, or what she calls 'removes' (2000: 5) to be both transparent and reflective, offering a window onto the world of the shop and creating a screen in which passers-by could see and be seen. Although concentrating on the exterior of spaces of shopping, Bowlby's argument is significant because she suggests that the shop window helps to create a new activity of window-shopping, which 'elicits the attention and the inattention, the passions and the boredoms, of single strollers and gathered crowds and distant onlookers' (2000: 51). The passers-by are

> anything but focused or directed in their behaviour. [...] [T]hey are not especially rational, but this is not to say that they are *irrational*: the alternatives simply do not apply to their intermediate state. They are literally neither here nor there. [...] In the common as well as the technical phrase, they are 'open to suggestion'.
>
> (2000: 66)

Bowlby argues that it 'is this indeterminacy that seems to make the passer-by the perfect candidate for the catching and latching of attention that the window is meant to secure' (2000: 66).

The indeterminacy that Bowlby points to creates two different ways in which the attention of the passer-by might be secured; one an instantaneous effect and the second a lasting impression. The former

> involves a collapse of time to the point where impression and desire come together at once – immediately and at the same time – to push the passer-by

into the store 'on the spur of the moment', the absolute automatic insistence of having to have it and *now*.

(2000: 66–67)

The latter involves a kind of 'time-lag' where 'the first impression, put away in the mind's own store, makes a second impression [...] when the appropriate occasion draws it out' (2000: 67).

While the shop windows that Bowlby discusses and the interactive mirrors at stake in this chapter are clearly distinct, in exploring the window in terms of reflection and transparency and in highlighting the temporalities of the impressions that the windows might have, Bowlby's points are helpful to think further about what I have argued is the intensive experience that the interactive mirrors create. In particular, while the interactive mirrors may well feature functions that allow customers to think about their purchases – StyleMe™ enables customers to 'send a shopping list and pictures to themselves via email or SMS' (Cisco 2011: 3) – as I have suggested, they are mainly framed in terms of encouraging customers to buy, *now*. In this way, shopping time becomes instantaneous, 'time is collapsed into the "immediate" urge of the present moment and the experience leaves no trace for another time' (Bowlby 2000: 68). It is in this way that I suggest that shopping is *intensive*; the virtual or potential future is brought into the actual concrete present. The virtual is (capable of being) actualized in and as the present.

Furthermore, taking up Bowlby's points about the indeterminacy of shoppers, the actualization of the virtual that the immediate urge to 'have it and *now*' indicates, can be understood in terms of the customer being open to suggestion. Being open to suggestion is, as Bowlby argues, not to suggest that bodies that get caught up in the intensive experience of shopping are irrational, but rather that they are 'intermediate', 'neither here nor there'. In the terms that I have developed in the book so far, being intermediate can be understood as being *in the process of change and transformation*. An effective shopping experience is an intensive time that engages the indeterminacy of the body *affectively*. Indeed, it is the intensive shopping experience – the leisure activity that is 'going shopping' – that creates and co-ordinates the open-to-suggestion customer. As Bowlby puts it, while '[d]oing the shopping involves definite articles, a necessary task; going shopping is out of the way, open-ended, a diversion' (2000: 32). To conclude this chapter, I want to return to the argument that power is increasingly working through intensity that I raised in the Introduction and Chapter 1 in order to begin to consider which bodies in particular are the indeterminate shoppers, that is which specific bodies feel and live out the affectivity of transformation that the interactive mirrors suggest.

Suggestion, difference and power

I have argued so far that the interactive mirrors require customers to not only view the images that they create but also to interact with them, to feel them and live them out. My attention has therefore been on the ways in which the mirror images are not so much 'read', rationally, but are affective, are felt in and as the body. What becomes clear, then, is that the interactive mirrors produce images that function in excess of representational texts, as intensive experiences. I have suggested that a focus on the relationship between the actual and virtual is one way in which sociology might make sense of the intensity of the interactive mirror images. Indeed, while the relationship between intensity and the virtual emerges through the case study of the mirrors, as I have discussed in the Introduction, it is also pointed to in the way in which social theory is arguing that power is now operating. For Lash, for example, power as intensive suggests that power is at once virtual; 'Intensities are virtuals or potentialities' (Lash 2010: 4). Such an understanding of power implies, at least, two inter-related issues. First, it indicates that contemporary society is becoming increasingly (organized around) the virtual. In this sense, an attention to the intensity of the mirror images is in itself significant; the mirror images indicate that images function as virtuals, as requiring interaction and doing with rather than, or as well as, reading. Second, it suggests that a consideration of how the virtual is actualized is at the same time a consideration of how power comes to be lived out in and as specific kinds of bodies. In what ways are the virtual images done with – and by whom?

To begin to answer these questions, it is necessary to think not only about how the virtual is conceived but also how the virtual, and its actualization, might be approached. A focus on the virtual requires the attention to the intensive, to sense, the immanent, emergent and processual. As I have suggested so far, images are not only texts to be read; approaches that treat images as a series of signs to be decoded for their underlying meaning cannot necessarily capture their experiential quality. For example, the images created by the interactive mirrors appeal to sense and imagination rather than reason, reading or meaning. An analysis of the interests and values of the businesses, organizations and design and artworlds involved in the creation of the interactive mirrors needs to attend to the ways in which they were designed specifically to appeal to immediacy and intensity; in the case of the in-store mirrors that have been my primary focus here, to create an 'enriched' and 'unique' experience for customers. While an 'external' approach might unpack the commercial interests of these examples and uncover their ideological meaning, they might miss their allure. This is not to celebrate the more playful or pleasurable aspects of the interactive mirrors but rather to trace how commercial interests and values resonate with the intensive and immanent interests and values of the bodies in front of the mirrors, as unique and varied 'museum goers, researchers, travelers, patients and students'. Power is working *through* such intensive experiences, not as an external series of structures imposed on the body but 'from within', as 'immanent in its objects and processes' (see Introduction).

To attend to power as intensity is not to overlook long-standing patterns that emerge but rather to examine how these patterns might be being made through intensity as well as extensity. For example, in what ways does the OMA's understanding of shopping as 'arguably the last remaining form of public activity' strengthen, as well as shift, the experience of the significance of commercialization? How does the intensification of shopping time reinforce the imperative of transformation? In particular, it is worth returning here to the ways in which the emergence of shopping was gendered as a leisure activity, appealing to women as, in Nava's terms, 'the arbiters of taste and interpreters of the new' (1997: 66). And, while the literature on the in-store interactive mirrors discussed here posits 'the consumer' or customer as gender-less, their emphasis is nevertheless on women: the images included in promotional material on FiveFaces' SocialEyes mirror are all of young women, with a particular emphasis on young white women, the IconNicholson mirror situated in Bloomingdale's was for the expensive women's wear designer Nanette Lepore, and the StyleMe™ mirror again only includes images of young white women in its promotional material and highlights the success of the mirror in trials with young women specifically. If as I have argued here then, the interactive mirrors are part of an attempt to revitalize shopping through the creation of an intensive in-store experience, it is important to note that the particular bodies that are seen as indeterminate or open to suggestion in such settings are gendered, raced, classed and aged.[23]

The association between women and affective experiences is significant, not only because of the ways in which shopping has historically been gendered, but also because of the relationship between women and *suggestion*. For example, in a discussion of Gabriel Tarde's work on the relationship between psychology and sociology which introduces a theory of suggestibility, Lisa Blackman (2007) argues that what is key in some of the ways in which Tarde's work was taken up by psychologists is the 'distinction between the effect of suggestion, and those who have the power or capacity to withstand suggestion' (2007: 586).[24] Perhaps unsurprisingly, this distinction works through gendered, racialized and classed differences. The ability for some to withstand suggestion is produced by them having been fortified by 'individualizing influences such as higher education, travel, self-direction, professional pursuits and participation in intellectual and public life' (2007: 586, reference omitted). In contrast, those who feel the effects of suggestion are associated with the 'so-called "mob susceptibilities" identified in women, and their alignment with the emotional rather than reason' (Blackman 2007: 586, reference omitted, see also Blackman and Walkerdine 2001).

It is helpful to understand the gendering, classing and racing of suggestion in light of my argument that the intermediacy of shopping can be seen in terms of being in the process of change and transformation. Being suggestible, being indeterminate, is one of the ways in which the imperative of transformation works through shopping and consumer culture. In terms of the examples of the intensive experiences that are created by the interactive mirrors at stake here, it is thus some bodies more than others who are susceptible to *feel* the intensive time of shopping, experience the 'collapse' of the future into the present and the affectivity of the virtual in the actual. In arguing that power works intensively through the interactive mirrors, I am therefore suggesting that, just as with a hegemonic understanding of power, where images as representations are part of the regulatory norms through which domination and oppression is produced and

Bringing the image to life 71

reproduced, images are a key way that ideas through which power operates today are circulated and made sense of. In the examples discussed here, the screens of the interactive mirrors bring images to life through the appeal of the intensive time of shopping to particular bodies. In setting up these ideas about the unequal distribution of the affectivity of images of transformation, the aim of the next three chapters is to unpack in more detail the ways in which images are involved in creating and re-creating social differences and power relations.

3 Becoming different
Makeover television, proximity and immediacy

> If you've spent years dealing with body issues and feel like you need a little help with loving yourself, here's an invitation to transform your life. 'How To Look Good Naked' wants to hear from you!
>
> (*How To Look Good Naked*, Living, USA)
>
> [T]ransformation stories that will make your jaw drop.
>
> (*What Not to Wear*, TLC, USA)[1]

Makeover programmes – involving the alteration of bodies, behaviour, spaces and things – have been a prevalent part of Western television schedules since the mid 1990s. Indeed, as Rachel Moseley (2000) describes, the late 1990s saw a 'makeover takeover' of British television that, in part, referenced 'the "things can only get better" ethos of the New Labour government', elected in 1997 (2000: 300). As Moseley goes on to argue, '[m]akeover television certainly suggests some possibility of change for the better – of home, of garden, or lifestyle generally, and even of self' (2000: 300). While early versions of the genre primarily concerned the makeover of homes and gardens (including in the UK *Changing Rooms*, 1996–2004, BBC1 and *Ground Force*, 1997–2005, BBC1), from the early 2000s these programmes extended from making over lifestyle to focus on improving the self. Taking up the trope of the 'before' and 'after', a familiar feature of women's magazines and magazine style television, programmes such as *What Not to Wear* (2001–2007, BBC2 and BBC1), and later, *How to Look Good Naked* (2006–present, Channel 4) and *10 Years Younger* (2004–present, Channel 4), concentrated on changing the self for the better through changing the body. Promising fashion 'rules' to 'take style-challenged individuals on a journey towards tailored self-esteem' (*What Not to Wear*, UK), or inspiration to 'show […] women how to look fantastic with their clothes on or off no matter what their body shape' (*How To Look Good Naked*, UK), the body is seen as the key to improving the self. Indeed, as the quotation above from *How To Look Good Naked* (USA) indicates, 'dealing with body issues' and 'loving yourself, is central to '*transform[ing] your life*' (my emphasis).

These programmes that focus on the body have, as I will discuss below, quite rightly attracted a good deal of academic attention, mainly from feminist theory that critiques the representations of appropriate feminine embodiment that they perpetuate. In particular, many critiques focus on makeover programmes as a form of neo-liberalism (Walkerdine 2003; Ringrose and Walkerdine 2008; Ouellette and Hay 2008; Weber 2009; Ticknell 2010); hence, they emphasize issues of governance, regulation and discipline, and how 'governance works' (Skeggs and Wood 2011: 18). Drawing on the concept of power that I've developed so far, where power is understood in terms of intensity and invention, in this chapter I consider how makeover programmes – and television more generally – operate as and through affect. Indeed, as I will discuss, the theories of affect that have recently become significant across a range of social sciences and humanities subjects have also been elaborated in relation to reality and makeover television.[2] Such theories have particular significance for thinking about images 'outside' of a model of representation. As Misha Kavka (2008) states, television

> evokes affective responses from viewers which are in excess of a controlled meaning-production. In the affective material generated by reality TV programmes we will find a way of moving beyond the semiotics of representation to the affect of presentation, which is linked to the way such programmes feel real.
>
> (2008: 7)

This chapter considers the way in which makeover television is affective through its production and circulation of images of transformation that are seen and experienced as proximate, immediate and actual.

The chapter draws on the previous case study on interactive mirrors and also sets up ideas that will be discussed in Chapters 4 and 5. In taking makeover programmes as its case study, the chapter unpacks the general themes of makeover programmes themselves and of the growing field of research on and theorizing of them.[3] While it analyses different scenes and conventions of makeover programmes, and the relationship between the programmes and viewers, it also attends to some of the dominant ways in which they are conceptualized in recent theoretical work on television, reality and makeover television.

The chapter explores the following questions: How is affect arranged and encouraged in and through makeover television? In what ways are makeover programmes an example of the imperative of transformation? What are the relationships between images and the bodies of those who are watching? If I am suggesting that images of transformation work through the promise of the future as potential, to which bodies does makeover television appeal? And what does this imply for the ways in which social and cultural differences are made and re-made? I address these questions through the concepts of proximity, immediacy and actuality, concepts that emerge in various accounts of makeover and reality television and that resonate with my focus on affect. I direct my attention towards the television *screen*. On the one hand, I consider how the television screen organizes the affectivity of images 'on screen', but I also discuss how these images are materialized or actualized, are felt and lived out 'off screen'. While there has been much textual analysis of makeover programmes, there has to date been little empirical research with audiences. I draw especially on the empirical audience research of Bev Skeggs and Helen Wood (2008) (Skeggs *et al.* 2008; Skeggs 2009, 2010; Wood and Skeggs 2011) and argue that makeover programmes involve a 'proximate' mode of viewing, at least for some bodies. The chapter focuses on this mode of viewing as a concrete experience and considers what this mode of viewing suggests for theories of television that have been interested in reading the image as a text so as to uncover the underlying ideological meaning of the image. Drawing on the conceptualization of images as affect, it concludes by offering a set of alternative concerns for understanding the relationship between makeover television as part of the imperative of transformation and contemporary power.

Makeover television, the body and affect

As I have indicated, makeover programmes which focus on the body are a prevalent part of contemporary television and are broadcast transnationally; for example, *What Not to Wear*, one of the first and best known programmes in the UK, has been shown in a number of countries including (among others) Australia, Sweden and Brazil, and an American version has also been made. The US programme, *Extreme Makeover* (2002–2007, ABC, USA), has been shown in countries including the UK, Belgium and Sweden, and a Bulgarian version has been made.[4] While makeover programmes obviously have their specificities, as a general rule they feature a range of 'experts' advising and transforming what is in the majority of cases a women's body in order to make her both look and feel better. In this sense, makeover programmes can be understood as a prime example of the imperative of transformation; as Tanya Lewis argues, '[t]he visual conventions of the makeover format are [...] centrally premised around the possibility of transformation and renewal' (Lewis 2008: 442). These transformations take place through learning guidelines for shopping and dressing stylishly, as in the case of *What Not to Wear* and *How To Look Good Naked*, through cosmetic surgery and medicalized interventions, as with *10 Years Younger* (2005–present, The Learning Channel and Oprah Winfrey Network, USA), *The Swan* (2004–2005, Fox, USA) and *Extreme Makeover*, and/or through healthy eating and exercise, as in *Supersize Vs Superskinny* (2008–present, Channel 4, UK) and *The Biggest Loser* (2004–present, NBC, USA; 2005–present, Living and ITV, UK).[5]

Changing the body in these programmes is therefore seen as an optimum means of improving the self, and many concentrate on the life stories of those who participate, suggesting that the poor self-esteem, lack of confidence, unhappiness and depression the women currently feel can be overcome by looking better. The *How To Look Good Naked* website, for instance, describes how 'each show follows one woman who is dissatisfied with her body shape, as stylist Gok

Wan shows her how to make the most of what she's got'. One episode from the first series follows 'body-loather' Claire, who 'spends her life hiding from the world'; 'Gok Wan has just four weeks to convince Claire to get out of her rut and start to strut'. In a similar vein, *10 Years Younger* takes participants whose lifestyles – drinking, smoking, stressful jobs, motherhood, etc. – have 'prematurely' tired them out and transforms their appearance in order to make them look younger and thus feel better. The programme involves members of the public judging participants' ages both before and after the makeover, with the aim of achieving a post-makeover age rating ten years below the initial poll age.[6] The *What Not to Wear* website also links the self to the body and, in an online 'style barometer' quiz asks, 'Are you prepared to delve into the deepest darkest depths of your psyche to reveal the sordid secrets of your wardrobe? [...] Do you know what not to wear?'

These examples highlight the ways in which improving the self is achieved through changing the body. As discussed in the Introduction, attending to the links between the improvement of the self through the improvement of the body has been a primary aim of research on what, over the last two decades, has been described as the increasing prominence and significance of the body in social and cultural life (see Featherstone 1991). While it is not new, then, to make these links between the self and the body, what can be identified in makeover television is an *intensification* of this relationship, so that the body comes to stand in for the self. For example, in her study of the relationships between makeover television, selfhood, citizenship and celebrity, Brenda Weber (2009) argues that makeover programmes work through a process of uncovering the 'true self' through transforming the body. Similarly, Sarah Banet-Weiser and Laura Portwood-Stacer argue in a discussion of *The Swan*, that there is an 'overt acknowledg[ment]' of 'the importance of *physical* transformation' in 'becoming a better "you"' (2006: 268). 'The underlying assumption made by these women [participants], and thus by these programmes', they suggest, 'is that appearance *is* one's character and capacity for achievement in all aspects of life' (2006: 268).

Feminist analyses of makeover programmes have been particularly insightful in pointing out the gendered and classed dimensions of such a focus on the body. For example, June Deery (2004) argues that makeover programmes are a 'spectacle, primarily, of female transformation' (2004: 212) and Angela McRobbie (2005) describes the programme *What Not to Wear* as 'largely a female genre of TV and the overall address is to women' (2005: 100, reference omitted). McRobbie explores the programme in terms of the symbolic violence that the (upper-) middle-class presenters enact over their working-class 'victims'; 'the message is that the poor woman would do well to emulate her social superiors' (2005: 100). Drawing on feminist theories of subjectivity, the abject and neo-liberalism, Jessica Ringrose and Valerie Walkerdine (2008) argue that while '[t]he positioning of the girl/woman as the site of self-transformation' is 'hardly new' (2008: 236), such positioning is further stressed by makeover programmes so that it is 'working class women [who] are the primary "vessels" of transformation' (2008: 242, reference omitted).

76   *Becoming different*

As both participants in and audiences of makeover television programmes, it is thus working-class women who are primarily involved in makeover television programmes. Rather than focus on a textual analysis of these programmes, my aim here is to explore how makeover television programmes work affectively to draw in the bodies of working-class women viewers. This focus on affect is, in part, to trace the ways in which, as a form of popular culture, makeover programmes are 'shaped by a logic of emotional intensification [...]: popular culture, at its best, makes us think by making us feel' (Jenkins 2007: 5). Tania Lewis (2008) for example, argues that makeover programmes have links with popular television genres including melodrama, sit-coms and dramas, which have previously dominated television programming, because of their emphasis on emotion (Lewis 2008: 442; see also Gorton 2009). She argues that

> [t]he documentary elements of reality TV and other popular factual formats are combined in the makeover format with many of the features of melodrama, with both the transformational process and in particular 'the reveal' being highly emotional experiences for the participant, their friends and family and even the show's experts.
>
> (Lewis 2008: 442)[7]

Moreover, if placed within the wider context of reality television, makeover programmes can also be seen as involved in the recent trend in television to heighten emphasis on affect, emotion and feeling (Gorton 2009): as the quotation from *What Not to Wear* (USA) with which I opened the chapter demonstrates, the 'transformation stories' at the core of makeover television 'will make your jaw drop'. Skeggs and Wood (2008) argue that, 'by sensationalizing women's domestic labour and emotional management of relationships', they 'display [...] the new ways in which capital extends into the "private", in which capital is engaged in the socialization of affective capacities' (2008: 560). Kavka (2008) sees reality television as emerging out of a 'mediascape that suddenly, in the latter half of the 1990s, discovered its own ability to propagate affective reality' (2008: 37). Discussing the death of Princess Diana in 1997, Kavka describes it as a 'real death' that was at the same time a media death, 'a death mourned *through* the media' (2008: 37). The mediation of the death produced and organized feelings of intimacy between mourners and a woman they had never met, feelings that Kavka argues fed into the 'broad appeal of reality television, an appeal whose roots lie in the fact that reality TV distils, or makes piquant, the affective capture that defines television as a medium' (2008: 48). While television has always been characterized by emotion and affect then, the dominance of reality television, of which makeover programmes are an important part, has been argued to further exaggerate and circulate the affectivity or emotionality of images. As Kavka argues, 'the work of (reality) television lies [...] in its production of affect' (2008: 5). In Chapter 1 I argued that the intensity of affect is organized and co-ordinated by the screen. In the next section I begin to consider the ways in which affect is produced and arranged by screens in makeover programmes.

Screens, mirrors, transformation

One of the ways to examine the relationship between the makeover television screen and affect is to explore what happens *on screen*, that is the conventions, tropes and themes through which makeover programmes work. One significant way in which transformation is organized 'on screen' is via the mirror. Analysing cosmetic surgery makeover programmes (including *The Swan*), Meredith Jones (2008a) focuses on the bodies of the women participants in these programmes, and argues that 'the bodies modified by CSRTV [Cosmetic Surgery Reality TV] are "media-bodies" that come about via "screen-births". They traverse boundaries between representation and reality, between skin and screen' (2008a: 515–516).[8] Her analysis of the cinematography of 'the reveal scenes' in *The Swan*, in which the woman stands in front of a covered mirror which when exposed will reveal 'the new body/self', is insightful for a consideration of the screen in relation to the argument concerning proximity and vision that I develop in this chapter. Jones suggests the cinematography of the reveal moves between 'transcendence' and 'immanence' (2008a: 517); for example, the camera moves from in front of the mirror, showing the mirror from the woman participant's perspective, to behind the mirror, to show the woman's reaction to her new image. Drawing on Mark Poster's Baudrillardian argument, Jones argues that the programme 'reconciles' 'flat', two-dimensional images and 'actual embodied' three-dimensional bodies; 'In the reveal body and body image are finally one: feeling, affect, and movement match – for once, and however briefly – appearance, exterior and reflection' (2008a: 517).

Jones' focus on the role of the mirror in *The Swan* is interesting, not only because in the previous chapter I explored the ways in which interactive mirrors can be understood as screens, but also because mirrors are a central trope in other makeover programmes. Early on in episodes of *What Not to Wear*, for example, after being selected for a style makeover participants were asked to select favourite outfits and view themselves wearing them from within a 360° mirror. The presenters of the programme ask the participant to critically analyse how their outfits make them look and offer their own views on how the clothes are suited, or not, to their body shape. This exchange forms the visual and experiential basis for the rules of appropriate clothing that the participant must follow on her shopping trip. As the series of *What Not to Wear* progressed, the mirror was used more explicitly to probe participants, not only about their style choices but also about their feelings about their bodies, as indicated above, through 'delv[ing] into the deepest darkest depths of your psyche'. Making over the body through selecting 'better' clothes was therefore offered to participants as the solution to *feeling* better about their body, and consequently about their selves.

In *How To Look Good Naked*, the mirror is also a prop for exploring participants' affects and emotions. In one episode with '38-year-old mum April Jewkes, a part-time ballet dancer who's far from impressed with the state of her body',[9] presenter Gok Wan removes April's jacket, positions her in front of three full-length mirrors and says 'tell me what you see when you look in the mirror'.

Following April's explanation of her disappointment with her body, and a short film of April at a ballet class (including an interview with her ballet teacher standing in front of a mirror), April removes her clothes down to her underwear, so she can 'face herself in the mirror'.[10] An exchange then takes place in which Gok asks April to 'really digest the three mirrors, have a really good look at yourself, and tell me what's going through your mind'. April opens up that she is disappointed in her body because it is boyish and has no shape, and that despite trying to tone her bottom, she cannot get rid of what she calls her 'bananas'. She also adds that she feels 'a fraud' about being unhappy with her body, because she is aware that she is slim. Gok's response to April's image of her body is to say that it lies with the death of her mother; her mother was her best friend, who offered her opinion on what April looked like. Gok suggests that April hasn't moved on from the death, so that she remains, mentally, a 'little girl'. Gok tells April that her 'body is near perfect' and that the programme is her chance to grow up. April, upset, agrees.

In this short clip from the programme, the mirrors function as an opportunity for April to 'really' see what she is thinking. It is through the mirror that April can 'really' see herself (see Chapter 2). There is a direct connection made between the physical and mental, where 'talking mentally' refers to what April feels about her body which provides, for Gok and the programme more generally the basis from which to justify the need for a makeover. That April is stuck in the past – she has a distorted image of her body because of her relationship with her mother – becomes the ground from which a self-transformation is necessary.

This need for transformation is explored by the programme through affect. The scene discussed here is shot through a series of close-ups of April's face, which is caught up with and reflective of Gok's account of her life and is increasingly more upset but also relieved or grateful. The soundtrack also supports this emphasis on April's emotions. Furthermore, as with Jones' explanation of the mirror in *The Swan* as providing a 'revelatory moment', in this scene the mirror image is conceived as showing April what she *really* looks like, if she will face (up to) it. The goal of the transformation is to make this mirror image of what April actually is, coincide with how she feels about her body. The transformation that April is about to go on, her better future that is promised, is thus brought into the present. The mirror image here is therefore both virtual – what might yet be – and actual – what April already is. The affectivity of the image – the potential living out of the image – works through *immediacy*, though making the virtual future the actual present. Jones argues that in *The Swan* the mirror becomes a screen in that mirrors collapse the distinction between body and body image, feeling and appearance, the actual and the virtual. In *How to Look Good Naked* the mirror also becomes a screen; a window onto a world that April might inhabit.

Immanence, immediacy and reality

In what I have discussed so far, the conventions and tropes of makeover programmes work *on screen* through an affective immediacy that brings together different images of what participants actually are and could be. However, I also want to think about the ways in which the immediacy and actuality of makeover programmes work *off screen*, that is, how the bodies of (certain) viewers may be engaged affectively by what they see on screen. Indeed, Jones' analysis of the 'screen-births' of participants in cosmetic surgery makeover programmes indicates that it is necessary to examine the ways in which their 'media-bodies' 'traverse boundaries between representation and reality, between skin and screen'. Jones argues that as a core genre of reality television, makeover programmes 'sit [...] at a nexus of transformed bodies that are at once fleshy and digital, three-dimensional and two-dimensional, on the screen and in the living world' (2008a: 515). For example, in the reveal scene, Jones tracks how the camera moves 'behind the mirror in order to film through it' (2008a: 518). In so doing she argues that *'the mirror literally becomes screen – the two are visually inseparable'* (2008: 518, my emphasis). This is a 'revelatory moment' not only for the contestant, but also 'between the contestant and the audience' (2008a: 518):

> As [the contestant] contacts the mirror with her fingertips, she simultaneously appears to be touching the inside of the television screen and almost seems to be reaching out to us, to be about to step out of the television world and into the real world. And, in a sense, this is what happens: after their makeovers 'inside' the television, contestants do step out into the world, but with newly formed media-bodies. Many declare 'I look like a movie star!' – and indeed, success in this format can lead to a continued suitability for life on and in the screen (the first Swan winner went on to be a television personality). This intense reveal scene, then, of mirror-screen symbiosis and of rebirth, is a demonstration of physical and media worlds meshing, of media-bodies coming into being, of actual screen-births.
>
> (2008a: 518)

For Jones here, the media-bodies created on screen 'step out into the world', so that their media or virtual body becomes physical or actual. Her analysis also draws attention to how the shots of the mirror/screen 'reach [...] out to us', the viewer, at home in the living world. In both cases, 'skin and screen', '[f]lesh and media combine' (2008a: 519); the bodies on screen are immediate and actual off screen.

In what ways does this immediacy and actuality, this combining of flesh and media, work through affect? Recent theories of vision and spectatorship have been exploring the relationships between bodies and images in terms of affect. In the context of reality television for example, Kavka identifies what she calls 'affective identification', which refers not so much to '*sharing in* the feelings of the other' (i.e. empathy) as to '*having* the feeling itself' (Kavka 2008: 42). Kavka argues that this is a form of transmission, that is 'part of the material productivity of affect' (2008: 42–43).[11] In their empirical audience research with working- and middle-class women, Skeggs and Wood attend to the specificities of the gendered and classed relations between images on screen and bodies off screen and explore what bodies not only share but *have* the feelings that they see on screen. In particular, they argue that there is a proximity to the viewing of reality television for working-class women which is not the case with middle-class women; reality television is 'more' intense, immediate and 'real', for working-class women. Discussing the ways in which the middle-class respondents tended to distance themselves from the programmes and offer 'considered responses' (Skeggs and Wood 2008: 15) of their engagement with them, Skeggs *et al.* (2008) argue that:

> overall, they were less closely involved with some of the details occurring in the lives of 'reality' television participants, showing less empathy with the protagonists and being less likely to immanently locate themselves within the drama. They often expressed concern over fair representation or the format of the programme, its manipulation of the 'real', and its potential for exploitation of participants.
>
> (2008: 15)

Analysing a female middle-class participant's response to realizing that she is watching reality television, Skeggs *et al.* detail the way in which,

> [t]hrough her ability to perform self-reflexively, Ann demonstrates that she is able to provide a contextualized and 'useful' educational reason for watching, while still being able to recognize the apparent flaws of the programme type – the 'reality aspect' – and demonstrate a considered opinion on exploitation.
>
> (2008: 10)[12]

Within the research then, the viewing of reality television by middle-class women was explained through 'a highly articulate display of reflexive telling' (2008: 10), as a distanced mode of viewing.

Significantly, the middle-class viewing practices described in the research were in contrast to the viewing by working-class women participants, whose

> approach to 'reality' television as entertainment did not require the mobilization of discourses of cultural value as a form of capital. Instead, their 'performance' was much less reflexive in relation to the display of their understanding of hierarchies of taste, and revolved around questions of *immediate pleasure*.
>
> (Skeggs *et al.* 2008: 11, my emphasis)

I will return to the issue of pleasure in the conclusion to the chapter, but here, it is the question of immediacy and its link with affect that interests me. The immediacy of responses to the television programmes is for Skeggs *et al.* 'performed' through affect: non-verbal noises – 'they gasped, laughed, tutted, sighed, "ooh'ed" and/or "aah'ed"' – or in the case of one participant, Saj, 'loud affective declarations of "*NO!*"' (2008: 17). Saj's response indicates that she 'did not have to self-consciously articulate her understanding of the programme; rather, she *demonstrated* how she experienced the programme' (2008: 17).[13]

The connection between immediacy and affect that Skeggs *et al.* identify here is interesting in light of the discussion in the previous chapter on intensity, where intensity was characterized as a 'direct', bodily feeling. The working-class women's experience of the makeover programmes is not reflexive but immediate, not rational(ized) but affective. The immediacy of the makeover programmes involved the working-class women participants 'respond[ing] to the "reality" television participants as if they were "real" – not representations' and 'demonstrating empathy and judgement through personal experience and ultimately *immanently positioning themselves* with the unfolding drama' (2008: 13). For these women, then, it is not so much that the images 'on screen' function as representational texts. Rather the images are engaged with in terms of their 'reality', in terms of what is 'really happening'.

There are two ways in which I want to think about this immanent positioning by working-class women with what they 'really' see: first in terms of the immediacy of television and the 'reality' of makeover programmes, and second, through the particular mode of vision that it implies. I address the second point below, but here it is worth considering how immediacy and reality is produced *through the screen*. While somewhat neglected in favour of analyses of the various kinds of everyday interactions that it is bound up with (Wood 2009) and the types of spectatorship or viewing it encourages, the television screen has, nevertheless, been of interest and/or concern since its emergence. In particular, in early debates about television, questions were raised – as they are today of the screens of computers and mobile phones – of whether and how television screens were disrupting the boundary between public and private/domestic. For example, drawing on Thomas H. Hutchinson's formulation of television as 'your window to the world', Thomas Keenan (1993) explores the conception of the television screen as a *window*. Taking up Hutchinson's formulation that television 'means the world in your home and in the homes of all the people in the world' (Hutchinson in Keenan 1993: 130, reference omitted), Keenan argues that not only does the television screen as a window pose key questions about how public and private spaces are constituted, it also re-works notions of distance and proximity, and of how vision might be conceived:

> In which direction does this window 'face'? Looking out *onto* the world, presenting a view of the distant (tele-vision)? Or does it intrude *into* the home, all the homes, transforming the space, transporting the 'world' into

the homes of the world – opening them up and facilitating the arrival of the image and the other?

(1993: 130)

Keenan's questions here indicate that television has been seen to blur the distinction between the world 'out there' and the people 'in here'; television faces both outwards and inwards, at the same time. I have already suggested that 'on screen' the mirror as screen functions as a window onto a world that both is and might yet be, and it is also interesting to consider further how the television screen of makeover programmes works as a window onto a world for viewers. Through what kind of screen do makeover television programmes offer a window onto the world?

What is seen as potentially so disturbing about television according to Keenan's argument is its ability to bring the world into the home, that is to bring the virtual into the actual. This disruption is at once both spatial and temporal in that the 'urgency of the "now"' is coupled with 'the proximity of the "here"' (Kavka 2008: 15). Television is thus concerned with and productive of liveness and presence, as Kavka goes on to argue,

> the present-ness of the television medium is an attribute not just of time but of space: the seeming 'liveness' of television collapses the time of action with the time of viewing, while the domestic setting of television viewing makes the set and its continuous programming a daily, ever renewable presence.
>
> (2008: 16)

Skeggs and Wood's research on working-class women's viewing of makeover television programmes develops what Helen Wood (2007) calls a 'text-in-action' method, which attempts to 'capture' this liveness, that is television 'as it is happening'.[14] The notion of television as 'alive' or 'happening' is expanded on further by Skeggs and Wood:

> What Lang and Lang call 'The unique perspective of television' refers to the way in which television's claims to liveness and immediacy create a sense of spatially and temporally 'being there', an experience which a phenomenologist such as Paddy Scannell would describe as an 'authentic' publicness through which we have direct access to the witnessing of events 'out there', or a kind of proximity without presence.
>
> (2008: 559, references omitted)

For Skeggs and Wood, then, television as 'live' and 'immediate' creates for the viewer an experience of 'being there'. This point is important because it highlights one of the ways in which the viewer is 'drawn in to' the image. Indeed, as I have discussed in Chapter 1 and develop further in the rest of the book, the affectivity of images works in part through appealing seemingly directly to bodies. Furthermore, in this rather lengthy quotation, Skeggs and Wood argue that proximity to the image is produced especially through reality television:

> However edited, scripted or formatted, 'reality' television presents the audience with the tension over an impossibly knowable 'what will happen next', making us part of the unravelling of the 'real' before our eyes. Whilst the staging of events on 'reality' television complicates any ontological claim to the 'real', it can make a claim to the 'actual' – the camera tells us this 'actually' happened as a response to an unscripted, if contrived, actual situation. According to Kavka and West (2004), the etymological genealogy of 'actual' is related to a temporal sense of 'now', rather than an ontological claim to truth, through which 'reality' television constructs a new sense of 'presentness', arguing that 'reality' television 'is curiously appropriate to its medium because of the way it manipulates time as a guarantor of both realness and social intimacy'. This is a process set in motion by the potential of the medium: 'The actuality strengthens the effect of immediacy; immediacy strengthens the effect of social community; and the community creates a sense of intimacy with performers'.
>
> (2008: 559, reference omitted)

While reality television is not 'real' it is 'actual', and this actuality constructs and confirms a sense of immediacy and intimacy; of 'being there' and experiencing with and what those 'on the screen' are. The virtual image is actualized through the television screen as a window onto a world. In general terms, this would be to argue that the virtuality of television images are actualized through modes of viewing. In this particular case of makeover television, the virtual image is actualized through the *proximate* mode of viewing that I have discussed, a mode of viewing that is direct, immediate and affective. In the next section I go on to consider further this proximate viewing and its suggestion that images are felt and lived out. In particular, I address the question of how the actualization of the virtual takes place through the promise of transformation.

Inclination, actuality and the better future

As a window on the world, I have suggested that makeover programmes organize and encourage, for working-class women, a proximate mode of vision where images are not viewed from a distance but are felt and lived out, that is where images are a *bodily experience*. Indeed, drawing on Vivian Sobchack's (1991) phenomenology of film – where film images are a sensuous bodily experience – Skeggs and Wood argue for a need to 'move beyond' seeing television 'as an object of vision, towards accepting [it] as a concrete experience of the viewer' (2008: 262). As such, television 'becomes open to dialogic interpretation as a sensuous experience rather than conceptualized or cognized through conventional sign systems' (2008: 262).[15] Concentrating on the ways in which the working-class women 'get carried away' (2008: 15) with the image is a method of capturing the affective relations between the programmes and the viewers (2008: 17) that become materialized in embodied practices; in this case through the embodied process of looking. These women are not independent from reality television but rather are 'absorbed' in it.

An understanding of the affective living out of makeover television images indicates that the action in the programme is not so distant but proximate. While it is not as straightforward as suggesting that affect always involves closeness – some affects might involve setting apart feelings, things, bodies, practices, deliberately or not – what emerges in Skeggs and Wood's work is an affective proximity between the working-class women viewers and reality television so that viewing becomes a concrete experience. For Laura Marks (2000), such a mode of viewing constitutes a form of 'haptic visuality'. Writing about film, Marks defines haptic visuality in distinction to 'optic visuality', a mode of perception that 'depends on a separation between the viewing subject and the object' (2000: 162). As such, for Marks:

> [w]hile optical perception privileges the representational power of the image, *haptic perception privileges the material presence of the image*. Drawing from other forms of sense experience, primarily touch and kinesthetics, haptic visuality involves the body more than is the case with optical visuality.
>
> (2000: 163, my emphasis)

Haptic visuality is thus a multi-sensory embodied experience of an image. It suggests that the image is not a representational text but rather a materiality. Haptic visuality *involves* the body – the image is experienced through the body; the image becomes material. Importantly, Marks' concept of haptic vision 'emphasizes the viewer's *inclination* to perceive' (2000: 162, my emphasis) what Marks calls 'haptic images'. Drawing on Deleuze's (2005) notion of 'optical images' in his work on cinema, and altering this to become her concept of 'haptic images', Marks defines haptic images as affective images 'connect[ed] directly to sense perception' (2000: 163). The haptic image 'forces the viewer to contemplate the image itself instead of being pulled into narrative' (2000: 163). Haptic images are in this sense immanent or immediate, rather than (only) being organized to make sense through a 'supplementary' narrative structure (see Chapter 4; Coleman 2011). The point of haptic *visuality* is that while any image might be haptic – affective, immanent – it is not necessarily the case that viewers will be *inclined* to perceive them as such. Haptic visuality, as an attention to this inclination, can therefore be understood as interested not only in the *content* of an image but in what that image *does*, that is in the kinds of inclinations that images produce, the kinds of materializations or actualizations that images might encourage and produce.

This notion of inclination is helpful to think through how it is that working-class women experience the images of makeover programmes in terms of immediacy and actuality. That is, as I have discussed above, while makeover programmes are part of a more general emotionalization of television, and thus work through what Marks would term 'haptic images', these images are not affective to all viewers in the same way. As we have seen, middle-class women have a reflexive relationship with them, explaining the ways in which the genre works through emotion and affect to manipulate reality and exploit unhappy relationships and ways of life. The bodies of middle-class viewers are not inclined to the affectivity of the images; indeed, they focus more on the content of the images and are not moved by them in the way that working-class women are.

I want to suggest that working-class women's inclination to the images of makeover programmes works in two, closely related, ways: on the one hand, there is a correspondence between the 'before' of the 'on screen' transformation, and on the other there is the promise that 'after' the transformation the future will be better. Both of these aspects of inclination are posited by the imperative of transformation that makeover programmes are involved in circulating and consolidating. They indicate that the images seen on screen are, for working-class women, not distant, do not belong to another life, but are *of their reality, of their immediate actuality*. The mode of viewing makeover television programmes is proximate for working-class women because the virtual images are 'real' or actual. The images are therefore not virtual in the sense of being distant but rather are virtual in that they are intensive; they are proximate to the specific actualities of working-class women's lives. For example, in immanently positioning themselves with what is happening on makeover programmes, Skeggs *et al.* argue that the working-class women 'dramatically enact their own life choice – making maternal and domestic sacrifices for the family – as the right choice, displaying and authorising their emotional labour' (2008: 13). The intensive immediacy of makeover programmes thus works through the actuality of the present; the presents of the working-class women on and off screen resonate.

Moreover, in immanently positioning themselves with the transformations that are central to makeover programmes, working-class women viewers incline towards the possibility of change, of a better future. Indeed, discussing the (financial and other) possibilities that are opened up for some participants of reality television, Skeggs *et al.* conceive a process whereby the working-class women in their research

> directly insert themselves into the lives that are on display on the television; they generate a fantasy of *not* struggling to provide for their families, projecting themselves into the comfort of the subject position of successful participant as a fantasy of a life lived without poverty and difficulty. 'Reality' television is not viewed as morally bad and exploitative [...], but as the remote and imagined possibility of a less constricted future: not as an ideological object but as a structure of opportunity.
>
> (2008: 19)

I return in the conclusion to the ways in which working-class women's viewing problematizes the positing of makeover programmes as an object of ideological

86 *Becoming different*

analysis. What is also suggested here is that, as an image of transformation, makeover programmes are affectively felt and lived out through indicating the future as potential. In Berlant's (2006, 2007, 2011) terms, they function as a 'cluster of promises' of 'the good life' (see Introduction). For those bodies and subjects that do not have access to (what is perceived to be) the good life, makeover programmes can be understood as offering a form of what Berlant calls 'aspirational normalcy' (2007), that is as promising to fulfil the 'desire to feel normal and to feel normalcy as a ground of dependable life, *a life that does not have to keep being reinvented*' (2007: 281, my emphasis). While working-class women's *presents* are constituted as in need of transformation, the 'promise' is that through transforming the body and the self, the future is a time when reinvention is no longer necessary.

Of course, as has become clear, makeover programmes – and the more general imperative of transformation – imply both that no area of life is exempt from the need to be reinvented, and that reinvention is a consistent and constant process. For example, concentrating only on those concerned with making over the body, programmes aim to alter age, weight, style, fashion, confidence and well-being – focusing on minute and intricate details, from the colour and texture of fabrics in *Mary Queen of Frocks* (Channel 4, 2011) and faeces in *You Are What You Eat* (Channel 4, 2004–2007), to appropriate foods to eat to correct health and illness in *The Food Hospital* (Channel 4, 2011) to surgical and non-surgical procedures to look thinner, more youthful and attractive. Such programmes therefore coincide with a wide range of 'actual' bodily 'problems' that are constituted as facing working-class women in particular (Skeggs 1997, 2009). This helps to explain the intimate and proximate mode of viewing that the programmes encourage: the images are 'real'; they correspond to the actual lives of the working-class women audience. The content displayed *on* the television screen is thus not contained *within* the screen but rather, as Jones describes, skin and screen, media and flesh combine. The television screen is thus not (only) a site of representation, but rather a space and time – a surface – of becoming.

In promising these processes of becoming different – better – makeover programmes can be understood as one of the ways in which the imperative of transformation is refracted in popular culture, and one of the reasons that they have become so pervasive and popular; they tap into and circulate the idea that the future can be different and thus they resonate with the imperative of transformation, with particular bodies' desires to become different.[16] As well as the specific practices and processes that each individual programme plans out, taken as a popular genre of mainstream television, makeover television is involved in the suggestion of the future as potential. That is, as well as the future being outlined as plans, the future indicated in makeover programmes also works in excess of a set of rules or practices to be learned and followed. The rules or practices suggest that the future unfolds, linearly, from present to future, seemingly smoothly and inevitably. 'Stick to the rules and you'll never be stuck for something to wear again', as the *How To Look Good Naked* website says. 'Look better for longer by protecting your skin' as the *10 Years Younger* website puts it. However, at the same time, the future that the transformation of bodies involves is less precise, more intangible. It is a future that functions as potential, as open, as fantasy. The affectivity of the images is not contained within the dieting or exercise plans, nor the rules of what to wear, nor the steps towards achieving satisfaction or contentment with one's body. Instead, the affectivity of the images connects to more general or more widespread socio-cultural themes and aspirations; in the case of makeover programmes, the impulse towards class mobility, the desire 'to feel normalcy as a ground of dependable life'. Tracing the materialization or actualization of virtual images is a way of analysing how the socio-cultural and bodily are connected through affect. It is to focus on affect as a way to attend to the relationship between the more general and more particular.

In order to discuss the relationship between the more general and more specific, to conclude the chapter, I return initially to the three shifts made by the turn to affect in social and cultural theory that I outlined in Chapter 1 as particularly significant to my argument in this book. These are an emphasis on relationality, a concern with the body as process and a re-working of representational thinking. In discussing these three main points I focus in particular on two issues that I think makeover television highlight: first, the necessity of attending to the creativity that is inherent in the working-class women's inclination to become different, and second the way in which concentrating on the affective immediacy of images implies an understanding of power that suggests an account of the surface of images.

Becoming better: television, affect, power

As I have discussed, 'the affective turn' in social and cultural theory is interested in a varied set of ideas and processes, some of which have been taken up in recent accounts of makeover television, and some of which I have been working through here. The first assertion made in the turn to affect that I am interested in takes up the emphasis on relationality and process in its understanding of contemporary social and cultural life as characterized by 'aliveness and vitality' (Clough 2007: 2), as 'changed and changing' and as 'exceed[ing] all efforts to contain it' (2007: 28). In terms of my focus in this chapter then, the images of transformation circulated in makeover television can be understood as affective because they are concerned with change; they are affective in their 'liveness' and emphasis on process. While I argue that images of transformation generally are processual and alive, issues of the 'liveness', intimacy and proximity seem to be especially significant to *television*, and to makeover television more specifically. It is the case, therefore, that the affective turn is not only a set of theories that have been applied to shifts in contemporary culture, but is also a series of current 'happenings' that have required new theories in order to be more adequately understood.

The second and third concerns of the affective turn that I identified regard the shift from conceiving bodies as entities to processes – bodies are in continuous process and change – and a re-working of images and representational thinking.

In this chapter, I have explored the ways in which makeover television programmes engage the body as process through the affectivity of images. However, it is also worth returning to Clough's argument that I discussed in Chapter 1 in order to develop further my focus on the screen. That is, *as a flat surface*, how is the screen involved in organizing the affectivity of images? It is helpful to take up Clough's analysis of the way in which the textual turn in the 1970s and 1980s rendered media and culture as 'flat' texts. Here, the notion of flatness refers both to the waning of affect in postmodern culture – namely, that culture becomes so integrated into capitalist production that it is no longer affectively or intellectually meaningful – and to the ways in which media and culture were read as a series of inter-linked texts. One way in which such an understanding of flatness could be developed in terms of the contemporary 'society of the screen' (Manovich 2002) would be to argue that as screens come to dominate socio-cultural life, as we come to access more and more of our information and images via screens, culture has become both textual and immaterial; culture has lost its materiality, its sensuousness, its profundity and its depth. In contrast to this conception of the implications of the flatness of the screen, what I have aimed to demonstrate in this chapter is that for working-class women, the screen of makeover television does not so much flatten out the affectivity of images as frame and arrange it. Indeed, it is *through the flatness of the screen* that affects are viewed, felt and lived out. The screen is thus a surface in the way that Adkins and Lury suggest, where co-ordination occurs not '"above", "behind" or "beyond"' it, but where 'the co-ordinating axes or categories of knowing are implanted [on or within the surface], producing a space of possible states' (Adkins and Lury 2009: 18).

Examining how images are felt and lived out through the flatness of the screen is relevant to the re-thinking of representation(alism). The textual approach that Clough identifies can be understood more broadly in terms of a model of representational thinking, a mode of analysis that has tended to focus on texts, discourse and ideology. For Clough, one of the consequences of a textual approach to images is an opposition between nature and technology, where technology (media, images) is seen to distort nature (the body). I would suggest that what a textual approach to makeover television does therefore is oppose the body and the image. The images of makeover television are seen to *represent* bodies, and are thus a text that can be read and deciphered for how far 'real' bodies are distorted by media technology. While technology is not synonymous with ideology, one of the ways in which the division between nature and technology has been played out is in theories of ideology, where the issue of distortion is key to what ideological analyses aim to uncover: how far is nature distorted by technology? How far are representations of bodies in images distorted by capitalist, sexist and racist ideologies? In other words, how can images be analysed as texts to be deciphered for their underlying ideological message? My argument here is not that such an approach to makeover television images is misguided; reading the ways in which makeover programmes fit into and reproduce capitalist ideologies – for example a neo-liberal imperative to transform in certain normative ways – is an important endeavour (see Introduction, and

Coleman 2011 for a discussion of the continued strategic usefulness of representational analyses). However, if what is focused on is the flat screen via which the affectivity of images is arranged, the notion of an ideological message that underpins the image is challenged; co-ordination of the image does not take place above, behind or beyond the image but *on the surface of the image, through the particularity of the makeover television screen.*

One of the specific ways in which I have identified that the makeover television screen works is as a window onto a(nother) world. To return to Manovich's genealogy of the screen, introduced in Chapter 1, television screens may seem to best belong to what Manovich terms 'the dynamic screen', that is a screen that shows moving images, is 'intended for frontal viewing' (Manovich 2002: 95) and strives for 'visual plenitude' (2002: 96); it requires the viewer to screen out their immediate environment and concentrate only on the moving image.[17] The proximate viewing that Skeggs and Wood's research indicates, suggests that viewing makeover television programmes is, for working-class women at least, an activity that involves a concentration on the screen. Indeed, pushing Manovich's genealogy further, if as I have argued the television screen functions as a window through which image and actuality mesh, it would also be appropriate to understand the makeover television screen in terms of one of the trends that Manovich argues occurs in the shift to computer screens, where the screen *vanishes*. As I outlined in Chapter 1, discussing VR, Manovich describes how 'the real, physical space and the virtual, simulated space [...] coincide' (2002: 97). While makeover television programmes are clearly not a form of virtual reality in the sense that Manovich explores, they are premised on and organized around reality (or actuality), so that the images are *experienced*, intensely, directly and immediately. In this sense, as Kavka argues, the 'TV screen is not a glass barrier between illusory and real worlds; instead, the screen is a join that *amplifies* affect and *connects* real people on one side with the real people, in another sense, on the other side' (Kavka 2008: 37). In the vocabulary that I have developed, the screen makes the distinction between the virtual and actual disappear.

If the connection between 'real people' on and off screen, between the virtual and actual, is *affective* it is therefore important to think through what a focus on the affectivity of makeover television images suggests for a conception of power. While I have argued that the images of makeover programmes work not so much as representations as affective materialities, this is not to overlook how the images are involved in the circulation and (re)production of power. Instead it is to examine the ways in which these images involve power as affect; through engaging the body directly and intensely the bodies of working-class women are affectively caught up in the images. In terms of the affective appeal of makeover television to working-class women, through immediacy and actuality makeover programmes are involved in the *constitution* of the category of working-class women. As is clear, the 'suggestibility' (Blackman 2007, see Chapter 2) of some bodies to images of transformation is uneven: not all bodies feel with images of transformation in the same way. Indeed, as Blackman points out, that reality and makeover television is so suggestive to working-class women (in my terms, that working-class women are inclined towards makeover television) is 'not simply evidence of working-class susceptibility or vulnerability to media influence, but rather [is] a technology of the social that works through encouraging intensity, intimacy, connection and belonging' (Blackman 2011: 239). What requires more engagement, then, is the ways in which 'mediated processes of self- and social (trans)formation [...] cannot be reduced to a neo-liberal psychotherapeutic logic' (2011: 247). As a socio-cultural impulse that is felt and lived out bodily, affect is thus unevenly distributed and is involved in the reproduction of inequality: there is an affective economy (Ahmed 2004) where 'value circulates and resides' and where 'affect is converted into judgement' (Skeggs *et al.* 2008: 18).

An understanding of power as affectively drawing in some bodies more than others suggests for me that an ideological analysis of makeover programmes is not the only way to understand their popularity and appeal. In particular, I would suggest that two inter-linked issues require attention, the first regarding the kind of – immanent, immediate, experiential – relationship between working-class women and makeover programmes, and second, the question of critique. First, to follow through on the point that makeover programmes are a refraction of the imperative of transformation and as such emphasize a future that might be better, to focus primarily on the ways in which makeover programmes are involved in the replication of standards and normative values is to potentially miss what it is about them that working-class women become so absorbed in, so inclined towards. If the imperative of transformation understands and addresses bodies as open-ended processes, what seems especially significant about makeover programmes is their suggestion of the potentiality that bodies might become better. Potential in this sense refers to the ways in which 'becomings' are involved in the making of something new, open or different, where this 'new' is not necessarily disconnected from the 'old' or the past (see Coleman 2009, 2011). It is the taking up of the spirit or force of an image, to become not like it but *with* it; to do (with) the image (Lash and Lury 2007). Of course, it could be objected that materializing images of transformation is not the creation of something new but the reproduction of the same old ideological values.[18] However, this would be to overlook the *empirical experience* of those bodies that are moved by and with such images. This is vital to note when images of transformation appeal most strongly to working-class women; it is necessary to both acknowledge this inclination and to understand how it works.

Furthermore, second, while working-class women get carried away with, and absorbed in, the images of makeover television programmes, at the same time, Skeggs and Wood argue that they are also critical of it.[19] For example, they draw on their interview with Lucy as she watches an episode of *What Not to Wear* and both 'goes along with' and criticizes the advice that Trinny and Susannah (two upper middle-class presenters) provide as inappropriate to the life of the working-class participant in the programme (2008: 263). One way to understand this criticism of the programme would be to see Lucy as forming a cool, distanced response; the kind of reflexive and considered responses of the middle-class women, for example. In this sense, criticism would operate through distance. However, Skeggs and Wood argue against the elision of criticism and distance, suggesting instead that it is *through the immediate and immanent experience of watching reality television that for working-class women criticism emerges*:

> What is important to note is that Lucy does not address the programme as if 'deconstructing' a textual representation of the characters as such, but is involved in a dialogic relationship with the text [...] potentially experienced more like an extended social realm. Her interactive engagement with the television programme in question is governed by the actuality of the setting and the self-representation of a 'real' mother. Thus, Lucy is immanently placing herself as adjudicator of this advice for her own life as well as that of the television participants, locating herself physically within the action: 'I don't want to be hand-washing etc.' We suggest that it is the focus on domestic labour and the labour of femininity that generates this connection, a gendered connection that also brings class relations into the conversation to assess authority (as seen in the dismissal of Trinny and Susannah as 'stuck up posh birds'). These types of responses were frequent in our data, where these programmes provoke recognition of the different types of labour and of the actual energy expended in the labour of femininity.
>
> (2008: 564)

Taking up this argument, then, for working-class women, images of transformation are not responded to through a distant or considered mode of spectatorship but rather are experienced – enjoyably *and* critically – through proximity. Through such proximity, the screen does not contain images but rather produces the possibilities of relating to, feeling with and materializing the images.

The conception of makeover television images as 'real' and absorbing therefore challenges how viewing practices have tended to be theorized through a model that works through spatial and temporal distance and rational 'reading'. For example, Kristyn Gorton (2009) argues that the emergence of the academic discipline of television studies out of film theory means that there is a prioritization of what she terms the concept of 'cool' distanced (psychoanalytic) desire. As such,

> there is a need to consider the emotional experience of spectators rather than place emphasis on a cool, detached or distanced response. The point worth making here is that distance must no longer be considered a necessary component to the spectator's critical response. The 'elision' made between 'distance' and 'intellect' and 'closeness' and 'sentiment' needs to be challenged.
>
> (2009: 77)

Gorton draws on Henry Jenkins' (1992) discussion of the discomfort shown at a viewer 'sitting too close' to the television screen: 'Surely, it can't be healthy

92 Becoming different

(morally, socially, ideologically, aesthetically, depending on your frame of reference) to give oneself over so totally to a television broadcast!' (Jenkins 1992: 60). In order to examine – and dispute – this unease with 'giv[ing] oneself over' to the television, Jenkins turns to Bourdieu's argument that 'contemporary bourgeois aesthetics consistently values "detachment, disinterestedness, indifference" over the affective immediacy and proximity of the popular aesthetic' (Jenkins 1992: 60, references omitted). For Bourdieu, bourgeois aesthetics privilege rational control over emotion and Jenkins identifies the dominance of critical detachment as the appropriate model to analyse popular culture. Jenkins argues that 'this discomfort with proximity has assumed a specifically political dimension within ideological criticism':

> the naïve spectator, drawn too close to the text emotionally, loses the ability to resist or criticize its ideological construction; critical distance, conversely, bestows a certain degree of freedom from the ideological complicitness demanded by the text as a precondition for its enjoyment. Within this formulation, distance empowers, proximity dominates.
>
> (1992: 61)

Jenkins' argument, that distance is the privileged position from which to analyse the ideological messages of a text, is crucial to the argument that I make in this chapter, and more generally in the book. Given the dominance and pervasiveness of this model in sociological and media and cultural studies accounts of the image, I argue that it is necessary to question, and challenge, the dichotomy between distance/privilege. This is necessary not only to correct, conceptually, the privileging of one side of the dichotomy over the other (distance over proximity) and the association of proximity, passivity and emotional over-identification with femininity and of distance, activity and rationality with masculinity (see Doane 1992; Jenkins 1992: 61). It is also necessary because, as I have argued, contemporary popular cultural images work not through 'cool' detachment but through close emotional and affective engagement. In order to understand how power works then, and in order to be able to develop appropriate forms of critique,[20] a focus on the ways in which affect functions through seemingly addressing the body directly, immanently, immediately, and through positing the body as in the process of constant change and becoming, is important. I return to the issue of affect and critique in the Conclusion, and in the next two chapters I continue to examine the affective appeal of images of transformation, by moving to consider those images that highlight the body, health and dieting as key ways of materializing the body differently.

4 Immanent measure

Interaction, attractors and the multiple temporalities of online dieting

> Weight Watchers is a flexible plan designed to fit in with your life, so you keep on living while playing the game and losing (weight, that is!).
> (Weight Watchers UK website, January 2012)

> Weight loss clicks when you play online.
> (Weight Watchers UK website, January 2012)

In the context of a concern with the ways in which the imperative of transformation is refracted across a variety of media, cultural and social sites and taken up through a range of bodily processes, a focus on weight is of primary interest. In this and the next chapter I explore how weight has become a 'problem' that must be fixed. The increasing significance and problematization of weight has been well documented in recent accounts of the body. While it is not correct to state that men or children are exempt from this imperative,[1] as feminists have long pointed out, the relationship between gender and bodily appearance is well established and it is women who are most involved in the concern around weight.[2] Feminist social and cultural research has focused on the problem of weight for women, tracing the logics of late capitalism to dieting and cosmetic surgery (Bordo 1993/2003), obesity (Colls and Evans 2009) and to a wider preoccupation with the healthy body (Sedgwick 1994). Attention has been drawn to the increase in, and experience of, obesity surgery (Throsby 2007, 2008, 2009), to the ways in which weight is associated with particular classed, raced and gendered positions (Skeggs 1997), to celebrity culture and, as explored in Chapter 3, makeover television programmes that aim to solve the ways in which over and underweight bodies are presented. While there is an increase in women undergoing surgery to lose weight (Throsby 2008, 2009), dieting is, as Susan Bordo suggests, 'the most popular form of "correction"' (2003: 202). Bordo and others point to the normalization of dieting within everyday Western cultures. Susie Orbach, for example, argues that '[n]o-one is much disturbed by statistics that show that 80 per cent of women in countries like the USA, the UK, New Zealand, Australia are dieting at any given moment' (1985/2003: xxiii). My focus in this chapter, then, is on dieting as an everyday, perhaps mundane, means of becoming materially different; slimmer, healthier and happier.

More especially, I explore the emergence and increasing popularity of *online* dieting plans and focus my analysis on the US and UK Weight Watchers websites, that, as the US site states, encourage existing and potential dieters to lose and 'keep weight off for the long haul'.[3] More specifically, Weight Watchers has developed an online dieting plan where, again according to the US site, 'state-of-the-art and easy-to-use interactive tools help you reach – and maintain – your weight-loss goals'. As the two quotations that open this chapter suggest, one of the ways in which online dieting is imaged and presented as an achievable means of successfully transforming the body/self is its capacity to 'fit in with your life'; so much so that dieting can be understood as 'playing the game', a game that 'clicks' when it is 'play[ed] online'. As the most popular form of 'correction' dieting is in this sense just another aspect of 'keep[ing] on living', a kind of 'second nature', as one current online dieter puts it and as I will go on to discuss. My interest here is in how the mode of living that (online) dieting organizes can be understood in terms of the imperative of transformation; as affectively and intensively future-oriented.

Indeed, in examining the ways in which Weight Watchers online dieting attracts and organizes the imperative of transformation through losing weight, what emerges as particularly significant is the temporalities that are produced. This chapter attends to the ways in which the linear temporality that successful dieting is often understood through – where dieters progress from overweight to ideal weight – is challenged and/or re-worked in online dieting by the co-existence of multiple temporalities. This is important to note given the recidivism rates of dieting; for most, dieting is not a one-off successful period of time but rather a process that is returned to again and again. Even when dieting is successful, this success is achieved through a 'lifestyle change' where, as the US website explains of its plans, 'what you learn will stay with you for a lifetime'. I argue that the temporalities of online dieting are involved in the creation of an agency that is not (only) repressed but *enabled*; the online plans indicate that dieting is – or should be – empowering, affirmative and life-changing. My focus on agency here thus emerges out of my conception of power as that which is intensive and inventive, rather than (just) repressive and restrictive – it is necessary, I suggest, to understand dieting not (only) as an oppressive regime imposed upon women, nor (only) as an unrestricted, individualistic agency. Instead, it is necessary to understand how agency is produced through interaction with the interface, where the multiple temporalities of the dieting website are affectively 'attracted' through a particular route (A. Wood 2007). As such, what becomes significant is the negotiation of multiple temporalities around a notion of a future idea(l) body weight that is potential (Adkins 2008) rather than planned for and measured in external and homogenous ways (Adkins 2009). Developing arguments introduced in previous chapters, this chapter suggests that the materialization of different kinds of bodies through dieting works through a logic of potential and the capacity to change.

In keeping with the focus of the book, in this chapter I examine the role of the computer screen in the ways in which online dieting is arranged as a series of images that indicate the possibility of the better future. In Chapter 2 I discussed how interactive mirrors function both in terms of a screen that disappears and a screen that is highly visible, that requires interaction. In Chapter 3 I examined the television screen as a window; the screen disappears so that makeover television images are experienced directly, immanently. My attention in this chapter is on the ways in which the computer screen becomes evident, that is, in Bolter and Gromala's terms, an interface 'reflecting the user and her relationship to the computer. The interface is saying in effect, "I am a computer application, and you are the user of that application"' (2005: 26).[4] In this way, I am interested in examining the ways in which the interface is not a neutral medium but actively shapes knowledges, understandings and experiences (A. Wood 2007); I analyse the ways in which online dieting is co-ordinated by Weight Watchers interfaces and the kind of dieting that interaction with its 'interactive tools' are seen to create and encourage. My argument here is that interaction is a means of exploring further the affective experiences of screens. Drawing from the ways in which I have discussed vision, experience and interaction in the book so far, I suggest here that through interaction with particular kinds of interfaces, particular kinds of bodies are materialized or actualized. I therefore ask; how do the modes of interaction that the Weight Watchers online dieting plans are organized around produce the ways in which images can be materialized? How is the interactive screen involved in materializing certain kinds of bodies? In what ways does the future as potential affectively attract and co-ordinate these materializations?

Weight Watchers, dieting and agency

Within the context of the normalization of dieting, a number of dieting clubs operate, of which Weight Watchers International, based in the United States for more than 40 years and the UK for almost 35 years, is perhaps the best known. According to the history pages of the Weight Watchers UK website, the company began in America in the early 1960s when Jean Nidetch, from Queens, New York, 'discovered the best way to control her weight was to be able to eat normal food and talk to her friends and other people who could understand, and support her'.[5] The US history webpage states that 'an estimated one million people, from Brazil to New Zealand, come together each week to help each other meet their weight-loss goals at Weight Watchers meetings. And now, Weight Watchers is reaching others via the Web at WeightWatchers.com'.[6] The role of the weekly meetings is to provide a regular form of monitoring of, and support for, weight loss; meetings are led by a trained leader who has previously lost weight through attending Weight Watchers meetings, there are confidential 'weigh-ins' and a different topic, such as making healthy food choices or eating out, is addressed each week. The meetings are described on the websites as building on the success of its leader through sharing her or his experience and

96 Immanent measure

expertise, as providing a supportive environment, and through the private weigh-ins, as enabling members to establish and maintain 'a commitment to yourself'; 'Once you've decided to lose weight, holding yourself accountable is essential to achieving success'.

In addition to the weekly meetings that the Weight Watchers plan was initially organized around, members can also follow a dieting plan via Weight Watchers Online. The Weight Watchers Online plan is described by David Kirchhoff, President and CEO of Weight Watchers International, as extending the 'singular mission' of the company 'to help people lose weight in a sustainable way by helping them adapt a healthier lifestyle and a healthier relationship with food and activity'. He goes on to state, '[t]o be successful, we must constantly find new ways to help more members and subscribers' and the online programme 'help[s] Weight Watchers successfully navigate into the new millennium by developing the best internet-based weight loss products anywhere'. As is clear, much feminist attention has been paid to weight and dieting, and overviews and discussions of this work are thorough and numerous (see for now classic examples, Bordo 2003; Davies 1995). Rather than rehearse such discussions here then, I draw on Cressida J. Heyes' (2006) characterization of feminist work on dieting in order to unpack some of the ways in which agency and temporality are typically conceived and to offer an alternative account. Although Heyes' Foucauldian approach does not refer to 'agency', I suggest that her argument facilitates a different way of understanding how dieting websites are involved in the invention of agency through temporality.

According to Heyes, 'existing critical accounts of dieting [...] typically rely on the central explanatory concepts of either "false consciousness" or "docile bodies"' (2006: 126), concepts that I suggest can be understood in terms of wider sets of debates concerning power, ideology and hegemony, and neo-liberalism, governance and discipline (see Introduction). Discussing the former explanatory concept of false consciousness and providing examples of the ways in which weight comes to be a 'stand-in for health' (2006: 128), of the 'myth that there is a standardized range within which each individual's weight must fall in order for her to be healthy' (2006: 128) and that 'a huge majority of diets will fail' (2006: 129), Heyes asks, '[c]an the widespread popularity of attempts to lose weight be understood only as the product of false consciousness – the result of systematically obscuring the truth about health, weight and recidivism?' (2006: 129). A notion of false consciousness rests upon the assumption that women diet 'because we have been ideologically duped by an oppressive set of beauty ideals: being thin will make us (hetero)sexually desirable, aesthetically pleasing to ourselves and others, and better able to build an image that is appropriately feminine' (2006: 127). While Heyes argues that her question '*can* be partly explained through ignorance and misconceptions' (2006: 129), not least because companies such as Weight Watchers 'obscure' (2006: 129) the labour of dieting through emphasizing 'lifestyle change' for example, the false consciousness model is inadequate in its focus on 'false beliefs about weight loss, or thrall to an oppressive aesthetic' to the detriment of considering dieting as 'an activity' (2006: 127).

Focusing on dieting as a bodily and embodied practice, Heyes suggests, is precisely what occupies feminist work that engages with Foucault's work on docile bodies, of which Sandra Bartky and Susan Bordo are 'the best-known advocates' (2006: 127). The notion of docile bodies suggests that power is not that which is simply imposed on us, without us necessarily being aware of it – as the false consciousness model implies – but rather is 'a ubiquitous relation within which multiple local forms of domination, discipline, or denial of self-government can occur' (2006: 131). Located within such an understanding, Bartky's and Bordo's work 'offer a number of more specific insights into the local practices of weight-loss dieting' (Heyes 2006: 133):

> Their Foucauldian accounts show how normalisation is enacted through ever-finer measurement and closer surveillance of the subject population. For example, standard height-weight tables are themselves a macro-tool for normalising the population – for taking a vast and diverse group of people and establishing a 'normal range' to which every individual bears some relationship. Deviation from the norm is then (falsely) read as proof of behaviours that can be pathologized, just as conformity is (falsely) taken as evidence of health and good conduct. Biopower here thus operates both at an epidemiological level and at the level of the production of a weight-based moral identity in the individual.
>
> (Heyes 2006: 133)

Heyes takes up these insights to examine the ways in which Weight Watchers' meetings and online and paper materials encourage and perpetuate such fine disciplinary work, for example through the notion of *watching* one's weight and recording the 'points'[7] value of food and exercise in diaries.

However, for Heyes, the focus on dieting as the production of docile bodies leads Bartky and Bordo to 'stress the *repressive* moments in the construction of the slender body, contra the *enabling* functions of the dieting process' (2006: 136). Heyes argues that, if dieting is so bleak it is necessary to enhance such accounts with a consideration of the question, 'why subject oneself to such a regime?' (2006: 136). Heyes draws on her own experience of participating in Weight Watchers meetings for ten months and on Foucault's later work concerning 'technologies of the self'[8] to examine this question. Technologies of the self, in Foucault's terms,

> permit individuals to effect by their own means or with the help of others a certain number of operations on their own bodies and souls, thoughts, conduct, and way of being, so as to transform themselves in order to attain a certain state of happiness, purity, wisdom, perfection, or immortality.
>
> (Foucault quoted in Heyes 2006: 138, reference omitted)

Importantly for Heyes, technologies of the self involve discourses of self-care that 'feminists have long encouraged' (2006: 126). That is, 'the care of the self is ontologically prior' (Foucault quoted in Heyes 2006: 143, references omitted) and is 'equated with taking care of oneself in the face of the gendered exploitation that characterizes many women's lives' (Heyes 2006: 143). 'The technologies of the self the process of dieting cultivates expand the dieter's capacities' (2006: 138), through offering 'the sense of self-development, mastery, expertise, and skill' (2006: 137). Consider, for example, the description on the homepage of the Weight Watchers UK website to 'Learn how to eat well, feel full and control your cravings, even when you're bored or stressed. So you lose weight week after week and discover a brand new you'. Similarly, in one of the Success Stories on the US site, Judy describes the effect of her meetings and states:

> The greatest benefit of my weight loss has been the opportunity to become reacquainted with myself. I forged a new relationship between my mind and body. I became mindful of the food I was consuming and, in turn, felt empowered by the good choices I made.

For Heyes, such examples demonstrate that dieting can – and must – be conceived as an expansive process of transformation as well as a disciplinary and regulatory process.[9]

While Heyes' argument is helpful for examining the kinds of notions that tend to circulate within feminist work on dieting, it is ultimately concerned with supplementing Foucauldian accounts by attending to Foucault's later work. However, for the purposes of this chapter, my concern is not to further develop the feminist Foucauldian approach that Heyes lays out, but rather to take up her identification of dieting as enabling and productive, and consider how this might work in relation to the argument I am making in this book that the imperative of transformation works through ideas about potential, change and intensity. In particular, I focus here on the notions of agency that are being suggested in work on digital media and the interactivity of the computer screen.[10]

For example, I suggest that the notions of false consciousness and docile bodies that Heyes identifies as operating within feminist work on dieting conceive women's *agency* as, in different ways, repressed and/or restricted through dieting; women's agency is regulated through (false) ideas, structures and/or discourses that encourage the achievement of an ideal(ized) body through dieting. Indeed, implicit or explicit in the critiques of dieting that Heyes outlines is a desire to expose and demolish contemporary Western culture's 'tyranny of slenderness'. Understanding dieting as a tyranny, as Heyes suggests, is to focus on the ways in which dieting is a regime imposed on women, a regime that, in my terms, determines women's agency in particular ways. My point here is not that slenderness is, actually, not tyrannous or that the tyranny of slenderness is, actually, a good or positive thing. Instead, I am interested in considering the ways in which the imperative of transformation in online dieting works through a notion of extended or expanded agency, rather than through a notion of an agency that is being repressed. Such a consideration draws attention to agency as, fundamentally, co-constituted through various engagements, entanglements or encounters

(Barad 2007; Suchman 2011). Moreover, such a consideration of agency in relation to dieting disrupts, or at least puts into question, the temporalities of dieting through which a repressive notion of agency works. As I go on to argue, this is important because online dieting is producing new temporalities that work through the generation of affect and potential.

Dieting, planning and the future

The notion of repressed agency, in terms of dieting, involves a relationship to a specific notion of temporality. The examples discussed above, whereby dieting involves a meticulous and constant observation, measurement and recording of calorific intake and output, suggests a temporality that is linear and progressive. That is, understood in terms of a notion of agency being repressed through dieting as a tyrannous regime, temporality is figured as that which inevitably moves forward. A closer consideration of the Weight Watchers Online plan is indicative here. As I have discussed, the original Weight Watchers plan that progressed through weekly group meetings has been 'extended' by a dieting plan that members can follow online. Weight Watchers Online is promoted as convenient, simple and personalized.[11] A key way in which the online plan promotes itself as successful is through its 'Don't take our word for it' features, where a quotation from a Weight Watchers member expands on and supports the company's characterization of itself. For example, on the main introductory webpage for the Weight Watchers US Online programme, online subscriber Taysha, explains her reasons for following this programme:

> Doing the plan online suited my personality. I boot up both at home and at work so I have access to WeightWatchers.com 24/7. I adore the POINTS Tracker. It helps me figure out my daily food and activity POINTS values.

On the UK site, Michele explains: 'I'm office based and use the internet for banking and shopping, so decided to use Weight Watchers Online. It proved to be convenient, simple and became second nature to me!' It is important for Weight Watchers to be able to characterize itself as convenient, flexible and simple as their weight loss programmes are intended to be sustainable ways of life – 'second nature'. The process of self-transformation – of becoming materially different – is thus ongoing. Weight Watchers' programme, Discover Plan™, for example, aims 'not just to help you lose weight but to keep it off for the long haul' and '[f]ollowing the plan online, you'll get a food plan you can stick with, plus guidance on incorporating exercise, becoming aware of your behaviour, and building a supportive environment. All online, all at your own pace'.

Subscription to the online plan includes tools and advice on eating well (for example, recipe and restaurant search facilities and customized meal plans), on exercise and staying active (for example, fitness video demonstrations) and on planning and tracking weight loss. This last online tool involves members keeping online food and exercise diaries that monitor calorie intake and output and provides charts that demonstrate weight loss progress. Online US subscriber Lisa states, 'Watching the line go in a downward slope of the Weight Tracker graph gave me the inspiration to keep at it and I loved what I was doing'. Weight Watchers Online, then, is depicted as a new solution to the problem of weight loss and, in extending the company's 'mission' and methods into 'virtual reality', it is seen to improve the convenience, ease and maintenance of weight loss. Losing weight online, 'at your own pace', involves a sense of a future body size and shape that is moved towards. Indeed, as the tools that monitor and track weight loss demonstrate, establishing a 'goal weight' is integral to Weight Watchers. The goal weight is thus an ideal(ized) image of what a body could – and should – become in order to be healthy and attractive and it thus operates as a point to which weight loss is directed.

For example, online subscriber Deborah, featured on the UK website's Success Stories pages, indicates the importance of the goal weight in motivating weight loss over a period of months: 'I always kept my goal in mind throughout my weight loss. With every pound I lost I knew I was getting closer to a pair of size 10 jeans!' Discussing the online tools that monitor progress, she explains how she is asked by 'Plan Monitor' to update her weight, even when her visit to the site wasn't with that intention. The continual tracking of her weight lost 'was a real incentive', and the weight loss rewards (stars, congratulatory messages) and 'tips if you've had a bad week and a gain' were 'very motivational'. It is worth noting here the ways in which Deborah describes the online tools; as personalized and anthropomorphized. However, my main point of concern is with the specific temporalities of dieting and weight loss that might be identified. The online tools are designed to track and monitor the progress, or not, of weight loss daily (through food and exercise journals) and weekly (through the graph), and a personal weight loss plan will be created for each subscriber (the Weight Watchers plans are designed to '[p]roduce a rate of weight loss of 1–2 lb per week after the first 3 weeks, during which losses may be greater due to water loss').

There is, therefore, a notion of progress built in to the online tools which might be understood to involve, what Helga Nowotny (1994) terms, 'the extended present', whereby 'the future mapped out in linear terms draws dangerously close to the present' (1994: 49–50):

> [The future] is increasingly overshadowed by the problems which are opening up in the present. The future no longer offers that projection space into which all desires, hopes and fears could be projected without many inhibitions because it seemed sufficiently remote to be able to absorb everything which had no place or was unwelcome in the present. The future has become more realistic, not least because the horizon of planning has been extended.
>
> (1994: 50)

Drawing on Nowotny's argument here, the temporalities produced by Weight Watchers website can be understood to indicate this notion of the future being

Immanent measure 101

drawn into the present. For example, according to Nowotny's point, the very concern with weight that the website, and the company more generally, is premised upon can be conceived as the future 'increasingly overshadowed by the problems which are opening up in the present'. That is, a concern with weight is a contemporary 'problem' – reproduced across a range of sites – which bears down on and comes to define the future as 'realistic' rather than as that which might be otherwise understood as 'sufficiently remote'.

For example, the goal weight can be conceived as making the future 'more realistic' in extending 'the horizon of planning'. The Weight Watchers' goal weight is set as a routinized probable, and preferable, outcome that can only be achieved through the monitoring and tracking of the progress of weight loss. Achieving the goal weight requires meticulous and personalized planning and maintenance, as evidenced by the tools designed for Weight Watchers Online: '[a]ssess your food and exercise habits with new and improved interactive tools', '[m]onitor your weight to see how your food and activity habits impact your progress', and '[g]et personalized goals based on your height and weight so you won't go hungry'.[12] In this sense, as Nowotny goes on to argue in ecological terms, '[t]he temporal category of the future is being abolished and replaced by that of the extended present' (1994: 51).[13]

For Nowotny, the extended present is a temporality in which the future is always already within the present; measured, planned for, determined, chosen in the present and, as such, is 'already taking place now, [...] being determined in the extended present' (1994: 51). Discussing the development of technology and its increasing embeddedness in the everyday, Nowotny argues that the extended present 'has chosen the future and not vice versa' (1994: 52). The Weight Watchers Online tools can be understood in a similar way, as bringing in to being a future that is determined through the embedding of technology in everyday life. In this sense, the possibilities of the future – the future as the not-yet decided – are closed off and pre-determined. The planning involved in the choosing of the future is repressive. Two dieters featured on Success Stories on the US site, for example, explain their reasons for following Weight Watchers plans in terms of their future: 'I knew the moment my grandson was born. I wanted to be able to run, play ball and ride bikes with him' (Lisa) and 'I was 27, too young to be out of breath after going up a flight of stairs' (Michelle).

While Nowotny's argument is important and interesting, and I return to them towards the end of the chapter, what is most significant here in terms of my argument so far concerning agency is that the planning involved in the choosing of the future by the (extended) present, or of the present being chosen by the future is repressive. That is, the potential and possibility of agency is also closed off; repressed through the tyranny of slenderness and the regime of dieting which involves a linear temporality progressing from an unsatisfactory present to a predetermined and planned for future. While the notion of an agency that is repressed is, clearly, one way of understanding the temporalities of dieting, I want to return to what I have suggested is the enabling agency that dieting produces to consider how both the Weight Watchers website and the Weight Watchers Online plan are

102   Immanent measure

not only extending and reinforcing dieting as a linear and progressive temporality but are also creating, or enabling, dieting temporalities that are *distributed, non-linear* and *non-singular*. This is to attend to the ways in which the website and online tools do not only repress agency but also constitute and enable agency through the 'choices'[14] that interaction(s) between the website and its user necessarily require. As I will argue, an exploration of the constitution of agency through interactivity necessitates an understanding of how temporalities are experienced and embodied affectively.

The interface, interaction and non-linearity

The point raised by Nowotny, that the embedding of technology in everyday life shapes or constitutes dominant socio-cultural temporalities, can be followed through in order to explore the temporalities that are constituted through contemporary everyday technologies, such as the computer and the world wide web. Recent work on technology and embodiment focuses on the screen as, in Aylish Wood's terms, 'a place where viewers interact with technological interfaces' (2007: 1).[15] Drawing on Wood's work in this section, I examine the Weight Watcher's website and online dieting plan through the modes of engagement and interaction that it produces and encourages. In other words, I explore Weight Watchers *as an interface*. While work on images has usually been concerned in analysing their content (for example images as representations or as story-worlds), Wood's approach is to 'step back from story-worlds' and,

> instead pay attention to the screen as an interface where viewers come into contact with technologies of image construction. It seems important to look more fully at this interface, as by thinking about how technologies are used to manipulate the different elements that make up an image's placement and transformation we can begin to see how the organisation of these elements is central to processes of viewing, playing a part in enabling and orchestrating engagements and identifications.
>
> (2007: 12)

For Wood, then, in order to understand how an image and a viewer are involved in particular engagements and identifications, it is necessary to examine not only the content of an image but also its technological construction and organization.

One of Wood's starting points is that the screen in digital culture is becoming increasingly split and fragmented (2007: 71). For example, television programmes, films, animations, contemporary art works, computer games and websites are characterized by images split up and distributed across a single screen. Wood argues that fragmented interfaces such as these produce new modes of engagement and interaction between the viewer and the image and that, as noted in the opening of the chapter, rather than being unobtrusive or transparent (as in the case of Hollywood continuity editing for example), the screen or interface becomes apparent. In this way, attention is drawn not only to what is on the

Immanent measure 103

screen but also to the methods, conventions, techniques through which images are organized and mediated. As I discussed in Chapter 1, the way in which images are framed is as important as what images are of. Wood points out how split screens are often supposed to create distracted and dispersed viewers whose 'ability to engage, identify with and take up a subject position [is] compromised in the absence of a centralising unified and embodied presence' (2007: 72). However, critiquing the notion of a passive viewer that tends to underpin such arguments,[16] she proposes an alternative way of understanding the interaction between interfaces and viewers, where 'a viewer's engagement with fragmented interfaces can be more productively understood by giving consideration to the *range of age*ncies available in such an engagement, and seeing in them a *generative potential* rather than only losses' (2007: 72, my emphases). That is, far from creating modes of distracted and passive engagement, the interactions that fragmented interfaces create involve activity, negotiation and (enabled) agency.

One of the ways in which Wood argues that fragmented interfaces create agency is through 'decisions' that viewers must make about which aspect of the interface to attend to. Wood compares fragmented interfaces to what she terms 'narrative films' and suggests that typical accounts of narration tend to emphasize 'an event-driven organisation […] of a linear chain of cause and effect' (2007: 84). Such narrative films are organized around a central character, who drives the plot, and 'the architecture[17] of the interface is transparent' (2007: 84). As such, these films encourage the viewer to take up one particular point of view (that of the central character(s)) in order to enter the 'story-world' and become absorbed in the narrative. Fragmented interfaces, on the other hand, are not so much transparent as 'reflective' (Bolter and Gromala 2005, see Chapter 2), that is, these interfaces highlight different areas of the screen at different points so that the decisions that the viewer is making are capable of becoming clear. Discussing the film *Pleasantville* (1998), for example, Wood explains that

> the gaudy use of colour creates a non-seamless structure, in which colour elements compete for a viewer's attention with characters – at key moments in the film, a colour change carries the narrative momentum as much as the character. At any moment of such an active colour transformation, a viewer's eye is drawn away from character action towards the colour 'action'. This splitting, or distribution, of attention results in a more complicated engagement with the imagery through the addition of another point of focus.
> (2007: 84)

Wood develops this notion of a more complicated engagement with fragmented interfaces in terms of temporality. She argues:

Where the cause and effects elements of a seamless text are usually understood in terms of a singular linearity, competing elements lead to a more complex linearity. If we imagine a singular linearity to involve an already complicated mode of engagement, in that viewers' dispositions bring their particular interests and histories into proximity with the structures of the text, the addition of competing elements brings another dimension to the engagement. Each time a competing element appears on the screen the singular linearity is deformed, as the competing element's ability to distribute attention puts pressure on the linear engagement of a viewer.

(2007: 84–85)

Wood's argument here is not that the linearity of a seamless text is singular (there are for example many seamless texts in which the plot is developed in a non-linear way) but rather 'that the emphasis within the image is singular' (2007: 170, n.12). An interface is non-seamless if it demands an engagement that involves competing elements and therefore a distributed mode of attention. An interface is non-seamless if it demands a non-linear, non-singular engagement.

Such an understanding of a non-seamless, fragmented interface has implications for the ways in which it is possible to understand the temporalities of the Weight Watchers Online website. One way of analysing the website would be to see it as a seamless text, that is as encouraging a linear mode of engagement whereby Weight Watchers Online potential or existing members are directed towards one specific outcome; the achievement of an ideal(ized) weight through successful dieting. Such an analysis might focus on the representations that are featured on the website, including smiling slim white women checking their laptop in a clean, clutter-free white bedroom (to signify the convenience, ease and simplicity of the Weight Watchers Online programme). Or, such an analysis might focus on the narrative pull of the Success Stories, where the successful end point of reaching the goal weight and/or the ease and appeal of changing an unhealthy lifestyle for the better is emphasized over the labour involved in losing weight. In this sense, the notion of the 'extended present' explored above in terms of the online monitoring and tracking tools would seem an appropriate way in which to conceive the temporality of dieting; there is a linear progression from the present into the future, and the future, as a particular goal, is decided in advance. The narrative singularity of dieting in these cases is in the ways in which this future is decided and (promoted to be) achieved are 'seamless'.

However, drawing on Wood's argument so far concerning the ways in which the interface is crucial in encouraging and structuring particular modes of interacting with digital media, Weight Watchers Online can *also* be understood to produce other temporal engagements with the notion of dieting. As a digital medium, it is clear that the Weight Watchers website is a non-seamless, fragmented interface. Both the Weight Watchers US and UK homepages, for example, are split into discrete sections that include images and text. These sections invite the viewer to navigate or negotiate the website by deciding whether to find out more about 'How Weight Watchers works', whether 'meetings or online' is 'right for you' or to 'Sign up now' to 'Get FREE recipes, workout tips and more'. There are a number of 'competing elements' on the interface and the emphasis on the screen is thus non-linear; attention is distributed across a range of options. While it may well be argued that the mode of engagement with this website involves a viewer who is passive and/or distracted (relative to the activity of the dieter who attends meetings in 'real life' for instance), Wood encourages an understanding of the website as opening up or complicating the notion of attention. Rather than encouraging inattention through its competing elements, the website creates 'a distributed mode of attention' which demands the viewer to make choices about what to give attention to. Following this through, it is possible to suggest that the temporality of dieting is not as linear as the Success Stories imply, but is distributed across a range of possibilities. Both of the Weight Watchers homepages are designed to be engaged with by a variety of viewers, those who may or may not be members already and, as such, those who may or may not have a goal weight established. This is important to note as a mode of distributed engagement is always already embedded into an online dieting temporality. One of the implications of this distributed engagement, as I go on to discuss below, is that the linearity of the cause and effect of dieting is disrupted.

Attractors, agency and temporality

It might seem, given the discussion so far, that Wood's approach to fragmented interfaces implies an unrestricted mode of engagement with the Weight Watchers website – viewers are free to choose to attend to whatever part of the website they like. It might also seem that this implies an agency that is conscious, intentional and located within an autonomous individual. In this way, it might seem, agency is extended or enabled to an unlimited extent. While Wood does suggest that the distributed attention prompted through engagement with fragmented interfaces can be understood in terms of 'how the text opens towards agency' (2007: 86), this agency is not unconstrained but rather is directed through 'attractors'.[18] Drawing on the idea discussed above that the colour changes in *Pleasantville* attract a viewer's attention towards the conventions through which the narrative is constructed, an 'attractor' can be understood as 'a significant influence in establishing [...] routes' through a text (2007: 87). For example, within the singular linearity of a seamless interface it is often that 'a character acts as an attractor within the system of narrative organisation' (2007: 87). That is, only 'particular routes of engagement' (2007: 87) are favoured through the role of the character as an attractor. However, Wood goes on to argue that,

> [i]n a non-seamless interface structured around competing elements, the character's position as an attractor is no longer singular as each competing element has the potential to exist as an attractor within any given system.
> (2007: 87)

The Weight Watchers website, then, as 'a non-seamless interface structured around competing elements', involves a number of possible attractors that may well demand attention. The banner across the top of the homepage, for example, which includes the options to find out more about 'How Weight Watchers

106 *Immanent measure*

works', 'Food and Recipes', 'Fitness & Health', 'Success Stories', 'Community' and/or 'Shop', can be understood as possible attractors in that they compete as elements for the viewer's attention. Compared to the meetings, which are described as dealing with one particular issue per session, the Weight Watchers website can be understood as a non-linear interface in that the engagement it requires is non-singular.[19]

Attractors are 'a virtual architecture of possible interactions' (A. Wood 2007: 91) which 'always influence [...] how a viewer reads a text, and opens up or closes off meaning to different degrees' (2007: 93). The options on the Weight Watchers homepage banner (or indeed the very many options on the rest of the page) structure the possibilities of interaction and open up and/or close off other possibilities. As Wood suggests then, '[w]ith more than one attractor the possibilities for agency expand' (2007: 87). That is, the attractors involved in the fragmented interface of the Weight Watchers website do not simply engage a viewer's agency that somehow pre-exists; rather *attractors are generative of agency*. The engagement produced through interaction with the website resides neither in the website nor in the viewer; rather, the non-singular distributed attention that Wood explains is produced *through the interaction itself*. What these points suggest is that agency is produced, or enabled, through interaction with attractors. In this sense, Barad's term 'intra-action' would seem more appropriate here than the more usual term 'interaction'. As Barad states, while inter-action assumes that there are two or more distinct things that pre-exist each other and can therefore interact, 'the notion of intra-action recognizes that distinct agencies do not precede, but rather emerge through, their intra-action' (Barad 2007: 33).

Furthermore, for Wood, attractors 'emphasize the different *temporalities* of competing elements' (A. Wood 2007: 9, my emphasis). For example, an attractor not only garners attention spatially – by highlighting different spaces of the screen as with the colour changes in *Pleasantville* – but also temporally, by highlighting the ways in which different temporalities are present on the same screen. Discussing attractors in films, Wood argues:

> In allowing themselves to co-operate with a text's organisations whether it is a narrative film or a more experimental one [...], viewers participate via the temporalities established with the interface. I do not mean by this in the sense of entering into the temporal world of a story, which can place us in a past, present or future, but in the sense that the images are experienced via the temporality established by the technological devices of the interface.
>
> (2007: 96–97)

Understood as an interface of attractors – temporalities of competing elements – the Weight Watchers website is constituted through a variety of dieting temporalities. It is important to note, as indicated previously, that the future is a crucial temporality of dieting, and that this future is in different ways brought into the present so as to seemingly dissolve the duration between the present weight and the goal weight. But this temporality is not singular or linear but multiple and fragmented. There are, for example, the pasts, presents and futures of those dieters featured as Success Stories and the recidivism of the vast majority of Weight Watchers members, and the temporalities of the (potential) dieters that viewers of the site 'bring with them'. Crucially, these multiple temporalities do not pre-exist or belong outside of the engagement with the website but rather are 'established *with*' (my emphasis) the 'technological devices of the interface' through intra-action. As such, 'temporal structure is not natural, but the consequence of an organisation' (Wood 2007: 96).

Wood's reference to 'temporal structure' here is interesting given my discussion above of what I term agency as often conceived as repressed in feminist work on dieting. In sociological literature, agency is typically understood as one part of a binary opposition involving structure: agency is restricted by (social) structures. For example, in my interpretation of the feminist work on dieting that Heyes discusses, in different ways, social and cultural preoccupations with body weight and shape, as well as capitalist concerns regarding profit (Weight Watchers as a business) and efficiency (healthy bodies are more productive than unhealthy ones), structure women's agency and encourage dieting. As I have argued, such an understanding of dieting as repressing agency works through and (re)produces temporality as linear, singular and progressive. However, what Wood's statement suggests is that the temporal structure of dieting, which works in a 'complicated' and generative relationship to agency, is not inevitable but is produced through its organization. Temporal structure in the Weight Watchers website and online dieting plan is organized as a more 'complex linearity' (A. Wood 2007: 85) whereby competing attractors 'within' the interface construct a route through the text. This understanding of Weight Watchers as an interface attends to the ways in which, despite the multiplicity of temporalities 'enabled' through the website, a particular route is favoured:

> Another way of thinking about the impact of an attractor is that it intercedes in our progression within a given spatio-temporal organisation. By progression I mean the way in which we establish linearity in our sense-making by connecting up different elements, including and excluding various pieces of information as we go along. Potentially, any spacetime is open to many progressions, but only a limited number occur, and attractors exert an influence over which progressions tend most frequently to occur.
>
> (2007: 94)

Indeed, as Manuel de Landa (2002) has argued in his discussion of science,

> different trajectories may be attracted to the same final state, [and] singularities are said to represent the inherent or intrinsic *long-term tendencies* of a system, the states the system will spontaneously tend to adopt in the long run as long as it is not constrained by other forces.
>
> (2002: 14)

108 *Immanent measure*

In the context of this chapter, then, within a 'sphere of influence', an attractor 'attracts' or 'engages' a multiplicity of trajectories or temporalities towards a 'singularity', or the 'long-term tendencies' of a system. In these terms, Weight Watchers, as a sphere of influence, can be understood to 'attract' the multiple temporalities involved and engaged with its website and online plan towards a singular tendency. In this sense, the route through the fragmented, non-linearity and non-singularity of the Weight Watchers website is a progression, in Wood's terms, in its singularity and linearity.

Online dieting temporalities and affect

Of course, it should be noted here that de Landa argues that these singularities are what the system will 'spontaneously tend to adopt in the long run', so long as that system is not 'constrained by other forces'. I am not suggesting here that, as a sphere of influence, Weight Watchers is unconstrained; as I have pointed out above, it is a business concerned with profit and efficiency among other things. However, drawing on the argument that agency is generated through interaction with the interface, rather than necessarily repressed by it, and on the argument that the Weight Watchers website engenders many different temporalities, the concept of the attractor attends to the ways in which its specific regime of dieting is attractive, or, in the terms that I've developed in the book so far, *affective* – experiential and intensive. That is, despite its enablement of agency and its multiplicity of temporalities, the Weight Watchers website 'attracts' a particular mode of dieting *through* interaction with its interface. Indeed, engagement with the Weight Watchers website indicates that agency is relational and constituted through interaction with the interface, and that the temporality of dieting is inherently multiple and distributed. As such, it dislodges an understanding of agency as that which is conscious, intentional and located within an autonomous individual.

This seems especially important, not only due to the critiques that feminists have made of such an understanding of agency (McNay 2000), but also given the current imperative *to diet* that I have discussed so far, whereby women, as autonomous subjects, are encouraged to utilize their will power, exercise their free will and achieve their goal weight. The Weight Watchers website promotes its plans through ideas such as 'stay in control', 'make smart choices' and 'lose weight while still enjoying your life'. In drawing attention to the multiplicity of dieting temporalities and to the way in which the future may figure in dieting as potential, my intention in this chapter has been to argue that dieting exceeds the straightforward progression from overweight to ideal(ized) weight. While it is clear that this temporality cannot be ignored – it is the dominant representation of and preferred 'route' through dieting after all – to *only* consider dieting in these terms is to overlook the different 'attractions' that dieting may have for many women. As Heyes argues, dieting is enabling, otherwise women would not so readily subject themselves to it. Focusing only on dieting as a linear progression is also to overlook what Throsby has described as the framing of the failure to lose weight 'as evidence of a moral failure of individual responsibility to care appropriately for the self, and by extension, to be a good citizen' (Throsby 2009: 201–202, references omitted). Attending to the temporalities that intersect with, or undercut, a linear temporality is also to make explicit the imperative to diet and to attempt to dislodge the seeming 'ease', 'convenience' and 'accessibility' that such an imperative implies.

While the sense of empowerment that Weight Watchers encourages can be understood to promote and produce a sense of careful planning in which the future is brought into the present in such a way that the future is pre-determined, it can also be understood as producing different temporal relations between the present and future. These, I would argue, cut through the individualizing effects of dieting critiqued by feminists and involve instead, what Claire Colebrook calls, 'more radically impersonal vital processes' (Colebrook 2008: 52). These forces include bodily affects, affects that, while felt in 'individual' bodies, are also collective in that they 'happen [...] across us' (Colebrook 2002: 39) and 'produce affective bodily capacities beyond the body's organic-physiological constraints' (Clough 2007: 2). Drawing on these ideas, I would suggest that dieting can be understood as an affective (social or collective) orientation to the future as the time and space whereby *things will be (materially) different*. For example, the constitution of the 'empowerment' that Weight Watchers online promises is a temporal orientation produced by and yet supposed to counteract uncertainty. Plans to 'stay in control', for example, create such uncertainty and anticipation through simultaneously indicating that present and future temporalities are 'out of control' and can be controlled by careful planning – an issue that I discuss in more detail in Chapter 5. According to such an understanding, it is not only, as Nowotny suggests, the (extended) present that has chosen the future as it is that the future has chosen the present. The online Weight Watchers tools function as part of the affective experience of the present whereby, as Adams *et al.* discuss in their analysis of anticipation as a 'defining quality' of contemporary social life, the present is oriented towards the future as if this were the only temporality that matters (see Introduction). For example, the online tools 'set the conditions of possibility for action in the present' (Adams *et al.* 2009: 249) by problematizing present body size and shape through an emphasis on a future ideal(ized) body shape and size: 'get started today'.

This affective orientation to the future in the present is, I suggest, a future that is not the linear progression that imperatives to diet imply, but a future that is *virtual*; always already 'within' the actual present as potential. While imperatives to diet suggest linear progression whereby the future is pre-determined by action taken in the present as the *only* temporality, my argument is that, as an affective state, dieting involves multiple temporalities that do not all move smoothly towards a logical outcome (a slimmer body for instance). The issue of recidivism seems to be worth returning to here, given that most Weight Watchers diets will fail and be taken up again. The diary entries of food and exercise, then, might very well include calorie intake which exceeds the points allowance, despite good 'intentions', and the graph charting weight progress might very well include peaks, troughs and plateaus as well as, or instead of, a downward trend. The 'long-term tendency' of dieting, then, might very well be failure rather than success, despite the route through dieting that the attractors might encourage. In this sense, the meticulous planning and the tracking of weight loss, and the notion of the extended present that I suggested that these tools might be understood through, is only part of the story. It might very well be the case that the future is brought into the present not only in terms of a plan that is successfully adopted, but also in terms of a future that remains what Nowotny terms 'sufficiently remote'. This is to see the future as an affective state that may or may not be achieved. In turn, this is to conceive the temporality of online dieting concerned with the future, not as open-ended or endlessly open, but neither as pre-determined through detailed planning. Rather it is to conceive the future as, in Lisa Adkins (2008) terms in the context of contemporary capitalist labour organization, 'engaged in the creation of potential' (2008: 194).

For Adkins, as I outlined in the Introduction, contemporary capitalism requires its labour to be not deposited in and derived from a commodity, such as a website, but as 'more open, as vital and alive' (2008: 195).[20] Discussing interviews with website designers, she argues that the value of the website is conceived by the designers not in terms of its hourly paid cost to build, nor in terms of its status as a commodity but rather in terms of 'a future which concerns potential leads, and more precisely, potential and not yet even existing customers' (2008: 194). While I do not want to speculate on the Weight Watchers designers' conception of the website, I think it is helpful to understand the website in terms of 'potential leads'; the attractors that I have suggested the Weight Watchers website interface includes indicate 'potential' futures to which the viewer might further attend: learn more about Weight Watchers, buy products to help you lose weight or subscribe to a plan now. These futures 'are engaged in the creation of potential' rather than establishing a pre-determined path to success. Indeed, it is interesting to note that while the Success Stories provide specific examples regarding how long it had taken for weight to increase (an 'unhealthy equation dictated my life for 10 years', Jennifer) and regarding how long weight loss has been maintained ('Elizabeth has now been maintaining for five years and still uses Weight Watchers Online as her "healthy eating tool"'), there is a vagueness about the time and labour involved in losing weight. The future is potential, then, through its elusiveness (as opposed to its meticulous planning) and through its assemblage with other temporalities.

However, while dieting involves potential, what becomes necessary at this point is a further consideration of how interaction with the Weight Watchers website does not necessarily escape the standardizations of ideal(ized) weight which feminists have argued that dieting is involved in, but re-works such standards through the ways in which the relationships between temporality, agency and dieting can be understood in terms of affect. That is, it is necessary to consider the ways in which affective potentiality is socially organized. For example, returning to the appeal of following the online plan 'at your own pace' seems significant here; highlighting that following the plan *online* allows dieting to become, more easily, 'second nature', suggests that the temporalities of the everyday life of *the dieter* are taken into account. Dieting, then, is not a homogeneous plan into which different dieters must be fitted, but rather is a programme – or *life* – set by the pace and agency of the dieter herself. What this points to is what Adkins (2009) has called a 'crisis' of measure, whereby homogenized and external forms of measure developed in industrial capitalism are increasingly unable to account for the 'productive activities' (Adkins 2009: 334) at stake in societies where a temporality of the future as potential is (becoming) dominant.[21] Crucially for Adkins, it is not that contemporary productive activities (of which website design might be one) therefore escape measure but that, while there may be 'a break with certain kinds of measure – especially those forms that operate externally to entities – this break may also involve the emergence of new kinds of measure, specifically ones whose co-ordinates may emerge from the entities themselves' (2009: 335).

Taking up this argument and understanding dieting as a productive activity fundamentally concerned with measure (that is, dieting as a process of potentially attaining an ideal(ized) 'goal' weight), what is involved in the temporalities of online dieting is precisely 'the emergence of new kinds of measure' that Adkins identifies. The 'measure' of online dieting emerges from the temporalities of the dieter, or, more correctly, measure emerges through the temporalities produced through the *intra-action* between the website and dieter. As such, the measure of a diet is not (only) the linear downwards trend of a chart from the progressive weight loss that is implied in the imperative to diet, but is also that which can incorporate the recidivism, the bad weeks and slip ups, that characterize dieting, because this measure emerges from the entity (the co-produced dieter and website) itself. This is therefore an understanding of the multiple temporalities of dieting not as a 'phenomena operating outside of the co-ordinates of time and measure, but *a material reworking of time itself*' (Adkins 2009: 335, my emphasis). Online dieting is not 'outside' of temporalities and measure per se, but rather, through interaction with the Weight Watchers website, online dieting is re-making temporalities and measure(s). As a mode through which contemporary power works, measure is here not so much an external repressive system imposed upon a dieter, but rather is *immediate*, *immanent* and *intensive*. These re-makings of time and measure are *material*; are registered in, on and through the materiality of the body, through the bringing to life via the screen of certain kinds of bodies.

Adkins' argument is also interesting here because it is made in relation to debates around the 'becoming woman' of immaterial labour. Debates about immateriality have also been played out in relation to digital culture where the physicality and 'fleshiness' of the body is seen as (capable of being) erased. However, just as such arguments have been challenged in the context of digital media (for example Sobchack 2004), Adkins' argument suggests the impossibility of uncoupling the body from the work that it does. While labour may be increasingly 'immaterial', the effects of this shift are materially felt. Although dealing with contemporary technoscience rather than immaterial labour, Adams *et al.*'s discussion of anticipation also draws attention to the ways in which changes in what they term 'temporal orientation' are materially felt and 'have affective dimensions' (2009: 260). My suggestion here is that online dieting should be considered in terms of these affective dimensions. The contemporary Western problem(atization) of weight (in relation to health for example) and the imperative to diet is a state that, as Adams *et al.* suggest, 'entails a forced passage through affect, in the sense that the anticipatory regime cannot generate its outcomes without arousing a "sense" of the simultaneous uncertainty *and* inevitability of the future, usually manifest as entanglements of fear and hope' (2009: 249).

What emerges through this 'sense' of the imperative to diet is that the attractors that Wood identifies as 'structuring' the 'routes through' the interface can be understood as modes of interaction that are constituted through affect. The attractors that, as Wood argues, work temporally to 'enable' a viewer's engagement with the interface are affective in that they 'attract' or 'appeal to' the temporalities that the viewer 'brings with them' and that 'structure' the viewer's interaction. This affectivity is co-constituted through the resonance between the temporalities of the attractors and the embodied temporalities of the viewer; the attractor and the viewer 'feel with' each other, immanently and intensively. It is not only the imperative to diet that is affectively felt then; it is that the very ways in which it is possible to become materially different are organized around and through affect. What this suggests is that the notion that digital media simply 'extend' the possibilities of agency and temporality 'in real life' requires challenging as it becomes crucial to attend to 'the emergence of new forms of time – time which is fused and unfolds with matter' (Adkins 2009: 334–335) which the engagement and interaction with online dieting produce. In the next chapter, I take up this focus on how weight becomes posed as an immediate, present problem and explore further the temporal dimensions of the ways in which the imperative of transformation affectively engages and organizes the living out of certain kinds of bodies.

5 Pre-empting the future
Obesity, prediction and Change4Life

> What is certain is that this epidemic of 'passive obesity' is unlikely to come to a natural end, i.e. without intervention.
>
> (Foresight 2007a: 17)

> It's never too early to get your baby on the right path to a healthy and happy future. Get started now!
>
> (Start4Life, Change4Life website, July 2011)

For the last three years the British government has been running a campaign called 'Change4Life',[1] which is, according to the Department of Health's website, 'a society-wide movement that aims to prevent people from becoming overweight by encouraging them to eat better and move more'. The campaign is described as both 'the marketing component of the Government's response to the rise in obesity'[2] and, more widely, as a '*social* marketing campaign' (Department of Health 2010: 13, my emphasis) so that '[r]ather than taking a top-down approach, the campaign set out to use marketing as a catalyst for a *broader societal movement* in which everyone who had an interest in preventing obesity [...] could play a part' (2010: 13–14, my emphasis). The campaign has thus involved a wide range of high profile activities across different platforms, including traditional forms of advertising, digital communications, relationship marketing and stakeholder engagement, and has been relevant to a variety of social groups. In this sense, the Change4Life movement has been a key way in which imagination, aspirations and promises about, and interventions in, contemporary British life have recently been organized. This chapter explores how Change4Life works through images of a better future that organize British socio-cultural life according to an emphasis on transforming the body. Following through the emphasis in the book so far on how transformation is affective, in this chapter I examine how the impetus for Change4Life is for images to be lived out in and as particular bodies. In order to be a successful societal movement, Change4Life images are *required* to move from being (virtual) images to being actualized. I consider the ways in which the societal movement therefore shifts from screens to 'real life', that is from advertising images to *embodied experiences*, and from a future danger to a present reality.

Much has been written about the increasing emphasis placed on what Deborah Lupton (1995) termed 'the imperative of health' where '"[h]ealthiness" has replaced "Godliness" as a yardstick of accomplishment and proper living' (1995: 4). Interestingly for my discussions of power in the book, Lupton conceives the imperative of health from a Foucauldian position, so that 'healthiness' is understood in terms of governmentality; 'incorporat[ing] both techniques or practices of the self – self-government – and the more apparent forms of external government – policing, surveillance and regulatory activities carried out by agencies of the state or other institutions for strategic purposes' (1995: 9). Conceived as such, the imperative of health is a form of neo-liberalism where power works in terms of governance 'directed at constructing and normalizing a certain kind of subject; a subject who is autonomous, directed at self-improvement, self-regulated, desirous of self-knowledge, a subject who is seeking happiness and healthiness' (1995: 11). Recently, the imperative of health has been argued by Karen Throsby (2007, 2008, 2009) to take place through the 'war on obesity', where 'health, slimness and bodily discipline are treated as synonymous' (Throsby 2009: 201). According to Throsby, there has been as 'a rapid proliferation of social and clinical weight loss interventions and programmes in which those who are medically categorized as obese are increasingly expected to engage in order to manage their body size' (2009: 201). Throsby argues that this 'war on obesity' is a 'morally and ideologically driven' project (2009: 201) where being overweight or obese in the first place, and failing to lose weight thereafter, is framed 'as evidence of a moral failure of individual responsibility to care appropriately for the self, and by extension, to be a good citizen [...]. Weight loss, in this context, is therefore not a choice, but an obligation' (2009: 201–202, references omitted).

One way to understand the Change4Life campaign, then, is as part of a wider neo-liberal trend within contemporary Western societies, whereby social problems are re-cast as individual's problems, and where the individual is increasingly responsible for the quality of their own lives (see Introduction). Indeed, recent articles on Change4Life have precisely addressed the campaign in these terms. For example, Bethan Evans *et al.* (2011) describe how the campaign seeks to conceive people as 'intercorporeal subjects', located within complex social relations and environments, where over (and under) weight cannot be reduced to an individual's free will. However, they argue that the campaign fails to follow through on this conception, and instead 'a neoliberal, rational model of embodiment in which a healthy body is seen as a product of conscious control persists as the assumed "healthy" model' (2011: 333). In line with the approach that this book develops, in this chapter I want to think about how Change4Life works not only through neo-liberal governance but also through a form of power as intensive and affective. This is not so much to critique what I have characterized here as those approaches to health as part of neo-liberalism – indeed, below I draw on many of their insights – but rather to examine how power is also working in excess of governance, that is, as I have discussed in Chapters 2, 3 and 4, is engaging the body *directly, immanently* and *intensely*.[3]

Pre-empting the future 115

In this chapter then, my aim is to examine how the 'imperative of health' functions as part of the *imperative of transformation*, in which socio-cultural life is organized around an affective dynamic of movement, change and transformation. Change4Life has emerged as a response to the notion – widespread throughout popular culture, medicine and policy – that there is an obesity problem now, and that this problem will only worsen in the future. This notion is clearly expressed in the quotation above from Foresight, 'a "horizon-scanning" centre' (Foresight 2007a, cited in Evans 2010: 22) within the Department for Business, Innovation and Skills that 'creates challenging visions of the future to ensure effective strategies now' (Foresight 2007a: i). The report (2007a) mapped, visualized and proffered scenarios for dealing with an increase in levels of obesity in the UK, and it is this report to which the Change4Life movement explicitly responds (see Department of Health 2010). According to Foresight, obesity is an epidemic that will spread – passively – unless an intervention is made in the present. Indeed, as the quotation above from the Start4Life campaign asserts, a healthy and happy future must be 'started now'. As I have set out in the book, I am interested in how affects are distributed unequally and therefore appeal to some bodies more than others; a central problem that I explore in this chapter is which bodies in particular feel the imperative to transform through the Change4Life movement? Which bodies live out the intervention that is being made *now*? I focus on the relationship between the Change4Life campaign and British society and culture in order to attempt to avoid some of the more general claims made about 'life' in some sociological theory. Although I concentrate on this specific focus, if, as I've suggested in the Introduction, the imperative to transform through the body emerges out of wider capitalist processes, the argument made here concerning transformation, bodies, affect and temporality may well be relevant to other international contexts. In relation to government health campaigns for example, the Foresight report cites campaigns in Finland dealing with heart disease and in France, Belgium and Spain on improving diet and exercise in children, as among the few examples of where '[s]ocieties have made significant and successful attempts to intervene in' health problems (2007a: 61).[4]

In the case of Change4Life, the campaign is a social *movement* that involves transforming the way in which many people in Britain live. Life is seen as changing, passively and almost inevitably, from a past that was relatively simple and healthy to a present and future that are technologically complex, sedentary and dangerous. As one of the campaign's television adverts puts it, '[o]nce upon a time, life was pretty simple'; we caught, killed and ate what we needed, exercising in the process. However it goes on, 'then, gradually, life changed. In many ways, it got easier. Nobody had to run around for their food, or anything else much for that matter' (*What's It All About?* television advert). This uncomplicated version of social and historical progress is seen to take place through the body, which has changed from the fit and healthy body required to hunt food to the overweight body of the present, to the dangerously obese body of the future. Eating and moving more now is therefore necessary to combat obesity – change *for* (a healthier and happier) life – and must become a constant and consistent modification to lifestyle habits – *change* for *life*. While such changes involve mundane and often boring daily practices, of monitoring calories in and out of the body for example, I argue that the imperative of transformation also functions in excess of these practices, as a series of images that promise the future as a better time, a time of potential. My focus here is on how Change4Life can be understood as a series of images that affectively resonate with and materialize particular kinds of bodies – the bodies of those who are categorized as overweight or obese and thus unhealthy – and particular ways of living healthier and happier lives. I argue that, in different ways, the campaign works affectively by bringing the future as potential into the present and requiring the future to be acted on in the present.

The chapter begins by providing some more background on the Change4Life movement and then places this campaign within a broader context of a concern with pre-empting an increase in levels of obesity. Discussing the predictions through which this increase in obesity levels is imagined, pre-emption is understood to involve an affective disruption of linear temporality, in that the present does not progress smoothly to the future, but is oriented around feeling and living out the future as if it were happening now (Massumi 2005; Adams *et al.* 2009). The next section explores the temporalities of pre-emption further through the notion of anticipation that I introduced in the Introduction and returned to in Chapter 4. In particular, I examine the role of images in producing, circulating and arranging affective anticipation as an everyday way of living. I argue that as affective intensity, power is increasingly working through potential, as that which not only restricts and constrains but also as that which brings to life. The final section thinks through the material implications and effects of the Change4Life movement as one of the exemplars of the imperative of transformation. If Change4Life is organized around the living out of images of the future as potential, which bodies 'feel with' the movement? In what ways is the intensive power of the movement materialized into particular kinds of bodies, and particular ways of life?

Change4Life

The Change4Life campaign was officially launched in January 2009 as a 'lifestyle revolution' (Secretary of State for Health, Alan Johnson, quoted in Donaldson and Beasley 2008). In their letter outlining the launch, Chief Medical Officer, Sir Liam Donaldson and Chief Nursing Officer, Dame Christine Beasley (2008) explain the campaign as a *movement*, 'bringing together a coalition of health and education professionals, the third sector, community groups, industry and the media with the shared aims of improving children's diets and levels of activity so reducing the threat to their future health' (Donaldson and Beasley 2008). With this in mind, the movement has involved schools, healthcare professionals and the local and regional National Health Service, charities (for example, British Heart Foundation, Cancer Research, Diabetes UK), supermarkets (for example Asda and Tesco), convenience stores and national brands (for example Kellogg's and British Gas), the Fitness Industry Association, community groups and interested individuals. In its first year, the movement included a number of different activities, such as: paying for advertising on television, in newspapers, on billboards and buses; direct and relationship marketing where 'customers' sign up to receive online and paper information[5]; digital communications including an interactive website, email marketing and online display advertising; public relations; partnership marketing where Change4Life partners distributed messages and offers; communications aimed at stakeholders including health and teaching workforces; and sponsorship of *The Simpsons* on Channel 4.

The initial focus of the movement was on 'families with children aged 5–11, [and] particularly on those whose current behaviours and attitudes indicate that their children are at increased risk of excess weight gain' (Department of Health 2010: 13). Since then the movement has targeted: Pakistani, Bangladeshi and West African communities with posters and booklets; parents with babies with a Start4Life campaign; children with a 'Let's Dance with Change4Life'[6]; and adults aged between 45–65 (of whom 71 per cent are classed as either overweight or obese) with a 'Swap it, don't stop it' TV, poster, promotional packs and online campaign. In the summer of 2011, a television and online 'fun generator' campaign was directed at families with children of school age to offer a 'helping hand' with suggestions of how 'to keep your kids active over the next few weeks'.[7] There are also a number of other 'sub-brands' (Department of Health 2010: 16), including Cook4Life, Walk4Life and Play4Life.

The movement was designed to be highly visible and, as the list of activities and branding exercises demonstrates, has had to appeal to a wide range of people. It features brightly coloured (blue, pink, green and orange) animated figures on a yellow background in movement; pushing shopping trolleys, riding scooters, flying kites, walking dogs, turning somersaults, hurrying to the table with dinner and so on[8] (see Figures 5.1a and 5.1b). The figures have a sense of pleasure and delight – life – about them, and the text that accompanies them supports this, with short, snappy phrases and questions: 'small swaps for a healthier you!'; 'all you need to get into gear'; 'hands up who wants our kids to live longer?'. Three television adverts broadcast from 2009 onwards similarly feature such messages, showing how our lives have become more technologized and sedentary (cars, computer games, processed food and large portions).[9] The three adverts enter into children's bodies through an insertion in their torso to discover the dangerous amounts of fat that could become stored there, and therefore encourage us to eat better and move more so that we can 'all live [...] happily, not exactly ever after, but more ever after than we had done' (*What's It All About?* television advert).

It's clear from this brief outline that the movement has been widespread. Rather than try to assess the success or efficacy of the campaign, either in terms of marketing or as a 'social movement',[10] what I'm interested in exploring is how the campaign is part of a wider social and cultural trend of transformation.

118 *Pre-empting the future*

(a)

(b)

Figure 5.1a–b Images from the Change4Life *What's It All About?* television advert. Permission for use of images kindly granted by the Department of Health on behalf of Change4Life.

How is the Change4Life movement part of an imperative to transform? In what ways is it an example of what social and cultural theory conceives as the movement, intensity and change of contemporary life? More specifically, how is Change4Life as a series of images involved in organizing, promoting and promising transformation? I examine the images of the campaign and analyse how they arrange a particular version of temporality where the future is prioritized and comes to shape present concerns. This chapter seeks to account for the ways in which images are experiences that require taking up and acting out. In the book so far I have explored the ways in which images are brought to life through a focus on the screen. As I have discussed, Change4Life involves images that are co-ordinated across a range of screens or surfaces – television, billboards and printed promotional materials. Drawing on my argument throughout the book, these images are not (only) representational texts but are (also) affectively felt and lived out. However, as a social marketing campaign, Change4Life directs attention to the living out of images through its events and activities.

Change4Life becomes a kind of mediascape as described by Lash and Lury, where images become things:

> There is such a thingification of media when, for example, movies become computer games; when brands become brand environments, taking over airport terminal space and restructuring department stores, road billboards and city centres; when cartoon characters become collectibles and costumes; when music is played in lifts, part of a mobile soundscapes.
> (2007: 6, references omitted)

In this chapter then, I examine how the images of the Change4Life campaign are both images organized across different screens or surfaces *and* are virtuals that move from these surfaces into 'real', physical life.

Such understandings of social marketing have recently been explored elsewhere (see Cronin 2010). For example, in her analysis of marketing 'other' than advertising, Liz Moor (2003) argues that activities such as events-based marketing and sponsorship are seen by marketing professionals as both 'a set of uniquely advantageous strategies in building longer-term relationships between consumers and brands' and 'are often organized around the promotion of brands rather than specific products or services' (2003: 40). Indeed, the Department of Health's (2011a) *Changing Behaviours, Improving Outcomes* document that outlines 'a social marketing strategy for public health' explicitly draws attention to how the aim of changing behaviour requires an approach where those targeted 'continue to interact with the brand for substantial periods of time' (2011a: 17). This is important, it argues, because in order to prevent (or pre-empt) future bad health, change must be for life, that it must be 'maintained over time' (2011a: 57). The Change4Life brand is thus discussed as a 'trusted brand', an endeavour that the *Change4Life: One Year On* report (Department of Health 2010) describes as attempting to be achieved by the Department of Health 'consciously decid[ing] to avoid government branding, since our research told us that people were keener to be part of a movement that was owned by all, rather than prescribed by the Government. Accordingly, one of our agency partners, M&C Saatchi, created the Change4Life brand, along with a suite of sub-brands (Walk4Life, Play4Life, Cook4Life, etc.) and toolkits which were made available to partners' (2010: 16). The notion that Change4Life is a social movement 'owned by all', is explained as operating both 'vertically', 'from understanding the problem and designing the solutions, to delivering and communicating products and concepts' and 'horizontally across types of intervention, and is not limited to narrow definitions of communications or marketing' (Department of Health 2011a: 11). As a social marketing campaign, Change4Life was thus deliberately designed to facilitate a network of partners from the public and private sectors, and to involve in particular 'communities' in disseminating information and tools to encourage healthiness. While narrow definitions of communications and marketing might prioritize screen-based advertising, Change4Life aspired to 'get people involved, not only to improve their own lives, but to improve the lives of others in their communities' (2011a: 17).

120 *Pre-empting the future*

Below I will return to discuss the specificities of the communities where lives need improving in order to consider how it is *certain* bodies that are required to be involved in this social movement. But here it is worth noting that Change4Life operates through a series of '"experiential marketing"' activities (Moor 2003: 40), including events for the sub-brands mentioned above. In Moor's terms then, Change4Life can be understood as an 'experiential brand', that is those brands 'built around "values and beliefs" rather than product-specific qualities' (2003: 44). Such brands are concerned with becoming not (only) a set of signs but '"a rich source of sensory, affective, and cognitive associations that result in memorable [...] brand experiences"' (Schmitt 1999: 21 cited in Moor 2003: 44). In the next section, I analyse how the affective experience of Change4Life both draws on and further consolidates what I have argued to characterize images of transformation: the future as potential.[11] Images function as potential in that they bring the potential of the future into the present; we can all live healthily and happily 'ever after' if we make a change to and for life now.

Obesity, prediction and pre-emption

As I have indicated, the Change4Life movement was initiated by the Department of Health to prevent a rise in levels of obesity. For example, the sentence immediately following the explanation of the campaign in Donaldson and Beasley's letter, cited above, states: 'Obesity is one of the biggest public health challenges we face', and this message is reiterated across different Change4Life publications and activities. The foreword, by the Secretary of State for Health, Andy Burnham, to the *Change 4Life: One Year On* report states that the campaign is '[r]esponding to an urgent need to tackle the alarming rise in obesity' (Department of Health 2010: 4), and the report goes on to assert that '[a]lready 30% of children and 61% of adults are overweight or obese. If the trend is allowed to continue, by 2050 nine out of ten adults could be overweight or obese' (2010: 11).

The statistics to which the Change4Life movement respond come from a report, *Tackling Obesities, Future Choices* (2007a), published by Foresight. According to Chief Scientific Advisor to the Government and Head of the Government Office for Science, Sir David King, this Foresight report was commissioned 'to examine the question, "How can we deliver a sustainable response to obesity over the next 40 years?"' and sought to 'challenge the simple portrayal of obesity as an issue of personal willpower' by emphasizing social environment (2007a: i).[12] The quantitative modelling of future trends in the Foresight report uses a dataset taken from the Health Survey of England between 1994–2004.[13] Beginning with this dataset that shows that in 2004, 23.6 per cent of men and 23.8 per cent of women were obese (2007a: 26), Foresight predict that by 2015, 36 per cent of adult males and 28 per cent of adult females will be obese; by 2025 this will rise to 47 per cent and 36 per cent respectively, and; by 2050 this could be 60 per cent and 50 per cent respectively (2007a: 35). Calculating future trends for children is 'controversial because of difficulties stemming from variation in normal patterns of growth, weight gain and changes in body composition' (2007a: 26). However, based on current levels of 8 per cent of males and 10 per cent of females who are obese, and taking into consideration the uncertain results of their methodology, the Foresight report suggests that by 2015, 15 per cent of under 20s are predicted to be obese, and by 2050, this could be 25 per cent (2007a: 36).[14]

It's worth noting here that the Foresight report focuses only on obesity whereas, for the Change4Life movement, it is the categories of obesity *and* overweight that are at stake.[15] This makes it difficult to trace how the Foresight prediction, that by 2050 obesity levels could be at 60 per cent for men and 50 per cent for women, map onto those stated by Change4Life, that 'by 2050 nine out of ten adults could be overweight or obese'. However, these higher statistics related to obesity and overweight are reiterated in various ways across the Change4Life movement: 'By the time we reach middle age, the majority of us could do with losing at least a bit of weight':

> kids need to do at least 60 minutes of physical activity that gets their hearts beating faster than usual. And they need to do it every day to burn off calories and prevent them storing up excess fat in the body.

Similarly, one of the television adverts circulates around the realization that if we don't do something now, 'nine out of ten of our kids would grow up to have dangerous amounts of fat built up in their bodies, which meant they'd be more likely to get horrid things like heart disease, type 2 diabetes, and cancer' (*What's It All About?* television advert).

Importantly, the *Change4Life: One Year On* report links this trend to future health and financial costs:

> [o]besity is not a cosmetic issue. Becoming overweight or obese increases an individual's likelihood of developing (among other conditions) cancer, type 2 diabetes and heart disease, leading to reduced quality of life and, in some cases, a life cut short.
> (Department of Health 2010: 11)

It also states that '[t]he annual cost to society of obesity-related illness could reach £50 billion by 2050 at today's prices' (2010: 11). It argues that it is particularly important to tackle obesity in children, to stop the '"conveyor-belt effect", whereby weight gained in childhood continues into adulthood' (2010: 11). My aim here is not to dispute the statistics (although there may be reason to do this). Neither is my aim to focus on whether or not a social marketing campaign is the most appropriate way of tackling obesity. Rather, I'm interested in unpacking how Change4Life *works* as part of a wider imperative of transformation. That is, taking seriously the movement's claim that change is *for life*, what does this emphasis on transformation *do* to contemporary British ways of life? More especially, what does an emphasis on transformation do to the *temporalities* of contemporary ways of life?

I have emphasized so far that the Change4Life movement pivots around a response to *predictions* of trends in obesity levels. Such predictions argue that obesity levels *will* increase and it is therefore imperative that this trend is intervened in *now*:

> There is an urgent need for action to halt the rapid current increase [in levels of obesity] and to develop a sustainable response.
> (Foresight 2007a: 5)

> 60 active minutes. Just one of the ways to change for life. Search Change4Life or call 0300 123 4567 for your free info pack. Now.
> (*60 Active Minutes* television advert)

As such, the remit of Change4Life is described as

> *preventative* not remedial: the programme was not set up to recruit overweight or obese children into weight loss programmes but to change the way all of us raise and nourish our children, with the aim of creating a cohort of 5–11 year olds who have a healthy relationship with food and activity.
> (Department of Health 2010: 13, my emphasis)

Prevention, according to Brian Massumi (2005), is associated with a mode of power underpinned by a linear temporality; it is rooted in the present and seeks to prevent an event happening in the future.

However, in contrast to being a preventative campaign, Change4Life might be better understood as *pre-emptive*. Indeed, this is what Evans (2010) argues in her discussion of the Foresight report. Pre-emption, Massumi argues, is performative in that it,

> does not prevent, it effects. It induces the event, *in effect*. Rather than acting in the present to avoid an occurrence in the future, preemption brings the future into the present. It makes the present the future consequences of an eventuality that may or may not occur, indifferent to its actual occurrence. The event's consequences precede it, as if it had already occurred.
> (Massumi 2005: 8)

The linear progressive temporality of prevention is thus re-worked with pre-emptive politics. Pre-emption 'suspends the place of the present in the traditional time-line' (2005: 9) and instead 'brings the future into the present' so that the future is an event – a *virtual* event – that exists and must be acted on in the present. As I discussed in the Introduction, this movement of the future into the present 'induces' the future event in the present; *whether or not* the prediction that in future 'nine out of ten of our kids would grow up to have dangerous amounts of fat built up in their bodies' is correct or will occur, it is brought into the present and effects the present, 'as if' the event 'had already occurred'.

What is more, this disruption of linear progression is *affective*. For example, projections always involve uncertainty, in that '[t]here is always an "if", since [projections] indicate trends rather than grounding laws' (2005: 3). While projections associated with prevention depend on the control of such uncertainty through linear progression (this past will result in this present and then in this future), with projections associated with pre-emption, uncertainty has been amplified. It is not that linear progression no longer remains integral to projections; the bringing of the future into the present in the Change4Life movement relies on linear progression, in that the campaign is an intervention in the present in order to stop a particular – obese – future unfolding seemingly passively. Rather it is that 'the trend is *characterized* by uncertainty' (2005: 3, my emphasis); uncertainty becomes not that which can be controlled but that which is affectively felt. Such uncertainty orients the temporality of contemporary sociocultural life around the future, as 'the centre of gravity' is shifted 'from the past-present axis describing trends whose arc will continue more or less predictably into the future, onto a present-future axis wobbling with uncertainty, trembling in anticipation of fear' (2005: 3). The anticipation of fear, Massumi argues, functions as a threat, 'an indefinite future tense: what may yet come' (2005: 3). Therefore, to be effective, to take uncertainty into account and to negate it with confidence, the political axis must '*act on the future*' (2005: 3).[16]

Drawing on Massumi's argument to explore the temporalities that are produced by the Foresight report, Bethan Evans (2010) argues that there are two different spatiotemporal logics at work. On the one hand, 'Foresight is explicitly pre-emptive in its engagement with the future (recognizing the multiplicity of possible futures)' (Evans 2010: 29). For example it recognizes the uncertainty of its predictions and acknowledges various scenarios that might unfold. However, on the other hand, the report relies on 'the linearity of biological time [which] means this complexity is often reduced to simplistic models and definitive predictions, within the report itself and associated documents' (2010: 29). As such, Evans argues,

> although the quantitative modelling exercise is premised with warnings about its limitations, the linear, deterministic concept of time it adopts means the future is produced as an extension from the present with a certainty that belies the complexity behind it. Thus, despite the wide margins of the 95 per cent confidence intervals [...], the summary reports that: 'By 2050, Foresight modelling indicates that 60% of adult men, 50% of adult women and about 25% of all children under 16 could be obese'. Moreover, in reproducing this statement, the press release (News Distribution Service 2007) and [the] Healthy Weight, Healthy Lives [report] remove the last trace of uncertainty by replacing could with will.
>
> (2010: 29–30, references omitted)

Evan's close analysis of the Foresight report demonstrates the ways in which the uncertainty that characterizes its pre-emptive politics is 'removed' in policy documents and in the circulation of policy in news reports. Her argument echoes the point made above, that the focus on obesity in the Foresight report is translated into obesity and overweight, and simplified to 'dangerous levels of fat' in the Change4Life campaign. While it is clearly the case that running alongside, and at times subsuming, the uncertainty that pre-emptive politics works through is linear progressive time, in the rest of this chapter I focus on the ways in which the future is brought into the present in and through Change4Life. That is, I concentrate on Change4Life as *pre-emptive*; as disrupting linear progressive temporality in requiring the future to be acted on now. As I explain in the following section, this is because I think, *as a series of images*, Change4Life functions through the affects of uncertainty and anticipation, bringing the future into the present as potential, a virtual that is felt and encouraged to be lived out.

The future as potential: images, affect and anticipation

The predictions made in the Foresight report are, I suggest, converted into *images* in the Change4Life campaign. Above, I have briefly described the Change4Life images in terms of what is represented; brightly coloured moving and lively figures for example. However, as well as representing particular ways of life, I want to argue that the Change4Life movement works through images that function as potential or virtuals. Such an understanding of images, I suggest, attends to (at least) two points. First, it focuses on how images work *affectively*, that is as 'more-than' (Thrift 2007; Hayden Lorimer 2008; Latham and McCormack 2009) or in excess of (Massumi 2002, Coleman 2009, 2011), representation. This understanding of images as affects focuses attention on the body, as images are seen as felt and lived out, in, through and as the body. As I have discussed previously in the book, as affects, images are intensive experiences; the 'shiver down the spine or the gut feeling' (Featherstone 2010: 195) – or, to pick up on the affects discussed above, in the case of Change4Life, the anticipation of and alertness to what danger might yet (be)come. As images, Change4Life engages the body, requires the body to feel and live out the imperative of transformation.

Second and relatedly, understanding images as potential or virtuals enables a consideration of the ways in which *the future* functions as essential in the Change4Life movement. I have argued that in the Change4Life movement, the future is brought into the present. In the Foresight report, this movement is necessary to avoid the threat that obesity poses in the future; the future is thus a catastrophe just waiting to happen.[17] However, as a social marketing campaign, the images of Change4Life are not dystopian but rather suggest the future as a time of potential.[18] *If* we change for life *now*, *if* we eat better and move more, the future will be happier, healthier and longer-lasting. This potential of the future is thus contained or anticipated within the present. Indeed, in the Introduction I discussed how the *anticipation* of the future in the present is pointed to by social theorists who also explore pre-emption in terms of the affective relations between the present and future. According to Vincanne

Pre-empting the future 125

Adams, Michelle Murphy and Adele E. Clarke (2009), anticipation comes to define contemporary life and is an affective state whereby the present is characterized by an orientation to the future 'as if the future is what matters most' (2009: 248). As I have previously indicated, in Lisa Adkins' terms the future as potential is 'open [...], vital and alive' (2008: 195). It is intensively felt and lived out.

The conception of the future as potential – as open, vital and alive – might seem to indicate that the future is a utopia, a time of unbounded liberation. However, as I have argued in the book so far, increasingly power is argued to be concerned with and involved in the production of potential. Power is 'a potentiality [with] an inherent capacity for growth, development or coming into being' (Lash 2010: 4). In this sense, power operates not only extensively – rationally, from the outside for example – but *intensively*. As intensive, power is thus productive; power necessitates change and transformation and indicates the prospect of other possibilities (methods of thinking, modes of embodiment, ways of living, etc.). Working as and through potential, power involves not only the concrete and material, but also the intangible, experiential and affective; *the virtual*. In previous chapters I have outlined the 'coupling' of the virtual and the actual, and have been concerned with tracing the relationship between intangible experiences or feelings and 'actual' things, or bodies. Importantly, understood as potential, power is organized and works not only through the actual but through the virtual, not only through concrete objects but through intangible potentials; images. In what sense can the images of the Change4Life campaign be understood as these virtual potentials? How are they actualized?

My understanding of the Change4Life campaign is that it works as a series of images. As I have argued, the future is brought into the present through the Change4Life movement. In these terms, the future/virtual is brought into the present/actual. Although the future is a virtual – intangible, not-yet – the present becomes oriented around this virtual so that the virtual becomes actualized in the kinds of feelings and ways of life that emerge and become dominant. In Brian Massumi's terms, the future 'remains virtual [...] but is real and present in its effects. The present reality of its effects mean that it can be responded to pragmatically all the while remaining virtual' (2005: 8). Whilst it is oriented around and made real in feelings, practices and actions, the future remains in excess of these actualizations; it remains as potential. It is this potential – the *image* that life can be better – through which the Change4Life movement works. For example, in the images included above, the image of the healthier and happier future (Figure 5.1b) is a virtual that might yet become actual if the horror at the realization of present ways of living (Figure 5.1a) affects the parent and child in the right way, that it moves them to move more and eat better. The future is thus both virtual, in that it is intangible and because it is brought into the present as an affect that must be acted on, made actual, now. Taking up the understanding of power as intensive potential, images work not only to restrict and regulate but also to produce and transform. The better future that the movement imagines is not an abstract calculation, but is materialized, is brought alive, in and through various attempts to produce healthier and happier bodies. Calculations are brought to life through images and 'essentially virtual notions [...] are able to take on flesh as, increasingly, the world is made in these notions' likeness' (Thrift 2005: 6). Moreover, this materialization of calculation happens through affect.

For example, the *Change4Life: One Year On* report states that '[c]ounting all postal, online, face-to-face and telephone responses, Change4Life generated 1,992,456 responses, exceeding the target of 1.5 million' (Department of Health 2010: 21).[19] The report also states that the campaign 'reached 99% of families [living in England] by the end of January 2009' and '[a]wareness of the advertising campaign peaked at 87% in March [2009] and remained high throughout the year' (2010: 17). Indeed, while sounding caution at the results of its tracking study, which interviewed 300 mothers of children aged between 0–11 years per month, the *Change4Life: One Year On* report states that

> The tracker shows a high degree of claimed change, with three in ten of those mothers who were aware of Change4Life claiming to have made a change to their children's behaviours *as a direct result of the campaign*. This equates to over 1 million mothers claiming to have made changes in response to the campaign.
>
> (Department of Health 2010: 60)

As the report itself recognizes, brand reach, awareness and response levels do not necessarily correlate with behaviour changes. However, there is clearly a high percentage of the English population who are aware, at the very least, that eating better and moving more are becoming important, in that there is a major campaign promoting them. While there may or may not be actual changes in behaviour, I would suggest that such awareness can be understood in terms of the affective anticipation of and/or alertness to the future. The future, as the virtual, thus becomes a key means through which power works. Furthermore, it is the *image* of the better future that is powerful. That is, power not only operates through the regimes and practices of eating better and moving more, but also through the *promise* of a better future – an intangible, affective virtual.

Conceiving the imperative to transform as an image of the future helps to understand how transformation has become a prevalent and appealing theme. The imperative of transformation indicates a future that, at once, requires living out – changing for the better – and that exceeds practice and exists as an intangible, affective anticipation of what might become. Change4Life exists as a series of changes to bodily behaviour that may or may not be taken up *and* as an image of what the future might yet be. In this sense, the movement and change that I have argued characterizes contemporary life, and that is made evident in the imperative of transformation, is organized temporally; around an image that the future is both what matters most and that can be made different to the

Pre-empting the future 127

present. The affectivity of images of transformation becomes movement and change, that is particular ways of life. It is therefore necessary to consider further the particular ways of life that images of transformation organize and encourage. Which bodies are most caught up in images of the imperative of transformation? Which bodies feel and move with Change4Life?

Temporality, bodies and the imperative of transformation

I have already indicated that certain groups are addressed by Change4Life: children, parents of babies and young children, ethnic minorities, adults aged between 45–65. Drawing on the argument developed so far, these groups can be understood as potential, that is as being the groups with the greatest capacity for change and with the greatest amount to gain from changing their future. Children in particular are imagined as a site of potential as they are seen as in the process of becoming.[20] Indeed, Evans argues in her discussion of the Foresight report that an emphasis on the future means that there is a 'disproportionate targeting of children in UK obesity policy, despite significant uncertainty surrounding the aetiology, diagnosis and implications of childhood weight for health (both during childhood and in future adulthood)' (Evans 2010: 23, references omitted). Furthermore, as an affective state, children are imagined as potential because 'childhood intensifies affects such as guilt, shame, fear and hope to make dystopian futures felt as present realities' (2010: 23).

In the Change4Life movement, children 'intensify affect' through the hope that is placed in them as the future, and through the fear of what contemporary lifestyles are doing to them. Evans *et al.* (2011) discuss how the movement's focus on improving children's weight and health targets mothers as 'gatekeeper of diet and activity' (Department of Health, cited in Evans *et al.* 2011: 332) and 'aims to produce healthy bodies through acting on intergenerational relations (2011: 331). For example, a mother is seen in one of the television adverts (*Me Size Meals*) as cutting short her son's life through love, so that '[e]xcess body fat therefore becomes the materialization of excess love/emotionality in the parent–child relationship' (2011: 334):

> Mum loves me. And thinks lots of food will make me big and strong. But she gives me enough to feed a horse. [...] She forgets I don't need grown up portions.

Children are also seen as a site of potential in that they can '"transmit" health education' to and between adults (Evans *et al.* 2011: 336), as this advert goes on to show:

> My teacher says, if we eat too much and do too little, food gets stored as fat in our bodies which means we could grow up to have heart disease, cancer, or type 2 diabetes. Nasty. So I told Mum not to fill me 'til I burst. Now I eat me size meals. Just the right amount for my tum.

These examples demonstrate how the Change4Life movement works through affect which engages the body and encourages it to move, to change. As I mention above, the three adverts all enter into a child's body through an insertion in their torso, to show the dangerous levels of fat within. Upon withdrawal back into the outside world, parents and children gasp with the horror and disgust at what they have seen and, literally, move to make changes to their diet and activity.

What I am suggesting here then, is that Change4Life is arranged around images that affectively *move us* to feel and to live out change. We are affectively appealed to to transform our lives, to *materialize* life into something better; healthier, happier and longer lasting. Of course, as the book has explored, affects are not distributed equally and some bodies are appealed to more than others. The Change4Life movement is arranged around appealing to specific bodies in particular, to those bodies that are calculated to be most at risk of obesity now and in the future. The social groups to which the movement appeals are explicitly targeted on the basis of their present or future weight. However, it is clear that classifications of obesity and overweight map on to categories of class, gender and race. Unsurprisingly those 'at risk' of having their lives cut short by poor diet and lack of exercise are concentrated in low income groups, or what the *Change4Life: One Year On* report calls 'clusters' of families, defined through eating and exercise habits, intent to change, consumption patterns and demographics (Department of Health 2010: 94). Both the Foresight report and the policy documents regarding Change4Life make a concerted attempt to avoid moral judgements that reinforce class and ethnic differences, hence classifying risk of obesity through these 'clusters' defined through habits and behaviour. However, as social theorists have long pointed out, habits and behaviour are intimately related to underlying social processes and categories and, as Evans *et al.* argue, Change4Life 'constructs a middle-class, white, nuclear family with stereotyped gender roles as healthy' (2011: 333).

As I have suggested above regarding the role of 'Mum' in the *Me Sized Meals* advert, and in line with the ways in which I discussed the appeal of makeover programmes to working-class women in Chapter 3, Change4Life addresses women in particular. As well as being appealed to as those who are capable of changing their own lives, women are also seen as key to transforming *the lives of others*. For example, despite the 'kids' exercise ideas' page of the Change4Life website being in the 'family' section, the examples featured from those who have changed their families' lives are from women; Lisa, who writes down ideas for activities for her children, and Emily and Sam, who walk rather than drive to the shops. Indeed, the *Change4Life: One Year On* report explains that women (or mothers) were explicitly targeted by advertising campaigns by three major health charities (Cancer Research UK, the British Heart Foundation and Diabetes UK) to support Change4Life. The charity campaign adverts asked the viewer to 'make [...] sure your kids are active for an hour a day. Reduce how much fat they eat' and were published in women's magazines, and '[t]he tracking study indicates that 23% of mothers recalled seeing the campaign'

(Department of Health 2009: 28). The 'How are the kids?' survey and Sugar Swapper interactive tool were also distributed in women's magazines (2009: 37, 52). The affective anticipatory logic of pre-empting future bad health is thus felt by women/mothers as the requirement to take care, not only of her own life but also of those around her.

Another 'cluster' 'at risk' of future poor health and thus addressed explicitly by Change4Life 'messages' are 'ethnic minority communities' (2009: 75). The necessity of these messages is explained by the *Change4Life: One Year On* report as based on '[a]nalysis of data from [the] National Child Measurement Programme [that] indicates that children from the Pakistani, Bangladeshi and black African communities are more likely to become overweight or obese than their white counterparts' (2009: 75). A 'bespoke' ethnic minority campaign was commissioned from a 'specialist ethnic minority marketing agency' and launched in Luton in late 2009. The programme included publishing materials in languages other than English, working closely with primary care trusts, local authorities, healthcare professionals and others working with communities, including 'engaging authority figures (such as faith leaders)' and 'working with respected celebrities from the communities' (including celebrity chef Ainsley Harriott and Olympian Darren Campbell) (2009: 76). Indeed, as I noted above, while the Change4Life campaign in general extended from published materials, and print and broadcast adverts into the 'real world', it is interesting to note the extent to which the more specialized ethnic minorities campaign emphasized the significance of this aspect.

In Luton, for example, Change4Life worked in partnership with the local Borough Council to organize a series of events, one of which was the Stockwood Family Fun Day in 2009, where local residents were invited to '[c]ome and experience a variety of taster sessions and activities in the park', and to find out more from 'a host of promotional standings, with health related advice and information'.[21] The Borough Council also initiated its own version of Change4Life, 'Take 3 4 Life', that encourages adults to be active at least three times a week for at least 30 minutes. In July 2011, the annual Take 3 4 Life event 'packed with free activities for the whole family' attracted over 4,000 people.[22] In Bradford, another area targeted by the Change4Life bespoke ethnic minorities campaign, local Pakistani and Bangladeshi community leaders attended a Change4Life conference in November 2009 to learn about the obesity problem in the locality, and to find ways to intervene in it. One activity included

> [c]onsultant nutritionist, registered dietician and best-selling author, Azmina Govindji, [...] demonstrat[ing] easy to follow steps to a healthier diet, giving traditional Pakistani and Bangladeshi meals a healthier twist and showing the audience a range of 'sneaky swaps' to incorporate the recommended 5-A-Day into their diets.[23]

These demonstrations were then taken up by community leaders in cooking workshops held in local communities, and local press continue to highlight supermarket offers on fresh fruit and vegetables and there is continuing support on healthy eating from the Department of Health, including in January 2012 YouTube cooking tutorials hosted by Ainsley Harriott and posted on the Change4Life website.

The images of what is required in order to pre-empt and intervene in the impending fact that 'children from the Pakistani, Bangladeshi and black African communities are more likely to become overweight or obese than their white counterparts' in these examples *become real or actual experiences*. The images are in this sense literally done with, lived out, felt and acted on. To conclude the chapter, I want to consider some of the implications of the insistence that Change4Life is not a traditional advertising campaign but is a *social movement*. If images are virtuals that are explicitly organized as events or experiences, what does this suggest for an understanding of power as affective potential?

Screens, potential, difference

In beginning to address the question posed above, it is helpful to return to consider the conception of the screen that Change4Life indicates. I would suggest that, in targeting the 'at risk' clusters described above, social marketing seems to particularly emphasize the need to engage *directly*, so that it is possible to suggest that screens are themselves seen as *distancing* the message of healthiness from those that it needs to reach. Such a conception of screens is evident in the Department of Health (2011b) Equity Analysis document that outlines the requirement of a social marketing campaign for health in England, of which Change4Life is one aspect.[24] Arguing that the 'majority of health problems fall disproportionately on individuals, families and communities that have lower incomes and lower education levels' (2011b: 2), and describing the '[r]educt[ion] of health inequalities [as] a matter of fairness' (2011b: 3), the document argues that a *social marketing campaign* can address how inequities of health are in part caused and reproduced by inequities of access to and understanding of information. For example, it describes how there is 'inequity in access to information, support and advice' that in part is organized around access to, and comfort and confidence with, screens and print materials:

> wealthier, better-educated people with managerial jobs are more likely to already have access to health information (for example via the newspapers they read or via employee wellness programmes), they are also more likely to seek out additional information (for example via websites) and to feel confidence in their own ability to use and act on that information.
>
> (2011b: 3)

In contrast:

> While access to new technologies has been growing rapidly, there are still nine million people in the UK who have never accessed the internet. These

people are more likely to be older, to have fewer qualifications and lower income than those who do use the internet. In addition, there are 4.8 million people living in Great Britain who report that they never read or even glance through a newspaper. Moreover, 4.4 million people report that they never watch any television news or current affairs programming. 785,000 people could be termed 'information poor' in that they fall into both groups.

(2011b: 3)

In the previous three case study chapters, I have traced the ways in which the imperative of transformation is organized through the screen. I have suggested that with different refractions of the imperative of transformation – shopping, makeover programmes, online dieting – and with different kinds of screens – interactive mirrors, television, computer – the affectivity of images of transformation appeals to (some) bodies through transparency and disappearance and/or reflection and being seen as evident. I have explored, then, how the immediacy of affect engages bodies seemingly directly through the screen. In the case of Change4Life however, screens are seen as only one way of providing information about and pre-empting bad health and, moreover, are seen as not a particularly helpful way of engaging with the bodies that most require that information; screen and paper based information may in fact function as a barrier. For this information to be effective, for these images to be actualized, the social movement *must intervene directly into the real, physical, actual life of the at risk clusters*. Images here become events; experiences that are brought to life through the actual living out of their virtuality.

One of the aims of this chapter, and the book more widely, has been to examine how images, as affect, are involved in the way in which power works. As a government funded health campaign, Change4Life addresses those bodies that have historically been categorized as at risk.[25] As such, Change4Life does not so much re-draw social differences as make social differences differently.[26] This is to argue that power as affect is not only regulating social differences but is *making or (re)inventing* difference. As an exemplary instance of the imperative of transformation, Change4Life impels some bodies to feel and move towards a better future. The imperative of transformation is therefore a materiality that is felt and lived out by *particular* bodies; those bodies that belong to the clusters classified as at risk of obesity and overweight. For these bodies, the future as potential is brought into, felt and lived out in the present. In this sense, the affectivity of power works through potential. Indeed, as the Department of Health describes in its account of the need for social marketing to tackle public health issues, Change4Life is a movement that has

> been prioritized because [it] address[es] those segments of the population who are greatest users of health services, because there is prior evidence that marketing can have an impact in these areas and/or because a strong case can be made that *people's lifestyles are amenable to change*.
>
> (Department of Health 2011b: 5, my emphasis)

The amenability to change – the capacity for transformation – has here become not only one of the aims of Change4Life but *one of the ways in which at risk clusters are themselves understood, categorized* and *targeted*. The capacity for transformation becomes a means of defining those bodies 'at risk' of future bad health. Change and transformation thus become not only an objective but also an immanent measure (see Chapter 4), that is a means through which social differences are understood and made.

As I have discussed then, Change4Life organizes social differences differently through the affective temporality of pre-emption, where the future as potential is brought into the present and is felt as necessary to be acted on, now. The effect of the virtual future in the present is that it is not only their futures but their presents that are imaged as difficult and dangerous. That is, the dangerous amounts of fat stored in their bodies in the future is imaged as a danger in the present. Through the anticipatory affects of love, guilt and fear, their presents become a state with 'weight', as Lauren Berlant (2006) puts it, 'an obstacle to living' (2006: 24). The pre-emptive politics of Change4Life as one site through which the imperative of transformation is organized and circulates raises questions concerning the possibility of living in the present *as it is*, without the future becoming the time that 'matters most' (Adams *et al.* 2009: 248). It also raises questions about the (im)materiality of contemporary social life, and the ways in which power works through intangible potential. In the case of Change4Life, I have argued that the future as potential is brought into the present through calculations and predictions that are then translated into and arranged as *images*, and as images that are *experiences*. In this sense, images become a central means through which 'theories and descriptions of the world come alive in new built form, new machines and new bodies' (Thrift 2005: 11). Through being felt in the ways that I have discussed above, images are actualized, in this case as ways of life that anticipate and are alert to the requirement to transform into a healthier, happier, longer-living (and hence more efficient and cost-effective) body. In the Conclusion to the book, I consider the relationship between images and the temporalities through which power works.

Conclusion
Transforming images – sociology, the future and the virtual

This book has tracked the way in which an imperative of transformation is circulated through images of a better future, and how these images are brought to life as particular kinds of bodies. It has argued that these images are actualized via the ways in which different screens co-ordinate the viewing of, interaction with and experiencing of the images. Central to the ways in which images are actualized is the affectivity of images where images are felt and lived out. In this concluding chapter, I want to draw together these themes through a focus on temporality, that is by returning to and teasing out the particular version(s) of temporality that the futures of images of transformation suggest. More especially, I think through the implications of the temporalities of images of transformation for sociology, and focus again on the concept of the future as potential, in terms of questions of difference, optimism (Berlant 2011) and critique. Taking up these themes I then consider ways in which the virtual might be a helpful concept through which sociology, and social and cultural theory more generally, can understand the future and its relationship to the present.

Time, difference, power

The case studies chapters have all argued that through specific modes of looking at, interacting with and experiencing the image that different screens organize, the future as potential is brought into the present. In this sense, the idea that time is (only) a linear progression from past to present to future is problematized. For example, in Chapter 2 on interactive mirrors, I suggested that mirrors have long been associated with transformation and the potential of the future that this transformation might bring. In the case of those interactive mirrors located within shops, the 'reflection' in the mirror indicates the ways in which the body and self might be improved in the future (for example, with the purchase of particular items). In this example, the virtual is brought into the actual temporally, in that the future becomes part of the way in which the present is experienced; and it is also the case that the virtual is brought into the actual spatially, through making virtual friends an important aspect of the in-store shopping experience. Both this chapter and Chapter 4, which focuses on online dieting, trace how customers' and online dieters' interaction with the screen establishes rhythms whereby at different moments the screen becomes apparent or disappears. In the case of dieting, the online plans complicate a linear and forward-moving version of time by enabling multiple temporalities to be imaged. A diet may not always – or indeed often – succeed. In this sense, the future as potential acts as a lure for dieting; it is that which exceeds the planning and practices of dieting.

In Chapters 3 and 5 I also discussed the ways in which the future as potential escapes a version of linear time. In Chapter 3 on makeover television, I argue that through the modes of viewing specific to working-class women, the television screen disappears and these viewers experience the better future affectively, through proximity and immediacy. The programmes highlight the processual quality of transformation and demonstrate that, for some bodies, the imperative of transformation is lived as an on-going awareness that change is necessary. Similarly, at stake in Chapter 5 on the Change4Life campaign is an attention to the specific bodies that are required to transform. Through this government initiative I argue that the future as potential is quite deliberately brought into the present in order to pre-empt what is framed to be the unfolding of a catastrophe of obesity and poor health. Running alongside each other then, are two versions of temporality; the assumption that time *is* linear and that this linear temporality that will inevitably unfold if nothing is done, and the pre-emptive version of temporality where the present becomes organized around particular versions of the potential future in order to ensure that the linearity of temporality *is not* inevitable (see Evans 2010). While in all of these examples I suggest that the future functions as 'potential', this potential is seen to indicate both the promise of the better future that images of transformation work through and something more uncomfortable and unsettling; that this potential is not necessarily achievable and that it comes to organize, for certain bodies more than others, present day concerns.

In focusing this book on how images of transformation bring the future into the present, I have drawn on different theoretical perspectives to consider the ways in which such non-linear temporalities are also being explored in other contexts: science and technology, for example (Borup *et al.* 2006; Van Lente 2000), politics and rhetoric (Berlant 2011; Massumi 2005), popular culture (Berlant 2011) and business and management practices (Thrift 2005; Adam and Groves 2007, see Introduction and Chapter 5 especially). While their positions differ, all of these theories think critically about what is at stake in the future being experienced in and as the present. In this chapter I want to consider some of the arguments that I have made about images of transformation in relation to a number of intersecting points from these various theoretical positions. This is to place my argument within a wider field of work on time and the future. In particular, I first return to the argument made in the Introduction and taken up in the rest of the book that the future is becoming the dominant temporality in contemporary socio-cultural life. In this sense, power is increasingly working by acting on the future, and is thus materially changing (linear) time (Massumi 2005; Adkins 2009). This point is important to consider as it suggests that social and cultural differences are being made and re-made through time; the second point I therefore examine is about the relationship between the future, power and difference. I then develop an understanding of this relationship with regards to a third point; what this might tell us about the present. These three points are further developed in the following section through a discussion of theory, critique and optimism.

The first point that I think is important to emphasize in the different theories of time and the future is the argument that the future is becoming an increasingly central part of everyday life. In the Introduction, I discussed how the science and technology sector is future-oriented (Borup *et al.* 2006; Van Lente 2000), and Thrift's (2005) argument that abstract predictions and calculations have become a key means through which the present is organized; these projections of the future come to take on flesh in and as the present. Chapter 5 explored this idea most explicitly, especially in relation to Massumi's argument, that the linear temporality of prevention (where predictions work from the present in order to intervene in an event in the future) exists at the same time as, and indeed is being replaced with, the affective temporality of pre-emption. This pre-emptive temporality is non-linear, in that future events are experienced in the present, as if they had already taken place.

Other social and cultural theorists have also argued in different ways that the future is now brought into the present so that an understanding of time as linear is disrupted. Melinda Cooper (2006) for example, has discussed catastrophic events such as climate change and terrorism, and argued that they seem to come 'from a future without chronological continuity with the past' (2006: 119). As such, they 'cannot be accounted for by traditional frameworks of risk management' (2006: 119), such as prediction and prevention, because the understanding of time as causal and progressive that underpins traditional risk management no longer holds up. Instead, Cooper argues that what the non-chronological relationship between the past, present and future 'provokes is [...] a state of alertness, without foreseeable end' (2006: 120). In this sense, the affective anticipation that Massumi and Adams *et al.* point to is relevant here, as bodies become attuned to uncertainty and the (potential) need to change. This alertness is an example of power working intensively: indeed, discussing how security has become a dominant mode of dealing with the uncertainty of the future, Ben Anderson (2009, 2010) has examined pre-emption as a means for liberal democracies to 'govern a range of events, conditions and crises' (2010: 779). For Anderson, the future comes to be understood as a disruption or surprise to what is imagined to be the smooth linear progression of time, and this engenders a form of 'anticipatory action', 'whereby a future becomes cause and justification for some form of action in the here and now' (2010: 778).

One of the issues that this book has begun to unpack is how affect is distributed unevenly, so that it is some bodies in particular that feel this state of alertness or anticipation. This argument that the temporality of anticipation and/or pre-emption is gendered – and classed, aged and raced – is the second point from the different literatures on the future that I want to highlight, and to consider in relation to my case studies. I discussed theories of anticipation and pre-emption in Chapter 5, where I argued that the Change4Life campaign generates an affective alertness to the need to transform the body for those bodies that are calculated and predicted to be most susceptible to obesity and poor health, and thus most in need of change: working-class, ethnic minority and mothers' (who take on primary responsibility for their children's health) bodies. Whether or not action is taken – that is whether or not obese bodies become slimmer and healthier – I argue that the campaign indicates that these and other bodies come to be aware of, or alert to, the potential need to change. This then has been my focus on the *imperative* of transformation, where changing the body becomes a way of life, for some especially.

While Chapter 5 explicitly focuses on the making and re-making of difference through affect, this was also a concern in other chapters of the book. In Chapter 2 for example, I explored the ways in which 'going shopping' can be an intensive experience that involves an indeterminacy of the customer, an openness to suggestion. Drawing on Blackman's (2007) work on suggestion, I argued that some bodies are more suggestive than others: those that do not have the privilege of background (in terms of class, gender or race), age or education. It is these bodies that are most intensely addressed by the better future promised via shopping. Taking this argument further is to examine how power is working through suggestion (see Orr 2006), that is through *affectively* (rather than rationally) addressing and engaging different bodies differently. Focusing on the case of interactive mirrors, one of the ways in which I examined the unequal distribution of affect was through exploring how shopping (and consumer culture more widely, see Cronin 2010; Moor 2003) works through the creation of intensive spaces and times. The interactive mirrors are seen as a means of 'revitalizing' shopping through bringing the virtual into the actual, and creating a 'timelessness' that encourages customers to buy more.

It is important to note that the stores for which the mirrors were initially designed were high-end, and that the impetus for the development of interactive mirrors is therefore to encourage these specific kinds of customers to spend money. This is to draw attention to the commercial reasons for the development of interactive mirrors, and to trace how this commercialism means that the mirrors will be interacted with by those who can afford to purchase products in the stores in which the mirrors are located. Indeed, the 'tourists' who visited the Prada Epicenter store in New York to view rather than to buy, are cited as one of the reasons for the problems with the changing-rooms and other interactive features; the technological features were 'too delicate' for the 'high traffic' that the store generated. However, designs for, and trials of, interactive mirrors suggest that they are now intended to be part of the high street shopping experience, in the UK in mid-range (though still resolutely middle-class) department stores such as John Lewis and in young(er) fashion stores such as Topshop, which in 2010 featured an interactive mirror as an installation in its flagship Oxford Street branch. Furthermore, in a television programme on the re-branding of struggling 'fast fashion' store Pilot, retail expert Mary Portas re-designed the worst performing store and placed an interactive Twitter screen in the changing-rooms – which themselves were restyled.[1]

I argued in Chapter 2 that the interactive mirrors appeal to young women in particular. The interactive mirrors are described by designers and retailers as resonating with young women because they find 'going shopping' (as opposed to 'doing the shopping', Bowlby 2000, see Chapter 2) fun, and the promotional materials for the mirrors all feature young white women. In the intensive shopping experiences created in part by interactive mirrors, time works non-linearly by bringing the future into the present for young women especially. I have argued that the better future functions as potential, and in addressing the bodies of young women specifically, I would also suggest that *the interactive mirrors see young women as a site of potential*. Young women are addressed as aspiring to and capable of materializing a better future; they are the ideal consumers of interactive mirrors. To return to McRobbie's (2008) point discussed in the Introduction, it is young women who today embody the capacity for experimentalism or transformation. In this case study then, the imperative of transformation works through the resonances between the potential of young women and the potential of the better future of shopping. As such, shopping may be understood as a site through which power (as intensive) works. As Adams *et al.* put it, '[g]irlhood is one site among many where distinctively gendered anticipatory regimes are at stake' (2009: 252).[2]

While the ideal consumers of the interactive mirrors are obviously those who will buy something, I would also suggest that the interactive mirrors are an example of how shopping and consumer culture might exceed use (or actual consumption, Lury 2011, see Chapter 2) and require a further thinking about transformation *as an image*. That is, as I discussed in Chapter 1, materialization is not a finished process and therefore the materialization of the future cannot be finally achieved through the purchase of a particular garment. Going shopping is open-ended. The better future shopping promises is thus a virtual image that is not exhausted. This understanding of the virtuality of going shopping indicates two issues. First, I suggest that the re-creation of in-store shopping as an *experience* recognizes this virtuality or open-endedness. It sees shopping as a leisure activity, where socializing with friends (on or offline) is key to its revival; shopping is about 'more' than 'just' buying things. Moreover, the technology of the interactive mirrors themselves recognize and draw attention to the virtual. An integral part of the close association between mirrors and transformation is that the mirror image shows not only what is (the actual) but also what might be (the virtual, that might yet be actualized). The increasing significance of interactive mirrors as part of the intensive shopping experience emphasizes, I think, the virtuality of shopping and highlights the way in which images are a key means through which power circulates.

It has also been one of my concerns in the other case study chapters to explore how the appeal of, or aspiration to, the better future is not necessarily materialized via 'actual' products (like clothing for example) but remains vaguer, as a set of feelings or inclinations. I have attempted to examine how the imperative of

138 Conclusion

transformation functions through the virtual and immaterial, and how transformation is an imperative for those bodies constituted as failing. Across all of the chapters is a focus on the gendering of the imperative of transformation. In Chapter 3 gender is considered in relation to class, in that I argue that it is the bodies of working-class women that are most strongly appealed to by images of transformation from makeover television. In Chapter 4 I explore the relationship between gender, weight and the materialization of a better future, and suggest that (over)weight is a problem that is felt most keenly by women. In Chapter 5 I develop this interest in weight and difference to examine how race and class are also made and re-made through the affectivity of images of transformation. To build on the second point made by theorists of time and the future, that the affectivity of anticipation and/or pre-emption works through and helps to constitute difference, the third point that I think is important in these theories is that, in working through the image of a better future, *the present* is experienced by some people as difficult.

In the Introduction, I posed the question of how the future as potential involves both changing a difficult present for the better, and a temporal orientation around the present as a 'compromised condition [...] of possibility' (Berlant 2006: 21). Berlant's framing of the present in this way is part of her concern with how optimism for a better life is 'cruel'; it is 'the condition of maintaining an attachment to a significantly problematic object' (Berlant 2011: 24). These attachments may be to many kinds of different objects – they could 'seem embedded in a person, a thing, an institution, a text, a norm, a bunch of cells, smells, a good idea – whatever' (2011: 23) – but they function as cruel optimism because 'the subjects who have x in their lives might not well endure the loss of their object/scene of desire, even though its presence threatens their well-being' (2011: 24). For example, an attachment to the achievement of a slimmer future 'threatens the [...] well-being' of a person because it arranges her present around a future ideal that may well not be achievable and that therefore casts her as failure.

In Chapter 4 I discussed the issue of failure in relation to the high rates of recidivism of dieting; in the context of Weight Watchers, the linear 'route through' dieting where a better future is achieved and maintained is almost never achieved. Nevertheless, despite this threat to well-being, the removal or loss of the object of attachment might not be 'well endure[d]' because, as Berlant goes on to indicate, 'whatever the *content* of the attachment is, the continuity of its form provides something of the continuity of the subject's sense of what it means to keep on living on and to look forward to being in the world' (2011: 24). In this sense, the promise of the better, slimmer future provides for the dieter the means of 'living on'. The present is made bearable through the slimmer future; the future offers the potential of transforming the difficult present so that the dieter can 'look forward to being in the world'.

Berlant considers the temporality of 'living on' in a discussion of food and obesity. She argues that while '[i]t would be easy and not false' to understand the 'crisis of obesity' and the advice given to combat it 'as an orchestrated surreality made to sell drugs, services, and newspapers, and to justify particular new governmental and medical oversight of populations whose appetites are out of control' (2011: 103), obesity is, nevertheless, a problem and moreover, there is an *experience* of eating and obesity. Berlant sees the rise in levels of obesity as 'ordinary people' responding to or living with the time of contemporary capitalism. Contemporary capitalism involves 'speed-up at work' (2011: 116), constant and ongoing life projects, and '[t]ime organized by the near future of the paying of bills and the management of children' (2011: 116). In this 'material context for so many' (2011: 116), where the future bears down on and comes to be felt in the present, '[f]ood is one of the few spaces of controllable, reliable pleasure people have' (2011: 115): eating (and its preparation and sharing) provides 'ordinary and repeatable scenes of happiness, if not health' (2011: 116). Interestingly for my argument that the imperative of transformation works through the image of the better future, Berlant argues that '[e]ating adds up to something, many things: maybe the good life, but usually a sense of well-being that spreads out for a moment, not a projection toward a future' (2011: 117).[3]

This sense of 'well-being that spreads out for a moment' is a helpful way of understanding the recidivism rates of dieting, and more generally the increase in those bodies categorized as overweight or obese that I discussed in Chapter 5. I have argued that the better future is a virtual image that exceeds the linearity of the plans that suggest ways of combating obesity. In this way, the virtual image is a means through which power works affectively and intensively; an image of the better future is not exhausted and it acts as an appeal that things might be different. Berlant's focus is slightly different, in that she concentrates on the present rather than the future (see below). In particular, while I have argued that the future is brought into the present in that the present comes to be organized around the future, Berlant suggests with the notion of the 'spread out' moment of eating, that the present may be a suspension of the future. However, there are connections to be made, I think, in relation to how it is the future that has come to be the temporality at stake in contemporary sociocultural life and how time is understood as non-linear. More specifically, there are connections to be made between Berlant's idea that eating is a spread-out moment, an 'interruption' (2011: 115) or 'small vacation' (2011: 116) from 'the body or life [as a] project' (2011: 116) and the notion of indeterminacy that I discussed in terms of going shopping above. Indeterminacy is a concept that Bowlby develops in relation to the timelessness of going shopping, where 'time is collapsed into the "immediate" urge of the present moment and the experience leaves no trace for another time' (Bowlby 2000: 68). In Chapter 2 I argued that this kind of time is intensive, and with shopping involves the virtual future being brought into the actual present. I would argue that the 'spread out moment' that Berlant describes can also be understood as intensive time, despite it operating in a way that she argues suspends the future, is 'not toward imaging the long haul, for example' (2011: 117). That is, the time of eating is intensive in that it disrupts the linearity of time, and works, at least in part, through affect; through pleasure and happiness for example rather than through what is known to be the rational healthy option.[4]

Eating and the obesity that it may well bring into being are for Berlant both a production of a difficult present and a means of making the difficult present bearable. In this sense it is an example of cruel optimism. Eating and obesity are also a means of thinking about the current emphasis on the future in both contemporary social and cultural life and theory. The effects and affects of this emphasis on the future in socio-cultural life are clear. For Berlant and I differently, the intensity of the future organizes the present as difficult, and as oriented around processes (or attachments) of actualizing a virtual potential (the good life, the better future). In the rest of this chapter, I want to consider the implications of an emphasis on the future for theory, in order to examine further the potential value of the concept of the virtual to sociology. Below, I return to the specific kinds of relationship between the present and future that I think a focus on the virtual and actual suggest. In the next section though I take up the theme of optimism that Berlant's work highlights, and develop this in relation to the issue of critique that I raised in Chapter 3.

'Inventing optimists': temporality, theory and critique

Berlant's focus is on the cruelty of optimism. However, despite its cruelty, this focus on optimism is a means of 'looking at the complexity of being bound to life' (Berlant 2011: 14). That is, Berlant is keen to emphasize that,

> [e]ven when it turns out to involve a cruel relation, it would be wrong to see optimism's negativity as a symptom of an error, a perversion, damage, or a dark truth: optimism is, instead, a scene of negotiated sustenance that makes life bearable as it presents itself ambivalently, unevenly, incoherently.
> (2011: 14)

In exploring how cruel optimism operates as a mundane lived reality for many in post-Fordist Western societies, Berlant is not suggesting that the people whose lives are made bearable by it are necessarily labouring under a false consciousness of it, or are misguided. As the example of eating demonstrates, enjoying the pleasures of what makes life bearable is to be understood in the context of what makes life difficult. The concept of cruel optimism is a means of attending to how the present might be a suspension of the over-bearingness of the future. In this sense, cruel optimism is

> a concept pointing toward a mode of lived immanence, one that grows from a perception about the reasons people […] do not prefer to interfere with varieties of immiseration, but choose to ride the wave of the system of attachment that they are used to, to syncopate with it, or to be held in a relation of reciprocity, reconciliation, or resignation that does not mean defeat by it.
> (2011: 28)

Cruel optimism then is a concept that is interested in how life is lived. That people might not 'interfere with varieties of immiseration, but choose to ride the wave of the system of attachment that they are used to' is an understanding of power and (the making bearable of) life that does not result in a negation or denigration of optimism.

For this book, it is important to take account of optimism because of the way in which images of transformation work through the idea(l) of the better future. Images of transformation function through optimism; they indicate the possibility of a better life. For example, makeover television can be understood to work though optimism in its promise of a better future that can be achieved through following particular practices and regimes, and that escapes these through existing as potential. As I discussed in Chapter 3, *How to Look Good Naked* provides 'tips on dressing for your shape, *whatever it might be*' (UK website, my emphasis), the BBC's *What Not to Wear* is described as the '[s]eries helping to make *all women* stylish, *regardless* of their shape, height or age' (BBC website, my emphasis), while a 2004 press release for *The Swan* describes the programme as 'turn[ing] a fantasy into reality by mirroring the classic fairy tale' in which 'a gaggle of self-proclaimed "ugly ducklings" will swim upstream to be transformed into a bevy of graceful beauties'. In framing the future as the better time that is aimed for by transformations, it is working-class women especially that are appealed to through the potential of the future. This potential constitutes the transformation in terms of looking *forward*, in terms of *optimism about the future*. In order to understand the popularity of these programmes and the ways in which the other images of transformation explored in this book work, theory thus needs to be interested in the ways in which this optimism is produced, not to see the optimism as 'a symptom of an error, a perversion, damage, or a dark truth' – even if it is cruel – but rather to take it seriously, to account for the appeal of the different and better time for working-class women. While Berlant proposes optimism as cruel in that it might not bring about the better future that it is attached to, she is not suggesting that 'we' should give up on optimism. The 'we' here refers both to Berlant's focus on the everyday and ordinary people, and to the theorists that her work can be seen as addressing. Even if the relationship between power and the making bearable of life are not fully clear or conscious to people, optimism must be engaged with.

Taking the optimism of images of transformation seriously, I suggest, is to see theory not as separate from the processes it describes but rather as inherently part of them, as immanent and inventive to them. As I have argued in previous chapters, theory is performative of the worlds it seeks to understand. This claim has two specific inter-related implications for theory: one is what happens to critique when theory is understood as inventive and the other concerns the ways in which theory might understand everyday optimistic processes of living. To develop the latter concern first, it is worth noting that, writing in an earlier essay and drawing on the work of queer theorist Sedgwick, Berlant (2002) argues that her development of the term 'optimism' is a response to a kind of cultural theory that deems scepticism 'the only ethical position for the intellectual to take with respect to the subject's ordinary attachments' (Berlant 2002: 72).[5] A cultural theory that prioritizes optimism rather than scepticism is not to be overwhelmingly positive, but rather to 'be aghast at the ease with which intellectuals shit on people who hold a dream. Dreams are seen as easy optimism, while failures seem complex' (2002: 72).[6]

Berlant is pointing out here how critique has come to be associated with negation and scepticism, where scepticism is allied with being serious, well-informed and knowledgeable. As such, optimism – both in ordinary everyday life and in theory – is framed as naïve or silly: optimism does not account for things as they 'really' are. Understood as a sceptical project, theory is about uncovering and critiquing the ways in which power works as hegemony, concealing or perverting the real conditions of life. One of the possible consequences of such a project is that theory can come to understand dreams and optimism as mistaken or foolish. As queer theorist Michael D. Snediker (2009) puts it in his work on queer optimism:

> optimism is imagined epithetically as 'premature': as though if the optimist at hand knew all that she might eventually know, she might retract her optimism altogether. Prematurity qualifies optimism as a temporary state of insufficient information. 'Woefully optimistic', on the other hand, implies that the knowledge that would warrant optimism's retraction might never arrive. As an epithet, 'woefully' (like 'hegemonic', 'dubious', or 'premature') subjects optimism to an outside judgment, the likes of which the optimist in question is profoundly unable to make.
>
> (2009: 1–2)[7]

Snediker characterizes optimism here as premature and/or woeful. Interestingly, both are understood temporally; 'premature optimism' as a 'temporary state of insufficient information' and 'woeful optimism' as an altogether misguided faith in a future that will never come to be. Moreover, both accounts of optimism are a form of 'outside judgement' which simultaneously sees 'the optimist in question' as 'profoundly unable to make' such a verdict and the judger (in terms of my argument here, the theorist) as the one who can really see what is going on.

The framing of optimism by theory as, ultimately, wrong has been challenged in this book through the argument that an understanding of theory as an external system or framework does not necessarily tell us very much about the *experience* of the better future indicated by images of transformation. That is, while theories interested in critiquing images of transformation are necessary in order to make clear the standards and ideals that the better future circulates – in Berlant's terms they are 'not false' – they, ultimately, see power as that which constrains and restricts; power is 'over' things. I have argued instead that power is (also) intensive; power is immanent, it produces and invents. Power works through the affectivity of images, where images are not separate to bodies but are 'directly' felt in and through bodies. In Chapter 3 for example, I examined how the proximate modes of looking that working-class women develop with makeover television, requires an understanding of these images not as separate to the audience but as resonating with the audience's present lives, experienced *through* working-class women's bodies. Another way in which I have addressed the immanence of power is through a re-thinking of how measure works. In Chapter 4 I discussed how measure is produced in online dieting. Drawing on Adkins' (2009) work, I argued that measure is not (only) an external, pre-existing framework into which bodies are then fitted but that it emerges out of interactions (or intra-actions) between bodies and images. An understanding of measure as such, helps to make sense of the ongoing appeal of dieting, even when so many women's (and men's) experiences of dieting is that it is not effective. Importantly, seeing measure as immanent is not to suggest that as a kind of material transformation, online dieting is somehow outside measure, but rather to suggest that immanent measure is one of the ways in which power as inventive, as intensive, operates. This, then, is not to see the women (and men) who diet as dupes of ideology, nor to see them as empowered but rather to think about the materiality of the body as produced through power as intensive.

To understand how power works in and through things – as *potentia* in Lash's (2010) terms – theory needs to locate itself within these processes. In Chapter 3 I raised the question of what this might involve for critique, which has often been understood as a way of deconstructing and/or of intervening in social systems or organizations that may be harmful or problematic. Characterized in this way, critique can be understood as a sceptical project – not necessarily because it 'shits on *people* who have a dream', but because it is interested in taking these dreams apart, in showing how they will not result in better futures or authentic happiness. However, in order to understand the appeal of optimism, I would suggest that it is also necessary for critique to be not so much sceptical as proximate to, involved in and immanent to, the processes it explores. Indeed, as Skeggs and Wood's work with working-class women viewers of reality television indicates, this would also be to attend to how 'optimists' are themselves involved in 'doing critique': the working-class women viewers were, at the same time, enjoying and critiquing the kinds of futures, and the routes to them, that makeover programmes organize.

More generally, for an approach towards images of transformation, what is suggested by the point that theory is immanent to that which it seeks to understand is that theory itself becomes 'optimistic'. As I have argued, optimism is not celebration or positivity, but rather is a means of engaging with how life is a process of 'living on'. It is a means of engaging with how the present and future are experienced and lived out. Indeed, Snediker's characterization of optimism as premature or woeful results, he suggests, in an 'antagonism between optimism and knowledge [that] has had the perhaps unsurprising effect of taking optimism out of critical circulation' (2009: 2). The consequences of this is not only that theory has, in general, come to deconstruct dreams, hopes and optimism, but also that theory has focused primarily on 'bad' affects and emotions, and in how life is limited or curtailed. While these are clearly crucial interests – and it is not my intention to repudiate them – what is also important is an attention to the ways in which knowledge and experience are also bound up with optimism, hopes and dreams, and in how life is *produced* (with all its limitations); in the cases in this book, with and through the appeal of the potential of the better future. Snediker also sees theory as inventive and, drawing on Deleuze, poses a productive direction for both queer theory and social and cultural theory more widely: he argues that theory may instead '"consist [...] in inventing a people who are missing"': 'optimists' (Snediker 2009: 13, reference omitted). In the final section, I want to take up this project of 'inventing optimists'. I return to the relationship between the virtual and actual as a means of thinking about what optimism might involve for sociology.

Sociology, the future and the virtual

One of the ways in which I think the concept of optimism is significant to the argument made in this book is in how it highlights both the pull of the future, and how this future is felt within the present. In this sense, optimism seeks to account for the *potential* of the future that I have been interested in. Both, Snediker and Berlant conceive optimism in terms of the present. They do this to shift theoretical attention away from the future, as they see a focus on the future as a deferral to the later. For example, Berlant is critical of theories that emphasize futurity because they 'enable a concept of the *later* to suspend questions about the cruelty of the *now*' (2011: 28), and she explains her concept of cruel optimism as a politics of presentism that disrupts the understanding of 'futurity as the primary lubricant for counter-normative political consciousness' (2011: 68). Both Berlant and Snediker make a distinction between optimism, as this focus on the present, and hope, which they see as a faith in (Snediker 2009: 28) or passive patience for (Berlant 2011: 13), the better future that will arrive.[8] I agree with Berlant's dissatisfaction with a deferral of problems of the now to later, and would argue that an attention to the politics of the present is necessary. However, my argument has been that the affectivity of contemporary sociocultural life involves the future not as later but as *now*, as *in the present*. In this sense, the future is not that which is *beyond* the present, a time that follows on from the present that must be waited for, but is folded into the present. It is thus crucial for theory to remain interested in the future because it is a central aspect of the present.

Throughout the book I have explored how the better future is brought into the present through the concepts of the actual and virtual, and I have discussed the ways in which the concept of the virtual has been taken up across different fields of study. For some (Lash and Lury 2007; Adkins and Lury 2009; Fraser 2009; Cronin 2010; Coleman 2009; Mackenzie 2005; Diken and Laustsen 2008), the concept of the virtual can be seen as having specific importance for contemporary sociology. This focus on the virtual works in (at least) two ways. First, the social is itself seen as (increasingly) virtual. As Bulent Diken and Carsten Bagge Laustsen (2008) argue '[w]hat makes the social is not only its actualized structures, stratifications and segments but also its virtual potentialities which are significant without becoming necessarily actualized (2008: 3). In terms of my argument this is to emphasize that potential, as Adkins points out, is 'not [...]

external to or outside of reality [...] but [is] *part of reality*' (2009: 336, my emphasis). Indeed, as I hope I have demonstrated, while this potential is immaterial and virtual, it is nevertheless crucial to the kinds of lives that are actualized in the present. In particular, I have argued that it is important to trace how the relationship between the actual and virtual is temporal, and that in the virtual future existing in and as the actual present, time itself has become an organizing principle of difference. The future as potential is part of the actualization of the present, that is, the future as potential is one way in which the actual is made and re-made. It is these processes of actualization, of making images of transformation material, that have been at stake in this book. I have explored how the ordinary, everyday and sometimes mundane ways in which images are looked at, interacted with and acted out are bodily experiences that become one of the ways in which lives are lived. Looking, interacting and acting are therefore all means through which images are materialized. This book has therefore been an attempt to extend those theories of visual and mediated culture that see practices of looking at and doing with images as ways of living (e.g. Haraway 1991), and to attend to the virtuality of contemporary socio-cultural life; a virtuality that I have argued involves the body through affect.

Second, the appeal of the virtual to sociology is because the virtual takes account of change, process and transformation. As I have argued, virtuals are in the process of actualization; the materialization of bodies is an ongoing process. The concept of the virtual accounts for the open-endedness of transformation. To continue to make sense of the social world, comprehending the virtual involves 'a willingness to understand Sociology's relationship with the empirical as an experiment of – or with – the yet to come' (Adkins and Lury 2009: 18). In terms of images of transformation, I have argued that the yet to come is so significant for some people because it indicates a better time, a better future. It indicates a time that is *different*, that does not unfold linearly from the present. For sociology, the yet to come might also be understood as that which is latent within the present but which might yet be actualized. This notion of the not yet is intriguing for sociology because it suggests that there may be a way of actualizing the social that is different to what the social is today. Indeed, for Mariam Fraser, the virtual indicates that the not yet might be actualized in ways that we don't yet know about, or can't quite yet anticipate. Discussing C. Wright Mills' (1958/2000) argument that the primary task for sociology is to make a connection between an experience in the here and now and its historical explanation, Fraser argues that while focusing on the actual/virtual does not overlook the relationship between the specific and more general, the here-and-now and the there-and-then, it is a shift away from the attempt to locate *explanations* in the form of structures. Fraser puts it in this way:

> Unlike Mills' social structures [...], virtual structures or patterns cannot do 'explanatory work' because they are not determining in the way that social forces, or the material sedimentation of such forces over time, are often understood to be in sociology. [Virtual structures] are not determining not

because the virtual has no relation to the actual (it is not an unintelligible outside), but because processes of actualization introduce many convergent divergences. [...] The virtual, in short, is not a blueprint (a pre-established theoretical formulation for example).

(Fraser 2009: 75)

Fraser here is pointing to the way in which, as potential, the virtual cannot be determining because its actualization cannot necessarily be known in advance. The virtual is not a 'blueprint' because it may be actualized in different ways. It is *potential* precisely because it is a capacity. As I have argued, this is not necessarily to celebrate potentiality, nor to suggest that anything might happen. There is a proximate, intensive relationship between the actual and virtual, so that the virtual is not infinite possibility but is embedded with the actual. It is though, to assert the significance of potential – in the form of optimism, hope, dreams and aspirations – within the present, to examine the ways in which the not-yet functions as an impulse or imperative of transformation.

Concentrating on the virtual as a potential within the actual is necessary in order for people whose presents are difficult to keep on living. For sociology, it is necessary in order to 'open up sociological accounts of how the social comes about' (Latimer and Skeggs 2011: 394), and of how the social *might* come about. It is to 'emphasize the importance of *imagination* for the politics of everyday life and experience' (2011: 394, my emphasis). I have argued that the social comes about, is actualized, via the affectivity of images that emphasize the importance of optimism about the future as different, as better.[9] To understand this optimism, sociology might find it helpful to expand the project of attending to the virtual, in so far as this might open up accounts of how optimism is felt, and also of how the social might be felt and done differently.

Notes

Introduction: transformation, potential, futures

1 In a radio interview with Berlant and Skeggs on cruel optimism, Skeggs pointed out the class-based assumptions of the argument that fantasies of the good life are fraying and suggested that for working-class people, the fantasy had always been unstable. She argued that in the United States and the UK, it is middle-class people who are currently most affected by the destabilizing of social mobility and aspiration. Listen to the edition of the BBC Radio 4 programme, *Thinking Allowed*, 13 February 2012, available at: www.bbc.co.uk/programmes/b01bm0pk which also includes an interview with Karen Throsby on obesity surgery. Last accessed 11 March 2012.

2 This tradition is interesting given the links Max Weber made between the religious notion of the calling and the Protestant work ethic that emerged under the modern capitalist system in the West, where the transformation involved in labour became inextricably linked to wider processes of rationalization and efficiency. As I will discuss below, the contemporary theme of transformation is not only relevant to individuals, but to capitalism more widely.

3 Interestingly, Heyes also points to a contradictory logic at work in the appropriation of feminist arguments into everyday capitalism;

> as Western feminism has urged women to look inside to find the authentic and diverse selves that patriarchy has denied and suppressed, this very gesture of self-discovery has been deeply implicated in emergent discourses that paradoxically take the disciplined and conformist body as a site of truth reflecting the self within. For women the elusive promise of self-determination often displaces its own radical intent with the poor substitutes of dieting, exercise regimes, cosmetic surgeries and makeovers.
>
> (2007: 5)

I discuss this argument in more detail in Chapter 4.

4 As I will argue below in contrast to Beck and Beck-Gernsheim, it is not so much that these categories are disintegrating as it is that they are being re-made.

5 One of which is that the life of one's own is 'completely dependent on institutions' (Beck and Beck-Gernsheim 2002: 23). Thus, as Rose and Miller also point out, while it appears that the neo-liberal individual is autonomous from state and institutional power, modern institutional guidelines 'actually compel the self-organization and self-thematization of people's biographies' (2002: 24).

6 Personal development workers include: 'management trainers, life- performance- business- and executive-coaches; learning consultants; personal development consultants; facilitators, and management developers' (Swan 2010: 1).

7 Skeggs and McRobbie are also concerned with arguments on individualization and 'reflexive modernization' that Anthony Giddens proposes (see Giddens 1991; Beck *et al.* 1994).

148 *Notes*

8 Skeggs goes on to note that this kind of sociology

> can thus be viewed as part of a symbolic struggle for the authorization of their experience and perspectives. In Giddens' case, these rhetoric ploys have powerful outcomes as they frame the shape of a new neo-liberal politics that influenced the governments of Clinton and Blair through the more general formulation of 'the Third Way'.
>
> (2004: 53)

As such, in addition to overlooking the findings of empirical sociology, which demonstrates that class remains crucial, far from being critical of them, such 'common-sense' sociological theories can feed into and further consolidate the neo-liberal practices and policies.

9 See Lash and Lury (2007: 12–13) and Lash (2010: 138).
10 Clearly, there are many differences between the critical cultural theory of Adorno and the cultural studies of the Birmingham School, not least because British cultural studies was quick to point out how culture was not only a sphere of relentless and meaningless commodification and standardization but also a site of resistance and identity formation. I do not wish to collapse these differences here, but rather point to the ways in which a central premise of how images have been understood as representational is currently being re-worked, both in theory and practice.
11 See Coleman (2009) for a development of the actualization of the virtual from a Deleuzian perspective in terms of the relationship between bodies and images.
12 See Coleman (2009) for how the past may also be a virtual.
13 In this sense there is an increasing interest in pessimism; see, for example, Tutton (2011). See the Conclusion for a discussion on optimism.
14 Massumi's discussion in this essay is focused on the neo-conservatism of George W. Bush's presidency. Neo-conservatism both draws on and is distinct from neo-liberalism: the possibility of neo-conservatism is paved by the 'open field' of neo-liberalism, but is characterized by 'command power', which 'joins disciplinary and biopolitical modes of power in complex interaction in a shared environment characterized overall by no one of these modes' (2005: 7). In addition, neo-conservatism is characterized by pre-emption, a notion I introduce in this chapter and return to in Chapter 5.
15 Massumi quotes George W. Bush here, as indicating that government must act on 'eventualities that may or may not occur' (2005: 4).
16 It is from Bush's 'favourite characterization of his presidential role' (2005: 6) as commander-in-chief that Massumi names his concept of command power.
17 As such, persuasion is replaced with 'the presumption of allegiance' (Massumi 2005: 6).
18 As Melinda Cooper points out, it is not so much the focus on the future that distinguishes Bush's neo-conservatism from Clinton's neo-liberalism as

> both economies mobilize speculative affect, attuning it to the emergence of the unpredictable. What has changed is the affective valence of "our" relation to the future – from euphoria to panic or fear, or rather alertness (a state of fear without foreseeable end).
>
> (Cooper 2006: 128)

Barack Obama's politics explicitly establish a relation of hope to the future, though this hopefulness can be understood as itself entangled with what Cooper terms alertness; a state of being alert to the potential danger of giving up on hope. See Coleman and Ferreday (2011).

19 For example, the invasion of Iraq by America and Britain in March 2003 was 'a foregone conclusion. When [the decision] arrives, it always seems to have preceded itself' (Massumi 2005: 5), as Donald Rumsfeld indicates: 'whatever it is that we do

substantively [...] will be known to you, *probably before we decide it*' (quoted in Massumi 2005: 6).
20 Both Lash and Massumi refer to 'facts': Massumi refers to the factual in contradistinction to the affective (Bush's form of command power works through affect rather than fact) and Lash to facts to indicate a shift from hegemonic to post-hegemonic forms of power. Despite the apparent tension in what facts refer to in their work, I think both Massumi and Lash are arguing that power be understood in terms of the intensive, the experiential, the material.

1 Screening affect: images, representational thinking and the actualization of the virtual

1 See Seigworth and Gregg (2010: 6–9) for more detail on other trends in affect theory.
2 While focusing on the body rather than on affect, see Grosz (1994) for her account of philosophies of the body that work from the inside-out and the outside-in.
3 It is important to note here that Clough is not critiquing textuality per se but rather the specific notion of textuality that emerges according to this Marxist tradition. See Clough (2000: Chapter 4 especially) for a discussion of (auto)ethnographic writing and text. Similarly, although I use the terms 'text' and 'reading' in this book to set my argument against, I am specifically referring to the tradition within cultural studies of treating images as ideological texts which are read. See below, and discussion of power, affect and intensity in the Introduction.
4 Jameson draws on Heidegger's distinction between *techne* and *physis*, or nature. See Clough (2000: 87–88) for a more detailed discussion.
5 My point in this book is not that images *do not* work as representations but that they *do not only* operate in this way. I am thus not arguing that representational analyses of images are no longer necessary but rather that sociological analyses of images could be opened up to examine not only what images are (of) but also what they do.
6 Law and Hetherington argue that this is one aspect of representational thinking in sociology, and this is the aspect that I concentrate on in this book. The other aspects are that sociology 'is literary in form; more or less linear in structure; [...]; mirrors or re-presents the world; builds a more or less coherent and consistent literary subject position' (1998: 2).
7 This concern with what is not 'caught' within representational thinking is also central to the material turn in feminist theory. As Stacy Alaimo and Susan Hekman (2008) argue, representational thinking has tended to read bodies as sites upon which cultural codes are inscribed and/or as culturally constructed through discourse: 'Focusing exclusively on representations, ideology and discourse', they suggest, 'excludes lived experience, corporeal practice, and biological substance from consideration' (2008: 4).
8 This then, is not a critique of representational analyses being misplaced in and of themselves, but an argument that theory must be adept at analysing the changes in the way in which images now work. As Lash and Lury outline, 'since the time of critical theory [the middle 1940s] *and* since the emergence of the Birmingham tradition in the middle 1970s – things have changed' (2007: 3).
9 See the contributions to the collections on affect referenced above for research in this area that is emerging. Brian Massumi (2002) proposes a comprehensive theorization of these and other concepts from a Deleuzian position. For how these concepts might be empirically researched in relation to bodies, see Coleman (2009).
10 Indeed, the emphasis that non-representational theory places on affect, images and bodies has necessitated the development of a range of social scientific methodological approaches. See for example the recent ESRC funded seminar series on researching affect and affect communication: www.cardiff.ac.uk/socsi/newsandevents/events/innovation/index.html, last accessed 11 April 2011.

11 Latham and McCormack's argument is part of a wider trend of non-representational theory within human and cultural geography. I have focused on Latham and McCormack's argument here, because of their interest in non-representationalism and images. For more general non-representational theory, including discussions of affect, see for example Thrift (2007); Hayden Lorimer (2005, 2007, 2008); Tolia-Kelly (2006); Jamie Lorimer (2008). For wonderful discussions of how the visual methodology of video might 'capture' the affective relations between humans and non-humans (in this case elephants), see Lorimer (forthcoming), and Renold and Mellor (forthcoming).

12 This point is interesting in terms of the relationship between cinema and television: whereas cinema fits into this definition of the dynamic screen, work on television argued that it is a medium that either requires or is awarded less concentrated and more distracted attention. See for example Ellis (1992) and Morley (1992). I return to the issue of 'distracted' or distributed viewing in Chapter 4 and in Chapter 3 I discuss the television screen as producing an absorbing rather than distracted mode of viewing. In this sense, it is also worth noting that issues of distraction tend to emerge in relation to new technologies; in contemporary discourse it is the computer screen rather than the television screen that leads to distraction (for example, in commentary on the low levels of concentration that children brought up with computer screens are often argued to have).

13 I have placed 'directly' in inverted commas here to draw attention to the debate that is ongoing in affect studies about the relationship between the biological and the socio-cultural that I introduced above in terms of the inner-outer or outer-inner relationship between bodies and the world. In this book, I draw upon the latter set of theories and aim to analyse the ways in which the 'direct' address of affect is mediated.

2 Bringing the image to life: interactive mirrors and intensive experience

1 Unless indicated otherwise, all websites accessed 13 September 2011. I am focusing on these examples here for brevity, rather than to suggest that these are the only examples that are noteworthy. For other recent examples of interactive mirrors as artwork, see 'Hereafter', by United Visual Artists (www.uva.co.uk/work/hereafter-2#/0), which was part of the Identity exhibition at the Wellcome Trust in 2009: www.wellcome.ac.uk/news/media-office/press-releases/2009/wtx056922.htm. In the context of health, see the interactive mirror designed by Ming-Zher Poh as a 'contact-free and remote way of measuring vital signs'; see www.guardian.co.uk/technology/2012/jan/22/medical-mirror-ming-zher-poh/print. Thanks to Celia Lury for bringing this to my attention. I discuss further examples of interactive mirrors placed in stores below.

2 I am not suggesting here that shopping and consumer culture are equivalent, nor that consumer culture can be collapsed into shopping. Rather, I am drawing on the relationship between consumer culture and transformation discussed in the Introduction and taking up my interest in this book on the organization of images of transformation via different screens to explore interactive mirrors.

3 Melchoir-Bonnet's focus is on Europe, and on France in particular.

4 Showing what man is and ought to be is one of the medieval and Middle Ages discourses of the mirror, and is held alongside another discourse where, '[w]hen the mirror was not reflecting the spotless divine model, it was the seat of lies and seductions, used by a cunning Satan to deceive men' (Melchoir-Bonnet 2001: 187). This alternative discourse, where the mirror is associated with sin, resonates with ideas of the mirror's role in creating a culture of narcissism.

5 Thanks to Monica Moreno Figueroa for this point.

6 With these two points, I am highlighting the cultural assumption that mirrors produce images 'naturally' and 'immediately'. I am not suggesting that mirror images are not created through technological processes, that other imaging technologies do not

Notes 151

involve the production of the image through the body standing in front of it, nor that the images captured in photographs and films remain in 'the past': see Coleman 2009 and Coleman and Moreno Figueroa 2010 for more detailed discussions of the temporalities of images.

7 It is interesting to note that while theories of the politics of representation have been keen to critique the notion of reflection, in order to re-think the representational understanding of images it is helpful to consider the processes of 'reflection' in more detail. I return to this issue below.

8 Rozin has also made interactive mirrors from other opaque materials. See: www.smoothware.com/danny/.

9 The 'epicenter' stores were part of a strategy by Prada in the 1990s to reinvent some of their stores as distinctive design spaces: stores in New York, Los Angeles, San Francisco and Tokyo were selected: the US stores were designed by the OMA (although the San Francisco store was never built), and Herzog & de Meuron designed the Tokyo store. For more on the interactive features of the store, see: http://digital-wellbeinglabs.com/dwb/concepts/prada-flagship-store-ny-2001/, which includes a short film and the 'Critical Cities' blog by Daniel Huppatz (Lecturer in Design, Swinburne University of Technology): http://djhuppatz.blogspot.co.uk/2009/08/muiccia-pradaomarem-koolhaas-prada.html.

10 Unless otherwise indicated, all quotations on the interactive mirrors in the Prada store are taken from: www.oma.eu/projects/2001/prada-new-york. The OMA is an international architecture, urbanism and cultural analysis business, with Koolhaas as one of its partners.

11 See also the discussion of Keenan's questions about the window in Chapter 3.

12 Indeed, the word 'perspective' has its roots in '*perspecitiva*', a Latin word meaning 'seeing through' (see Friedberg 2006: 39).

13 See: http://trendwatching.com/trends/12trends2012/?screenculture, accessed 7 February 2012. Thanks to Carla Banks for this link.

14 See the trendwatching.com Retail Renaissance briefing (2011): http://trendwatching.com/trends/retailrenaissance/, accessed 7 February 2012.

15 Indeed, 'offline' experiences of shopping are moving online, as a recent initiative by the supermarket Tesco's clothing line, Fred and Florence demonstrates. In February 2012, Tesco launched a virtual fitting-room where customers can upload either, two photographs of themselves or their body measurements and a photograph of their face in order to 'try before you buy'. Customers enter the virtual fitting-room through 'liking' the application on Facebook and can see what a selected range of clothes would look like on their virtual body. Measurements and images remain confidential, unless customers decide to share images of themselves wearing Fred and Florence clothes with friends on Facebook; to coincide with the launch of the virtual fitting-room, in late February 2012, Tesco were running a competition to win a £50 voucher by sharing 'looks'. See: www.facebook.com/Clothingattesco?sk=app_261347243942251 for more details. Last accessed 29 February 2012.

16 As indicated, this is framed in terms of the 'convenience, the ability to hear other consumers' experiences, total price transparency, and virtually endless choice' for the customer. One example provided in the Retail Renaissance Briefing is 'a shopper in Sears, who when faced with an in-store price $3 higher than Sears' online store, simply pulled out his smartphone, bought online, selected in-store pickup and walked over to collect his purchase'.

17 See: www.fivefaces.com.au/files/FiveFacesSocialEyes.pdf. All information on this mirror is taken from this promotional literature. Thanks to Matt Moran for bringing this to my attention. Last accessed 31 January 2012.

18 See: www.nytimes.com/2007/03/18/fashion/18mirror.html. All quotations on the mirror are taken from this article. Last accessed 31 January 2012.

19 See: www.cisco.com/web/about/ac79/docs/retail/StyleMeEngagementOverview_120

152   Notes

611FINAL.pdf. All quotations on the mirror are taken from this promotional material. Last accessed 31 January 2012.

20 Cisco puts it as such:

> As online apparel sales continue to grow, retailers should take the opportunity to reinforce and integrate their store and web channels to avoid cannibalization. Forrester Research predicts online fashion retail will grow at a compound annual growth rate (CAGR) of 10 percent versus just 3 percent for in-store sales. In the United Kingdom, 35 percent of shoppers buy apparel online. By combining the virtual and physical worlds, Cisco StyleMe allows retailers to use their stores to capture and even enhance online sales. Cisco IBSG's initial work also shows that mashop concepts such as Cisco StyleMe can drive cross-channel sales, increase conversion rates, and grow wallet share.
>
> (2011: 1)

21 As I have discussed, while mirrors in general have been linked to transformation, my focus in the rest of this chapter on shop mirrors is intended to flesh out my interest in this book on the imperative of transformation.

22 Indeed, as Nava argues, department stores were not only a space for women to shop but were also a site of employment for women as shop assistants (1997: 67–68).

23 It is perhaps important to note that the interactive mirrors are being designed for high street rather than designer shops. In addition to the mirrors that I have discussed here, see for example the installation of SHOWstudio's interactive mirror, *Mirror Mirror* in Topshop's flagship Oxford Circus store for five days in May 2010 as part of the launch of the brand's new make-up line. The mirror 'dispensed sartorial advice that appeared written, as if by magic, across the mirror's surface' to customers from 'over thirty top fashion creatives'. See: http://showstudio.com/project/mirror_mirror, accessed 7 April 2012.

24 Blackman's discussion here is focused on explaining how Tarde's work was taken up by early twentieth-century psychologist, Edward Ross to explore the idea of social influence and transmission. See also Blackman (2011).

3 Becoming different: makeover television, proximity and immediacy

1 Both of these quotations were taken from the relevant television station websites. These, and the other websites referred to in this chapter were accessed on 8 June 2011. The first quotation is taken from a 2008 call for participants for the US version of *How To Look Good Naked*, Living TV (see: www.accesshollywood.com/_article_9295?&__source=rss%257Cah_Latest) and the second from an overview of the US version of *What Not to Wear*.

2 These terms – reality television and makeover programmes – are complex ones. While, on the one hand, they designate different genres (programmes such as *Big Brother* and *I'm a Celebrity, Get Me Out of Here* are reality programmes but not makeover programmes – although they do share some of the same features, including the participants going on a journey of self-transformation) on the other hand reality television is an umbrella term which includes makeover programmes (given their inclusion of 'real' people who are followed in 'real life' situations). Bev Skeggs and Helen Wood (2008), for example, who analysed makeover programme *What Not to Wear* as part of their research on reality television state, '[w]e used the generic term "reality TV" to explore the increased use of working-class women to display the performance of different aspects of self-work' (Skeggs and Wood 2008: 561, see also Skeggs and Wood 2011). In this chapter I am interested in makeover programmes as a form of reality television and I explore the relationship between them. I use the term 'makeover programme' to refer to programmes which are explicitly concerned with the transformation of (mainly) women's bodies (rather than on transformation through being placed in unfamiliar environments,

such as *Wife Swap* and *I'm a Celebrity*), and which draw on conventions associated with the makeover, including 'the reveal', and 'before' and 'after' scenes. I provide more information on the makeover genre below; for more on reality television see Murray and Ouellette (2004) and on reality television and class, Wood and Skeggs (2011).

3 Indeed, it is difficult to do justice to the vast field of work on makeover programmes, particularly if these programmes are placed in the context of reality television (see note above) and are seen as part of a wider shift in television to emphasize emotion (see Gorton 2009).
4 On reality television in Slovenia and Hungary, see Volcic and Erjavec (2011) and Imre and Tremlett (2011) respectively.
5 There are also video game versions of *The Biggest Loser* for the Nintendo Wii and DS, and for the Xbox 360.
6 Interestingly, then, it is not so much biological age that is at stake in this programme but the age at which 'the public' judges a particular participant to be.
7 Lewis also makes links between makeover programmes and 'early forms of modern advice culture, looking as far back as nineteenth-century Victorian England where the dramatic social upheavals that accompanied the industrial revolution saw the emergence of a plethora of taste, etiquette and domestic advice manuals (2008: 442).
8 For her analysis of cosmetic surgery more generally, see Jones (2008b).
9 Quotation taken from the following webpage, where the extract of April, Gok and the mirror is also available: www.channel4.com/programmes/how-to-look-good-naked/video/series-5/episode-14/meet-april, accessed 10 January 2012.
10 See: www.channel4.com/programmes/how-to-look-good-naked/video/series-5/episode-14/meet-april, accessed 10 January 2012.
11 See also Blackman (2011) and Walkerdine (2011) on affect, transmission and reality television.
12 Skeggs *et al.* are keen to point out that these middle-class responses, which 'were reproduced with surprising regularity' (2008: 10), should be understood in the context of the research interview, and that such distancing

> does not necessarily mean that the middle-class women are definitely not drawn into a relationship with those on television, but rather it shows that, [...] in the interview, they display their ability to be reflexive, often abstracting from the particular scenario on television to wider social debates.
>
> (2008: 15)

13 Saj was watching *Supernanny*, a British 'reality' programme which aims to transform children's bad behaviour through changing the parents' skills. The programme was shown on Channel 4 from 2004–2009, which has also had an American version. See here for more information: www.supernanny.co.uk/. Although Skeggs *et al.* discuss the programme in terms of 'reality' television, I would also argue that it is a makeover programme in that its primary concern is the improvement of parenting skills. See note above on the relationship between reality and makeover television. For a more detailed discussion of *Supernanny*, gender and class, see Jensen (2010).
14 For Helen Wood, such a method is necessary because technological developments in television, including an increased number of channels and increased interactivity with the screen and with the programmes (2007a: 486) demand new modes of empirical enquiry. In particular, Helen Wood explains that she developed the method of

> 'text-in-action' because it brought the 'nowness' of the television text alive in the time and place of consumption as a mediated communicative exchange, rather than relying entirely on the retrospective accounts of viewers that are the staple of the interview or focus group in traditional text-reader research.
>
> (2007a: 494)

15 Similarly, in a discussion on morality Tim Dant (2010) develops a phenomenology of television whereby 'the way in which the viewer relates to what is shown depends on making sense of it through a process that Husserl and Schutz call "appresentation"' (2010: 3). Dant argues that the viewer *experiences* television rather than 'seeing television as a medium carrying encoded messages' (2010: 3).

16 It may also be one of the reasons why makeover programmes are becoming less popular. While the imperative of transformation remains firmly embedded within social and cultural life, the 'things can only get better' ethos of progressive governments has been disrupted, at least in the UK, by the financial crisis. Polls conducted in late 2011 suggest that large sections of the British population no longer believe in a better future but rather envisage their children's future as worse than the present.

17 This is an interesting categorization of television because it is in contrast to classic audience studies of television viewing which suggests that television viewing is, for women in particular, a 'fundamentally social activity involving ongoing conversation, and usually the performance of at least one other domestic activity (ironing, etc.)' (Morley 1986: 150; see also Ellis 1992 on the difference between cinema and television viewing).

18 Indeed, in terms of Deleuze's work, it is generally the case that it has been taken up in relation to art which in some way critiques, explicitly or not, a capitalist system (see Coleman 2011 for a discussion of this).

19 Thanks to Maureen McNeil, whose questions on different versions of this chapter suggested that I should think more about criticism and critique.

20 In this sense, there are resonances here with Latour's (2004) argument that critique has 'run out of steam' because of its belief that there was no efficient way to criticize matters of fact except by 'moving *away* from them and directing one's attention *toward* the conditions that made them possible' (2004: 231). The implications of this distancing is twofold: first it involves an understanding of critique as deconstruction, which in Latour's terms is destructive. Second, it treats matters of fact as primary ('accepting much too uncritically what matters of fact were' (2004: 231)) and as all that there is. In contrast Latour argues, 'Reality is not defined by matters of fact. Matters of fact are not all that is given in experience' (2004: 232). While Latour shifts his attention from 'matters of fact' to 'matters of concern', in this book it might be argued that I am attempting to shift attention towards affect, potential and the virtual as a means to account for what else there might be of the actual. See in particular the Conclusion.

4 Immanent measure: interaction, attractors and the multiple temporalities of online dieting

1 For example, as I discuss in Chapter 5, the British government's 'Change4Life' programme, launched in 2009 through the NHS, is, according to its website, directed at changing families' eating and exercise habits based on the premise that '9 out of 10 kids today could grow up with dangerous amounts of fat in their bodies', and Reebok's 2001 'Belly's Gonna Get Ya' television advert targeted men through depicting exercise as the means to lose the 'beer belly'.

2 Culturally at least. That is, the examples of Change4Life and the Reebok advert seem to suggest that where men are involved in the concern with weight, this is focused around issues of health, rather than appearance.

3 These websites (www.weightwatchers.com/ and www.weightwatchers.co.uk/Index.aspx respectively) were accessed between July 2009 and January 2012. Where possible, I have indicated in the main body of the text the specific pages of the website where quotations are taken from.

4 Here, I use the terms 'user' and 'viewer', although I do not want to suggest that these terms are interchangeable or equivalent. Indeed, from the perspective of sociology and media and cultural studies, the term 'user' can be critiqued for being a term

devoid of social and cultural difference, including, but not restricted to gender, class, race, sexuality or disability. As the chapter develops, I prefer to use the term 'viewer' to indicate that I am drawing on Aylish Wood's argument (who uses 'viewer') and to refer to the tradition within sociology and media and cultural studies that deals with the viewer and involves debates concerning, for example, activity/passivity and rationality/emotionality. See for example Bolter and Gromala (2005) on the 'user' in the context of interaction design and from a science and technology studies perspective, see Wilkie and Michael (2009).

5 Given this history comes from the website, it is clearly partial and incomplete. It is not so much my intention here to provide a more objective account of Weight Watchers, but rather to explore the ways in which the site is involved in presenting the company and, as I will discuss, involved in producing particular dieting temporalities.

6 Which is not to say that those who lose weight maintain this weight loss. Indeed, Sue Thompson argues that there is a 98 per cent failure rate for the dieting industry in general (http://anybody.squarespace.com/anybody_vent/2007/1/13/exploiting-women-help-us-create-a-case-against-weight-watche.html, accessed 15 July 2009) and Susie Orbach suggests that Weight Watchers has a 97 per cent recidivism rate (www.marieclaire.com/health-fitness/news/articles/diet-fat, accessed 15 July 2009).

7 'Points' here refers to the Weight Watchers programme that designates a particular value, evidenced by 'points' for the calorific and fat content of each type of food. Thus, the main webpage for the Discover Plan™ indicates that '2 slices of toast' equals '3 points' and '1 large slice thin crust pizza topped with vegetables' equals '6 points' (www.weightwatchers.co.uk/plan/eat/plan.aspx). Weight Watchers food and cookbooks all include the points value as well as the nutritional values usually published.

8 In this chapter, 'technologies of the self' is focused on rather than 'technologies of power', as Heyes argues that it is through the latter concept that the concept of docile bodies is developed (Heyes 2006: 138).

9 As I will go on to discuss, Heyes is keen to point out that the enabling dimensions of dieting do not necessarily increase freedom – although they are 'often interpreted by a liberal political tradition simply as the increase of autonomy' (2006: 136) – but intensify power relations.

10 In making this move from Heyes' Foucauldian position to an exploration of agency, I am not suggesting that Heyes' emphasis on dieting as enabling and productive is equivalent to the agency that I examine as produced through interaction with the Weight Watchers website. That is, I am not suggesting that Foucault's work attends to agency and that Heyes' argument necessarily implies an account of dieting as generative of agency (Heyes' Foucauldian argument that dieting is productive of and for the subject is not the same as arguing that dieting involves agency).

11 And in this way, Weight Watchers' promotion of its online services is in-line with other companies, such as banks, supermarkets and home-energy companies, who advertise their internet services in terms of 'flexibility', 'convenience', 'speed', 'ease' and 'security'.

12 Accordingly it is clear to see the reasons that feminists have found it so helpful to approach dieting through a Foucauldian perspective.

13 It should be noted here that Nowotny's point concerning the extended present is developed through what she argues, again in ecological terms, is the collapse of a notion of progress. While I do not want to follow Nowotny's argument that progress is not important in the context of dieting – indeed I think it can be argued that progress, becoming a 'better' weight, is integral to the notion and process of dieting – I do think the notion of the extended present, and the linear temporality it suggests, is helpful here.

14 I place 'choice' within inverted commas here to indicate that I later discuss how choice is organized in terms of the concepts of attention and attractors; see below.

15 Wood discusses 'images' and 'viewers' as her analysis is concerned with moving images. While the Weight Watchers website primarily involves still, rather than moving, images

156 *Notes*

16 and written text, and it is debateable whether those who interact with the website are viewers in Wood's sense, I think that Wood's argument as I discuss it here is relevant and helpful to an understanding of the temporalities produced in the dieting website.
16 See also the discussion in Chapter 3 on the supposed distracted and passive television viewer.
17 Although I do not have space here to develop this further, it is worth noting that 'architecture' is a key term for Wood and is defined as the 'spatio-temporal organisation' of 'a viewer's embodied encounter with interfaces' (2007: 9). Wood suggests that the concept of architecture emphasizes the spatial dimension of this encounter and introduces another term, attractor, to emphasize the temporal dimension (2007: 9). I discuss the concept of the attractor in more detail below.
18 Wood also develops the notion of an agency which is inevitably constrained, rather than unbounded, through Bourdieu's work on habitus and dispositions. Thus, as indicated in a quotation above, Wood argues that 'viewers' dispositions bring their particular interests and histories into proximity with the structures of the text' (2007: 85).
19 This is not to suggest that Weight Watchers meetings are necessary linear – there may well be interruptions to the topic that is being dealt with, and questions and discussions may well move the topic in a different direction. Rather, it is to suggest that, in relation to the website, meetings can be understood as 'seamless' in their singular motive and the website can be understood as non-seamless and non-singular, at least in its design. It is this understanding of how dieting is generative, rather than only repressive, that I pull through from Heyes' argument.
20 And here, consider the discussion in Chapter 3 of television as 'alive' and 'happening'.
21 Adkins' argument is developed in relation to the productive activity of labour and, more specifically, to accounts which see women's socially reproductive labour as immeasurable by clock time in industrial capitalism as a basis for understanding contemporary capitalism's 'immaterial labour'. Despite the focus of Adkins' argument, I think it is a helpful way of exploring the kinds of 'measure' of ideal(ized) weight that are produced through interaction with the Weight Watchers website, not least because of debates surrounding the (im)materiality of the body in online space and time.

5 Pre-empting the future: obesity, prediction and Change4Life

1 All websites accessed 27 July 2011. The Change4Life campaign operates in England and Wales and it is this campaign that I focus on in this chapter; similar campaigns run in Scotland (Take Life On, One Step at a Time) and Northern Ireland (Get a Life, Get Active). See: www.nhs.uk/Change4Life/Pages/links-resources.aspx.
2 This and the previous quotation taken from: www.dh.gov.uk/en/Publichealth/Change4Life/index.htm.
3 As I noted in the Introduction, this is more complex than a repudiation of Foucault's argument about power, given that his concept of bio-power indicates how power becomes immanent to bodies and is concerned with making up bodies. I am focusing here, then, on the ways in which the imperative of transformation cuts across bodies and socio-cultural life more widely. See Chapter 4 for a discussion of how Foucault's work has most readily been taken up in relation to discipline and repression and the Introduction and Conclusion for more detailed discussions on power.
4 Thanks to Carolyn Pedwell for elucidating this point to me.
5 I signed up for such materials in 2010 and have received emails alerting me to offers in supermarkets and to new online tools on the Change4Life website and information packs detailing the 'Swap it, don't stop it' initiative, including a wipeable wall chart to monitor weekly food, drink and exercise swaps, an Owners Manual with tips on swaps, a Self-MOT test and a Self-MOT window sticker to set the date for my next self-MOT.

6 This specific part of the campaign involved Diversity, the dance troupe that won the ITV1 programme, *Britain's Got Talent* in 2009, and a YouTube competition.
7 www.nhs.uk/change4life/Pages/change-for-life.aspx.
8 The television adverts feature 'claymation' figures by Aardman Animations, who also made Wallace and Gromit. In still images, such as in paper promotional materials and online, the figures resemble these clay figures and are also similar to Keith Haring graffiti figures (see the Change4Life website which includes the television adverts discussed below).
9 It's worth noting here that the three adverts feature voiceovers from a man, a girl and a boy, all with Northern English accents, a likely response to the Foresight report which states that incidence of obesity is 'generally greater in Scotland and the north of England' (Foresight 2007a: 30). The depiction of video games as central to current weight problems was refuted by the video games industry. A 2009 print advert featuring a boy sitting on the floor in a poorly lit room playing a PlayStation 3 under the caption, 'Risk an early death, just do nothing', resulted in a complaint to the Advertising Standards Authority by the Market for Computer and Video Games (MCV) on the grounds that the advert was 'unrepresentative of the positive effect video games have on the UK's youth', and was dangerous to small businesses (www.mcvuk.com/news/read/mcv-complains-to-asa-over-anti-games-government-ad). The complaint was not upheld, but later television adverts featured children playing video games that involved activity, such as dance mats and those played on the Nintendo Wii.
10 See for example Piggin and Lee (2011).
11 See Cronin (2008b) for a discussion of how outdoor advertising brings the future into the present through modes of calculation and vitality.
12 An aim that, as Bethan Evans (2010) and Bethan Evans *et al.* (2011) expertly point out and as I discuss further below, is not successfully achieved.
13 The Health Survey of England

> records BMI [Body Mass Index] and other measurements such as waist and hip size, which makes possible the monitoring of the increasing prevalence of obesity in the population and its distribution across age groups, gender, socioeconomic status and region. Although BMI needs careful interpretation on an individual basis, it provides a meaningful picture at the population level.
>
> (Foresight 2007a: 25)

14 The Foresight *Modelling Future Trends in Obesity and Their Impact on Health* (2007b) report cites slightly different statistics:

> the proportion of those who are obese in the under-20 age group, will rise to approximately 10% by 2015. By 2025, around 14% of the under-20s (with a slightly higher percentage in females than males) will be obese, and by 2050 this will be around 25%.
>
> (2007b: 15)

15 The categories of obese and overweight are calculated according to the measurement of BMI. BMI is calculated by dividing an individual's weight in kilograms by their height in metres squared (weight kg/height m^2). The table below shows the BMI categories for the Caucasian population:

Underweight	<18.5
Normal weight	18.5–24.9
Overweight	≥25.0
Pre-obese	25.0–29.9
Obese Class I	30–34.9
Obese Class II	35–39.9
Obese Class III	≥40.0

16 This shift is, for Massumi, part of a wider shift from neo-liberal power to 'command power', which 'joins disciplinary and biopolitical modes of power in complex interaction in a shared environment characterized overall by no one of these modes' (2005: 7): See Introduction.
17 For example, in a discussion of climate change, John Urry (2010) describes present excessive consumption patterns as sending the earth 'catastrophically careering at full speed, it seems, to the edge of the abyss' (2010: 207). My comparison of the future of obesity levels with the future of climate change is not accidental. According to the Foresight report,

> [t]here are strong parallels between climate change and obesity. In both issues, failure to act early will lead to serious adverse consequences in just a few decades. Delay in agreeing remedies and acting on them raises the real possibility that reversal of the trends may cease to be an option for both. Similarly, disagreement about the causes of a complex issue will marginalize a multiple approach to remedial change.
>
> (2007a: 17)

18 In this sense, they are distinguished from images circulated in previous and current public health campaigns in the UK, for example on smoking (from 1998 onwards) and on HIV/AIDS (in the 1980s) which focus on fear; diseased lungs, childhood asthma, tombstones, etc.
19 These responses include families registering their details by telephone, post or on the website, posting in 'How are the kids?' questionnaires and interacting with the website (see Department of Health 2010: 21).
20 The theme of the child as a site or state of potential has been taken up recently in critical theory. For Lee Edelman (2004), this fantasy of the child, whose appeal seems impossible to refuse, should be resisted by queer theory, which should instead organize itself around a version of temporality that refuses the future and around the figure of the queer as negativity. See Muñoz (2009) for an alternative theorization of queer temporality, where queerness is argued to be a phenomenon of futurity. I will address this issue in forthcoming work. See also the recent special issue of *Feminist Theory*, edited by Erica Burman and Jackie Stacey (2010) on the child and childhood.
21 Quotations taken from www.thebestof.co.uk/local/luton/events/183169/family-fun-day, accessed 22 January 2012.
22 www.luton.gov.uk/internet/references/news/news%20digest/_id1138ac77_/july/26_07_11%20-%20record%20turn%20out%20for%20take%203%204%20life%20, accessed 22 January 2012.
23 www.phn-bradford.nhs.uk/NR/rdonlyres/A265A98B-A9A9-42F5-AFD9-95E243CF3B87/0/Event201109.pdf, accessed 22 January 2012.
24 The other aspects are social marketing campaigns – Smokefree programme, an integrated campaign targeted at older people and their carers on seeking medical diagnosis and advice quickly and a programme directed at younger people to 'influence behaviours such as smoking, binge drinking, experimenting with drugs and risky sexual behaviours, that form part of a pattern of risk-taking in the transition from the child to adult self' (Department of Health 2011b: 5).
25 Making a similar point, Evans *et al.* argue that 'as a form of public pedagogy [Change4Life] [...] seemingly respond[s] to criticisms of former health education campaigns which highlighted the problems of an individual, blame based approach, whilst this remains an implicit driver of the intervention' (2011: 331).
26 Social categories and differences are thus sustained through the power of the future as potential; the past is not erased but rather endures (see Coleman 2008). I am grateful to Carloyn Pedwell for a discussion on this point.

Conclusion: transforming images – sociology, the future and the virtual

1 Mary Portas: Secret Shopper, Channel 4, 19 January 2011. See: www.channel4.com/programmes/mary-portas-secret-shopper/episode-guide/series-1/episode-1.
2 Adams *et al.*'s argument is developed through an understanding of neo-liberalism and, I think, works through an understanding of power as repressive and regulative (rather than as inventive, as I have attempted to develop here). I do not want to focus on these different modes of power here, but rather highlight the idea that girlhood is involved in anticipatory affects.
3 And she goes on to note, that '[p]aradoxically, of course, at least during this phase of capital, there is less of a future when one eats without an orientation toward it (Berlant 2011: 117).
4 I say 'at least in part' as Berlant argues that there may well be conscious and/or deliberate choices in eating; 'eating involves many kinds of self-understanding, especially in a culture of shaming and self consciousness around the moral mirror choosing pleasures so often provides' (2011: 117).
5 Berlant's argument here is in a collection of essays on the work of Eve Sedgwick. It is Sedgwick who suggests that cultural theory has become sceptical and it is Berlant who argues for the need to take optimism seriously.
6 See also the special issue of *Critical Inquiry*, Winter 2004, on critique.
7 There is a wider discussion to be had here on the debate within queer theory on the future, optimism and hope, and in particular the work of Lee Edelman (2004) and José Esteban Muñoz (2009). I will explore this in a future article in relation to the child.
8 See note 7 above: again this distinction between hope and optimism is beyond the scope of the book, but is an issue I will explore further in a future article.
9 Whether this image of the future as better remains today in the West in the context of the financial crisis is an open question.

References

Adam, A. and Green, E. (2001) *Virtual Gender: Technology, Consumption and Identity Matters*, London: Routledge.
Adam, B. and Groves, C. (2007) *Future Matters*, Leiden and Boston: Brill.
Adams, V., Murphy, M. and Clarke, A. E. (2009) 'Anticipation: technoscience, life, affect, temporality', *Subjectivity*, 28(1): 246–265.
Adey, P. (2010) *Aerial Life: Spaces, Mobilities, Affects*, Chichester: Wiley-Blackwell.
Adkins, L. (2002) *Revisions: Gender and Sexuality in Late Modernity*, Buckingham, Philadelphia: Open University Press.
Adkins, L. (2008) 'From retroactivation to futurity: the end of the sexual contract?', *Nordic Journal of Feminist and Gender Research*, 16(3): 182–201.
Adkins, L. (2009) 'Feminism after measure', *Feminist Theory*, 10(3): 323–339.
Adkins, L. and Lury, C. (2009) 'What is the empirical?', *European Journal of Social Theory*, 12(1): 5–20.
Adorno, T. (1991) *The Culture Industry: Selected Essays on Mass Culture*, London: Routledge.
Agger, B. (2004) *The Virtual Self: A Contemporary Sociology*, Oxford: Blackwell.
Ahmed, Sara (2004) *The Cultural Politics of Emotion*, Edinburgh: Edinburgh University Press.
Ahmed, S. (2010) *The Promise of Happiness*, Durham, NC and London: Duke University Press.
Alaimo, S. and Hekman, S. (2008) 'Introduction: emerging models of materiality in feminist theory', in Alaimo, S. and Hekman, S. (eds) *Material Feminisms*, Bloomington, IN: Indiana University Press, pp. 1–22.
Anderson, B. (2009) 'Security and the future: anticipating the event of terror', *Geoforum*, 41: 227–235.
Anderson, B. (2010) 'Preemption, precaution, preparedness: anticipatory action and future geographies', *Progress in Human Geography*, 34(6): 777–798.
Banet-Weiser, S. and Portwood-Stacer, L. (2006) '"I just want to be me again!" Beauty pageants, reality television and post-feminism', *Feminist Theory*, 7(2): 255–272.
Barad, K. (2007) *Meeting the Universe Halfway: Quantum Physics and the Entanglement of Matter and Meaning*, Durham, NC and London: Duke University Press.
Beck, U. (1992) *Risk Society: Toward a New Modernity*, London: Sage.
Beck, U. and Beck-Gernsheim, E. (2002) *Individualization*, London, Thousand Oaks, New Delhi: Sage.
Beck, U., Giddens, A. and Lash, S. (1994) *Reflexive Modernization: Politics, Tradition and Aesthetics in the Modern Social Order*, Cambridge: Polity.
Benjamin, W. (1992) *Illuminations*, London: Fontana Press.

Berlant, L. (2002) 'Two girls, fat and thin', in Barber, S. and Clark, D. (eds) *Regarding Sedgwick*, New York: Routledge, pp. 71–116.
Berlant, L. (2006) 'Cruel optimism', *Differences: A Journal of Feminist Cultural Studies*, 17(3): 20–36.
Berlant, L. (2007) 'Nearly utopian, nearly normal: post-Fordist affect in La Promesse and Rosetta', *Public Culture*, 19(2): 273–301.
Berlant, L. (2008) *The Female Complaint: The Unfinished Business of Sentimentality in American Culture*, Durham and London: Duke University Press.
Berlant, L. (2011) *Cruel Optimism*, Durham, NC and London: Duke University Press.
Blackman, L. (2007) 'Reinventing psychological matters: the suggestive realm of Tarde's ontology', *Economy and Society*, 36(4): 574–596.
Blackman, L. (2011) ' "This is a matter of pride": *the choir* – unsung town and community transformation', in Wood, H. and Skeggs, B. (eds) *Reality Television and Class*, Basingstoke and New York: BFI/Palgrave, pp. 237–249.
Blackman, L. and Venn, C. (2010) 'Affect', *Body and Society*, 16(1): 7–28.
Blackman, L. and Walkerdine, V. (2001) *Mass Hysteria, Critical Psychology and Media Studies*, Basingstoke: Palgrave Press.
Bolter, J. D. and Gromala, D. (2005) *Windows and Mirrors: Interaction Design, Digital Art and the Myth of Transparency*, Cambridge, Massachusetts and London: The Massachusetts Institute of Technology Press.
Bordo, S. (1993/2003) *Unbearable Weight: Feminism, Western Culture and the Body*, Berkley and Los Angeles: University of California Press.
Borup, M., Brown, N., Konrad, K. and Van Lente, H. (2006) 'The sociology of expectations in science and technology', *Technology Analysis and Strategic Management*, 18(3): 285–298.
Bowlby, R. (2000) *Carried Away: The Invention of Modern Shopping*, London: Faber and Faber.
Brown, N. and Michael, M. (2003) 'A sociology of expectations: *retrospective prospects* and *prospecting retrospectives*', *Technology Analysis and Strategic Management*, 15(1): 3–18.
Bryant, A. and Pollock, G. (2010) (eds) *Digital and Other Virtualities: Renegotiating the Image*, London and New York: I. B. Tauris.
Burman, Erica and Stacey, Jackie (eds) (2010) 'The child and childhood', *Feminist Theory*, 12(1).
Burns, P. and Novelli, Marina (eds) (2008) *Tourism and Mobilities: Local-Global Connections*, Wallingford: CABI.
Buscher, M., Urry, J. and Witchger, K. (eds) (2010) *Mobile Methods*, London: Routledge.
Butler, Judith (1993) *Bodies That Matter: On the Discursive Limits of Sex*, London: Routledge.
Carrier, J. and Miller, D. (1998) (eds) *Virtualism: A New Political Economy*, Oxford and New York: Berg.
Clough, P. T. (2007) 'Introduction', in Clough, P. T. with Halley, J. (eds) *The Affective Turn: Theorising the Social*, Durham and London: Duke University Press, pp. 1–33.
Clough, P. T. (2000) *Autoaffection: Unconscious Thought in the Age of Teletechnology*, Minneapolis, MN: University of Minnesota Press.
Clough, P. T. with Halley, J. (2007) (eds) *The Affective Turn: Theorizing the Social*, Durham and London: Duke University Press.
Cisco (2011) 'Cisco StyleMe™ virtual fashion mirror: how new consumer behaviors are enabling retailers to revitalize their stores by combining the virtual and physical

References

worlds', available at: www.cisco.com/web/about/ac79/docs/retail/StyleMeEngagement Overview_120611FINAL.pdf, last accessed 8 February 2012.

Colebrook, C. (2002) *Gilles Deleuze*, London and New York: Routledge.

Colebrook, C. (2008) 'On not becoming man: the materialist politics of unactualized potential', in Alaimo, S. and Hekman, S. (eds) *Material Feminisms*, Bloomington, IN: Indiana University Press, pp. 52–84.

Coleman, R. (2008) 'A method of intuition: becoming, relationality, ethics', *History of the Human Sciences*, 21(4): 102–121.

Coleman, R. (2009) *The Becoming of Bodies: Girls, Images, Experience*, Manchester: Manchester University Press.

Coleman, R. (2011) ' "Be(come) yourself only better" self-transformation and the materialization of images', in Guillaume, L. and Hughes, J. (eds) *Deleuze and the Body*, Edinburgh: Edinburgh University Press, pp. 144–164.

Coleman, R. and Ferreday, D. (2011) (eds) *Hope and Feminist Theory*, London and New York: Routledge.

Coleman, R. and Moreno Figueroa, M. (2010) 'Past and future perfect? Beauty, hope and affect', *Journal for Cultural Research*, 14(4): 357–373.

Colls, R. and Evans, B. (2009) 'Questioning obesity politics: introduction to a special issue on critical geographies of fat/bigness/corpulence', *Antipode*, 41(5): 1011–1020.

Coole, D. H. and Frost, S. (eds) (2010) *New Materialisms: Ontology, Agency, and Politics*, Durham, NC and London: Duke University Press.

Cooper, M. (2006) 'Pre-empting emergence: the biological turn in the war on terror', *Theory Culture Society*, 23(4): 113–135.

Cresswell, T. and Merriman, P. (eds) (2011) *Geographies of Mobilities: Practices, Spaces, Subjects*, Burlington, VT: Ashgate.

Critical Inquiry, 30(2), Winter 2004.

Cronin, A. (2008a) 'Mobility and market research: outdoor advertising and the commercial ontology of the city', *Mobilities*, 3(1): 95–115.

Cronin, A. (2008b) 'Calculative spaces: cities, market relations, and the commercial vitalism of the outdoor advertising agency', *Environment and Planning A*, 40: 2734–2750.

Cronin, A. (2010) *Advertising, Commercial Spaces and the Urban*, Basingstoke: Palgrave Macmillan.

Dant, T. (2010) 'Morality and the phenomenology of television', Unpublished paper.

Davies, K. (1995) *Reshaping the Female Body: The Dilemma of Cosmetic Surgery*, London: Routledge.

De Beauvoir, S. (1949/1997) *The Second Sex*, London: Vintage.

De Landa, M. (2002) *Intensive Science and Virtual Philosophy*, London and New York: Continuum.

Deery, J. (2004) 'Trading faces: the makeover show as prime-time "infomercial" ', *Feminist Media Studies*, 4(2): 211–214.

Deleuze, G. (1992) 'Ethology: Spinoza and us', in Crary, Jonathon and Kwinter, Sanford (eds) *Incorporations*, New York: Zone, pp. 625–633.

Deleuze, G. (1993/2003) *The Fold: Leibniz and the Baroque*, London and New York: Continuum.

Deleuze, G. (2005) *Cinema 1: The Movement Image*, London: Continuum.

Department of Health (2010) *Change4Life: One Year On*, London: Central Office of Information, 2nd edition, available at: www.dh.gov.uk/en/Publicationsandstatistics/Publications/PublicationsPolicyAndGuidance/DH_112529.

Department of Health (2011a) *Changing Behaviour, Improving Outcomes: A New Social*

Marketing Strategy for Public Health, London: Central Office of Information, available at: www.dh.gov.uk/en/Publicationsandstatistics/Publications/PublicationsPolicyAnd-Guidance/DH_126409.

Department of Health (2011b) *Equality Analysis: Social Marketing Strategy for Public Health in England*, London: Central Office of Information, available at: www.dh.gov.uk/en/Publicationsandstatistics/Publications/PublicationsPolicyAndGuidance/DH_126409.

Diken, B. and Laustsen, C. B. (2008) *Sociology through the Projector*, London and New York: Routledge.

Doane, M. A. (1992) 'Film and the masquerade: theorising the female spectator', *The Sexual Subject: A Screen Reader in Sexuality*, London: Routledge, pp. 227–243.

Donaldson, L. and Beasley, C. (2008) 'Launch of Change4Life, a national movement to tackle childhood obesity', available at: www.dh.gov.uk/en/Publicationsandstatistics/Lettersandcirculars/Dearcolleagueletters/DH_089671.

Edelman, L. (2004) *No Future: Queer Theory and the Death Drive*, Durham, NC and London: Duke University Press.

Elliott, A. and Urry, J. (2010) *Mobile Lives*, London and New York: Routledge.

Ellis, J. (1992) *Visible Fictions: Cinema, Television, Video*, London: Routledge and Kegan Paul.

Evans, Bethan (2010) 'Anticipating fatness: childhood, affect and the pre-emptive "war on obesity"', *Transactions of the Institute of British Geographers*, 35: 21–38.

Evans, Bethan, Colls, Rachel and Hörschelmann, Kathrin (2011) '"Change4Life for your kids": embodied collectives and public health pedagogy', *Sport, Education and Society*, 16(3): 323–341.

Featherstone, M. (1991) 'The body in consumer culture', in Featherstone, M., Hepworth, M. and Turner, B. (eds) *The Body: Social Process and Cultural Theory*, London: Sage, pp. 170–196.

Featherstone, Mike (2010) 'Body, image and affect in consumer culture', *Body and Society*, 16(1): 193–221.

Featherstone, M., Thrift, N. and Urry, J. (eds) (2005) *Automobilities*, London: Sage.

Foresight (2007a) *Tackling Obesities: Future Choices – Project Report*, Department of Innovation, Universities and Skills, 2nd edition, available at: www.bis.gov.uk/foresight/our-work/projects/published-projects/tackling-obesities.

Foresight (2007b) *Tackling Obesities: Future Choices – Modelling Future Trends in Obesity and Their Impact on Health*, Department of Innovation, Universities and Skills, 2nd edition, available at: www.bis.gov.uk/foresight/our-work/projects/published-projects/tackling-obesities.

Foucault, M. (1977/1991) *Discipline and Punish: The Birth of the Prison*, London: Penguin.

Fraser, M. (2006) 'The ethics of reality and virtual reality: latour, facts and values', *History of the Human Sciences*, 19(2): 45–72.

Fraser, M. (2009) 'Experiencing sociology', *European Journal of Social Theory*, 12(1): 63–81.

Fraser, M., Kember, S. and Lury, C. (eds) (2005) 'Inventive life: approaches towards a new vitalism', *Theory Culture and Society* 22(1). Re-printed as Fraser, M., Kember, S. and Lury, C. (eds) (2006) *Inventive Life: Approaches Towards a New Vitalism*, London: Sage.

Fredriksson, C. (1997) 'The making of a Swedish department store culture', in Falk, P. and Campbell, C. B. (eds) *The Shopping Experience*, London: Sage, pp. 111–135.

Friedberg, A. (1994) *Window Shopping: Cinema and the Postmodern*, Berkeley, Los Angeles and London: University of California Press.

References

Friedberg, A. (2006) *The Virtual Window: From Alberti to Microsoft*, Cambridge, MA and London: The Massachusetts Institute of Technology Press.

Gibbs, A. (2010) 'After affect: sympathy, synchrony, and mimetic communication', in Gregg, M. and Seigworth, G. J. (eds) *The Affect Theory Reader*, Durham, NC and London: Duke University Press, pp. 186–205.

Giddens, A. (1991) *Modernity and Self-Identity: Self and Society in the Late Modern Age*, Cambridge: Polity.

Giddens, A. (1992) *The Transformation of Intimacy: Sexuality, Love and Eroticism in Modern Societies*, Cambridge: Polity.

Gill, Rosalyn (2007) 'Postfeminist media culture: elements of a sensibility', *European Journal of Cultural Studies*, 10(2): 147–166.

Gorton, K. (2009) *Media Audiences: Television, Meaning and Emotion*, Edinburgh: Edinburgh University Press.

Graham, S. (2001) *Splintering Urbanism: Network Infrastructures, Technological Mobilities and the Urban Condition*, London and New York: Routledge.

Gregg, M. and Seigworth, G. J. (eds) (2010) *The Affect Theory Reader*, Durham, NC and London: Duke University Press.

Grosz, E. (1994) *Volatile Bodies: Toward a Corporeal Feminism*, Bloomington, IN: Indiana University Press.

Hall, S. (2003) *Representation: Cultural Representations and Signifying Practices*, London, California and New Delhi: Open University Press.

Hannam, K., Sheller, M. and Urry, J. (2006) 'Editorial: mobilities, immobilities and moorings', *Mobilities*, 1(1): 1–22.

Haraway, D. (1991) *Simians, Cyborgs and Women: The Reinvention of Nature*, London: Free Association Books.

Harvey, D. (2007) *A Brief History of Neoliberalism*, Oxford: Oxford University Press.

Heyes, C. J. (2006) 'Foucault goes to Weight Watchers', *Hypatia*, 21(1): 126–149.

Heyes, C. J. (2007) *Self-Transformations: Foucault, Ethics and Normalized Bodies*, Oxford: Oxford University Press.

Huppatz, D. (2009) 'Miuccia Prada/OMA/Rem Koolhaas: Prada Store', *Critical Cities: Reflections on 21st Century Culture*, blog, 6 August 2009, available at: http://djhuppatz.blogspot.co.uk/2009/08/muiccia-pradaomarem-koolhaas-prada.html.

Illouz, E. (2009) 'Emotions, imagination and consumption: a new research agenda', *Journal of Consumer Culture*, 9(3): 377–413.

Imre, A. and Tremlett, K. (2011) 'Reality TV without class: the post-socialist anti-celebrity docusoap', in Wood, H. and Skeggs, B. (eds) *Reality Television and Class*, Basingstoke and New York: BFI/Palgrave, pp. 88–103.

Jameson, F. (1984) 'Postmodernism, or the cultural logic of late capitalism', *New Left Review*, 146 (July–August): 59–92.

Jenkins, H. (1992) *Textual Poachers: Television Fans and Participatory Culture*, London and New York: Routledge.

Jenkins, H. (2007) *The Wow Climax: Tracing the Emotional Impact of Popular Culture*, New York: New York University Press.

Jensen, T. (2010) 'What kind of mum are you at the moment? Supernanny and the psychologising of classed embodiment', *Subjectivity*, 3(2): 170–192.

Jones, M. (2008a) 'Media-bodies and screen-births: cosmetic surgery reality television', *Continuum: Journal of Media & Cultural Studies*, 22(4): 515–524.

Jones, M. (2008b) *Skintight: An Anatomy of Cosmetic Surgery*, Oxford and New York: Berg.

Kavka, M. (2008) *Reality Television, Affect and Intimacy: Reality Matters*, Basingstoke and New York: Palgrave Macmillan.

Keenan, T. (1993) 'Windows: of vulnerability' in Robins, B. (ed.) *The Phantom Public Sphere*, London, Minneapolis: University of Minnesota Press, pp. 121–141.

Knowles, R. D., Shaw, J. and Docherty, I. (eds) (2008) *Transport Geographies: Mobilities, Flows and Spaces*, Malden, MA and Oxford: Blackwell.

Kuhn. A. (2009) '*Screen* and screen theorizing today', *Screen*, 50(1): 1–12.

Lacan, J. (1977) *Écrits: A Selection*, London: Tavistock.

Lash. S. (2010) *Intensive Culture: Social Theory, Religion and Contemporary Capitalism*, London: Sage.

Lash, S. and Lury, C. (2007) *Global Culture Industry: The Mediation of Things*, Cambridge: Polity.

Latham, Alan and McCormack, Derek (2009) 'Thinking with images in non-representational cities: Vignettes from Berlin', *Area*, 41(3): 252–262.

Latimer, J. and Skeggs, B. (2011) 'The politics of imagination: keeping open *and* critical', *The Sociological Review*, 59(3): 393–410.

Latour, B. (2004) 'Why has critique run out of steam? From matters of fact to matters of concern', *Critical Inquiry*, 30(2): 225–248.

Law, J. and Hetherington, K. (1998) 'Allegory and interference: representation in sociology', Lancaster: Department of Sociology, Lancaster University, available at: www.lancs.ac.uk/fass/sociology/research/publications/papers/law-hetherington-allegory-interference.pdf, last accessed 24 February 2012.

Lewis, T. (2008) 'Introduction: revealing the makeover show', *Continuum*, 22(4): 441–446.

Lindsay, G. (2004) 'Prada's high-tech misstep', *Business 2.0*, March, available at: http://money.cnn.com/magazines/business2/business2_archive/2004/03/01/363574/index.htm, last accessed 24th February 2012.

Lorimer, H. (2005) 'Cultural geography: the busyness of being "more-than-representational"', *Progress in Human Geography*, 21(1): 83–94.

Lorimer, H. (2007) 'Cultural geography: worldly shapes, differently arranged', *Progress in Human Geography*, 31(1): 89–100.

Lorimer, H. (2008) 'Cultural geography: non-representational conditions and concerns', *Progress in Human Geography*, 32(4): 551–559.

Lorimer, J. (2008) 'Counting corncrakes: the affective science of the UK corncrake census', *Social Studies of Science*, 38(3): 377–405.

Lorimer, J. (forthcoming) 'Witnessing and evoking moving animals: a Deleuzian methodology for more-than-human visual analysis', in Coleman, R. and Ringrose, J. (eds) *Deleuze and Research Methodologies*, Edinburgh: Edinburgh University Press.

Lupton, D. (1995) *The Imperative of Health: Public Health and the Regulated Body*, London: Sage.

Lury, C. (1997) 'The objects of travel', in Rojek, C. and Urry, J. (eds) *Touring Cultures: Transformations of Travel and Theory*, London and New York: Routledge, pp. 75–95.

Lury, C. (1998) *Prosthetic Culture: Photography, Memory and Identity*, London: Routledge.

Lury, C. (2011) *Consumer Culture*, 2nd edition, Cambridge: Polity.

Mackenzie, A. (2005) 'Is the actual world all that must be explained? The sciences and cultural theory: review essay of Manuel Delanda, intensive science, virtual philosophy (2002) and Isabelle Stengers, the invention of modern science (2000)', *Journal for Cultural Research*, 9(1): 101–116.

McNay, L. (2000) *Gender and Agency: Reconfiguring the Subject in Feminist and Social Theory*, Cambridge: Polity.

McRobbie, Angela (2005) 'Notes on *what not to wear* and post-feminist symbolic violence', in Adkins, L. and Skeggs, B. (eds) *Feminism After Bourdieu*, Oxford and Malden, MA: Blackwell, pp. 99–109.
McRobbie, Angela (2008) *The Aftermath of Feminism: Gender, Culture and Social Change*, London: Sage.
Manovich, L. (2002) *The Language of New Media*, Cambridge, Massachusetts and London: The Massachusetts Institute of Technology Press.
Marks, L. (2000) *The Skin of the Film: Intercultural Cinema, Embodiment, and the Senses*, Durham, NC and London: Duke University Press.
Massumi, Brian (2002) *Parables for the Virtual: Movement, Affect, Sensation*, Durham, NC and London: Duke University Press.
Massumi, Brian (2005) 'The future birth of the affective fact', *Conference Proceedings: Genealogies of Biopolitics*, available at: http://browse.reticular.info/text/collected/massumi.pdf, last accessed 14 July 2011.
Melchoir-Bonnet, S. (2001) *The Mirror: A History*, London: Routledge.
Mills, C. Wright (1958/2000) *The Sociological Imagination*, Oxford: Oxford University Press.
Moor, L. (2003) 'Branded spaces: the scope of "new marketing"', *Journal of Consumer Culture*, 3(1): 39–60.
Morley, D. (1986) *Family Television: Cultural Power and Domestic Leisure*, London: Routledge.
Morley, D. (1992) *Television, Audiences and Cultural Studies*, London: Routledge.
Moseley, R. (2000) 'Makeover takeover on British television', *Screen*, 41(3): 299–314.
Muñoz, J. E. (2009) *Cruising Utopia: The Then and There of Queer Futurity*, New York and London: New York University Press.
Murray, S. and Ouellette, L. (eds) (2004) *Reality TV: Remaking Television Culture*, New York and London: New York University Press.
Nava, M. (1997) 'Women, the city and the department store', in Falk, P. and Campbell, C. B. (eds) *The Shopping Experience*, London: Sage, pp. 56–91.
Nowotny, H. (1994) *Time: The Modern and Postmodern Experience*, Cambridge: Polity.
Orbach, S. (1985/2003) *Hunger Strike: Starving Amidst Plenty*, London: Karnac Books.
Orr, J. (2006) *Panic Diaries: A Genealogy of Panic Disorder*, Durham, NC and London: Duke University Press.
Ouellette, L. and Hay, J. (2008) 'Makeover television, governmentality and the good citizen', *Continuum*, 22(4): 471–484.
Piggin, J. and Lee, J. (2011) '"Don't mention obesity": contradictions and tensions in the UK Change4Life health promotion campaign', *Journal of Health Psychology*, online publication, 1 April 2011.
Probyn, E. (2005) *Blush: Faces of Shame*, Minneapolis, MN: University of Minnesota Press.
Renold, E. and Mellor, D. (forthcoming) 'Deleuze and Guatarri in the nursery: towards an ethnographic multi-sensory mapping of young gendered becomings', in Coleman, R. and Ringrose, J. (eds) *Deleuze and Research Methodologies*, Edinburgh: Edinburgh University Press.
Ringrose, J. and Walkerdine, V. (2008) 'Regulating the abject: the TV make-over as site of neo-liberal reinvention toward bourgeois femininity', *Feminist Media Studies*, 8(3): 227–246.
Rose, N. (1989) *Governing the Soul: The Shaping of the Private Self*, London and New York: Routledge.
Rose, N. (1996) *Inventing Our Selves: Psychology, Power and Personhood*, Cambridge: Cambridge University Press.
Rose, N. (2001) 'The politics of life itself', *Theory, Culture and Society*, 18(6): 1–30.

Rose, N. and Miller, P. (1991/2010) 'Political power beyond the state: problematics of government', *The British Journal of Sociology*, 61(60th Anniversary Issue): 271–303.
Rozin, D. (2001) 'Wooden mirror', *IEEE Spectrum*, available at: http://labspace.open.ac.uk/file.php/4287/Wooden.pdf, last accessed 23 August 2011.
Rozin, D. (no date) 'Wooden mirror', available at: www.siggraph.org/artdesign/gallery/S00/interactive/thumbnail16.html, last accessed 8 February 2012.
Savage, M. (2000) *Social Class and Social Transformation*, Milton Keynes: Open University Press.
Schmitt, B. (1999) *Experiential Marketing: How to Get Customers to Sense, Feel, Think, Act, Relate to your Company and Brand*, New York: The Free Press.
Sedgwick, E. K. (1994) *Tendencies*, London and New York: Routledge.
Sedgwick, E. K. (2003) *Touching Feeling: Affect, Pedagogy, Performativity*, Durham and London: Duke University Press.
Sedgwick, E. K. and Frank, A. (1995) 'Shame in the cybernetic fold: reading Silvan Tomkins', in Sedgwick, E. K. and Frank, A. (eds) *Shame and Its Sisters: A Silvan Tomkins Reader*, Durham and London: Duke University Press.
Seigworth, G. J. and Gregg, M. (2010) 'An inventory of shimmers', in Gregg, M. and Seigworth, G. J. (eds) *The Affect Theory Reader*, Durham and London: Duke University Press.
Sheller, M. and Urry, J. (eds) (2004) *Tourism Mobilities: Places to Play, Places in Play*, London and New York: Routledge.
Shields, R. (1996) *Cultures of the Internet: Virtual Spaces, Real Histories, Living Bodies*, London: Sage.
Shields, R. (2002) *The Virtual*, London and New York: Routledge.
Skeggs, B. (1997) *Formations of Class and Gender: Becoming Respectable*, London: Sage.
Skeggs, B. (2004) *Class, Self, Culture*, London and New York: Routledge.
Skeggs, B. (2009) 'The moral economy of person production: the class relations of self-performance on "reality" television', *The Sociological Review*, 57(4): 626–644.
Skeggs, B. (2010) 'The value of relationships: affective scenes and emotional performances', *Feminist Legal Studies*, 18(1): 29–51.
Skeggs, B. and Wood, H. (2008) 'The labour of transformation and circuits of value "around" reality television', *Continuum*, 22(4): 559–572.
Skeggs, B. and Wood, H. (2011) 'Introduction: real class', in Wood, H. and Skeggs, B. (eds) *Reality Television and Class*, Basingstoke and New York: BFI/Palgrave, pp. 1–32.
Skeggs, B., Thumin, N. and Wood, H. (2008) ' "Oh goodness, I *am* watching reality TV": how methods make class in audience research', *European Journal of Cultural Studies*, 11(1): 5–24.
Snediker, M. D. (2009) *Queer Optimism: Lyric Personhood and Other Felicitous Persuasions*, Minneapolis, MN: University of Minnesota Press.
Sobchack, V. (1991) *The Address of the Eye: A Phenomenology of Film Experience*, Princeton, NJ: Princeton University Press.
Sobchack, V. (2004) *Carnal Thoughts: Embodiment and Moving Image Culture*, Berkeley, Los Angeles and London: University of California Press.
Suchman, L. (2011) 'Subject objects', *Feminist Theory*, 12(2): 119–145.
Swan, E. (2008) ' "You make me feel like a woman": therapeutic cultures and the contagion of femininity', *Gender, Work and Organization*, 15(1): 88–107.
Swan, E. (2010) *Worked Up Selves: Personal Development Workers, Self-Work and Therapeutic Cultures*, Basingstoke: Palgrave Macmillan.
Swan, E. and Fox, S. (2009) 'Becoming flexible: self-flexibility and its pedagogies', *British Journal of Management*, 10(S1): S149–159.

Thrift, N. (2005) *Knowing Capitalism*, London: Sage.
Thrift, N. (2007) *Non-Representational Theory: Space, Politics, Life*, London: Routledge.
Throsby, K. (2007) '"How could you let yourself get like that?" Stories of the origins of obesity in accounts of obesity surgery', *Social Science and Medicine*, 65: 1561–1571.
Throsby, K. (2008) 'Happy re-birthday: weight loss surgery and the "new me"', *Body and Society*, 14(1): 117–133.
Throsby, K. (2009) 'The war on obesity as a moral project: weight loss drugs, obesity surgery and negotiating failure', *Science as Culture*, 18(2): 201–216.
Ticknell, E. (2010) 'Tears at bedtime: the television make-over show and the reconstruction of femininity under neoliberalism', in Gill, R. and Scharf, C. (eds) *New Femininities: Postfeminism, Neoliberalism and Subjectivity*, Basingstoke and New York: Palgrave Macmillan, pp. 83–98.
Tolia-Kelly, D. (2006) 'Affect: an ethnocentric encounter? Exploring the "universalist" imperative of emotional/affectual geographies', *Area*, 38(2): 213–217.
Turkle, S. (1995) *Life on the Screen: Identity in the Age of the Internet*, New York: Simon & Schuster.
Tutton, R. (in press, 2011) 'Promising pessimism: reading the futures to be avoided in biotech', *Social Studies of Science*, 41(3): 411–429.
Urry, J. (1995) *Consuming Places*, London and New York: Routledge.
Urry, J. (2007) *Mobilities*, Cambridge: Polity.
Urry, J. (2010) 'Consuming the plant to excess', *Theory, Culture and Society*, 27(2–3): 1–22.
Van Lente, H. (2000) 'Forceful futures: from promise to requirement', in Brown, N., Rappert, B. and Webster, A. (eds) *Contested Futures: A Sociology of Prospective Techno-Science*, Aldershot: Ashgate, pp. 43–64.
Volcic, Z. and Erjavec, K. (2011) 'Fame on the farm: class and celebrity on Slovene reality TV', in Wood, H. and Skeggs, B. (eds) *Reality TV and Class*, Basingstoke: Palgrave Macmillan, pp. 73–87.
Walkerdine, V. (2003) 'Reclassifying upward mobility: femininity and the neo-liberal subject', *Gender and Education*, 15(3): 237–248.
Walkerdine, V. (2011) 'Shame on you! Intergeneral trauma and working-class femininity on reality television', in Wood, H. and Skeggs, B. (eds) *Reality Television and Class*, Basingstoke and New York: BFI/Palgrave, pp. 225–236.
Weber, B. (2009) *Makeover TV: Selfhood, Citizenship, and Celebrity*, Durham, NC and London: Duke University Press.
Wilkie, A. and Michael, M. (2009) 'Expectation and mobilization: enacting future users', *Science, Technology & Human Values*, 34(4): 502–522.
Wood, A. (2007) *Digital Encounters*, London and New York: Routledge.
Wood, H. (2007) 'Television is happening: methodological considerations for capturing digital television reception', *European Journal of Cultural Studies*, 10(4): 485–506.
Wood, H. (2009) *Talking with Television: Women, Talk Shows and Modern Self-Reflexivity*, Urbana, IL and London: University of Illinois Press.
Wood, H. and Skeggs, B. (eds) (2011) *Reality Television and Class*, Basingstoke and New York: BFI/Palgrave.
Woodward, K. (1997) 'Concepts of identity and difference', in Woodward, K. (ed.) *Identity and Difference*, London: Sage.

Index

actual, the; and virtual, the 17–18, 22–6, 41, 45–6, 49, 50, 59–60, 62, 64, 67, 69–70, 78–9, 87, 89, 125, 131, 133, 137, 140–6; and television 73, 83–5, 91
actualization *see* actual, the
Adam, A. and Green, E. 17
Adam, B. and Groves, C. 19, 134
Adams, V. *et al* 2, 23, 45, 109, 112, 116, 124–5, 132, 135, 137
Adey, P. 12
Adkins, L. 2, 10, 23, 24, 94, 110–12, 125, 134, 144–5; *see also* Adkins, L. and Lury. C
Adkins, L. and Lury, C. 39–40, 88, 144, 145; *see also* Adkins, L.; Lury, C
Adorno. T. and Horkheimer, M. 14, 16
affect 39
affective turn, the 29–30, 30–9
affect and theories of the body 31, 33
affect and biology 31–2
affect and relationality 32–3, 87
affect and process 32, 45, 87; *see also* materialization; materialization of images
affect and technology 33–6, 88
affect and television 33–6
affect and representational thinking 36–9, 87–8
affect and intensity 38
affect and sensation 38
affect and methodologies 39
affect and the virtual 39
affect – theories of 30
agency 94–9, 101–2, 103, 104–9
Agger, B. 17
Ahmed, S. 10, 22, 90
Alaimo and Hekman 45
Alberti, L.B. 55–6
alertness 135, 136

Anderson, B. 135
anticipation 23, 116, 135
attractors 106–8

Banet-Weiser, S. and Portwood-Stacer, L. 4, 33, 75
Barad, K. 45, 106
Bartky, S. 97
Beck, U. 6, 9, 10; *see also* Beck, U. and Beck-Gernsheim, E
Beck, U. and Beck-Gernsheim, E. 6–7, 9, 10
Berlant, L 1–2, 25, 86, 132, 133, 134, 138–44
Blackman, L. 48, 70, 89–90, 136; *see also* Blackman, L. and Venn, C
Blackman, L. and Venn, C. 26, 31, 33, 36, 37, 39; *see also* Blackman, L
Bloomingdales 62
Bolter, D.J. and Gromala, D. 27, 52–3, 55–7, 59, 95; *see also* interaction; mirrors; screens
Bordo, S. 4, 93, 96, 97
Borup, M. *et al* 20–1, 134, 135
Bourdieu, P. 92
Bowlby, R. 47, 67–8, 137; *see also* shopping; screens
brands 14
Brown, N. and Michael, M. 19, 20
Bryant, A. and Pollock, G. 17
Burns, P. and Novelli, M. 12
Buscher, M. *et al* 12
Butler, J. 45

calculation 120–2, 126, 135, 157n11
Carrier, J. and Miller, D. 17
Cisco Internet Business Solutions Group 62–70; *see also* mirrors
Change4Life 113–32, 136; and mothers 127–9; and ethnic minorities 129–31

Index

Clough, P.T. 33–6, 38, 87–8, 109; *see also* Clough, P.T. with Halley, J
Clough, P.T. with Halley, J. 31; *see also* Clough, P.T
Colebrook, C. 109
Colls, R. and Evans, B. 93; *see also* Evans, B
command power 24
consumer culture; *see* transformation and consumer culture
consumer culture and emotion 30
Coole, D.H. and Frost, S. 45
Cooper, M. 135
Cresswell, T. and Merriman. P. 12
critique 90–2, 133, 141–4
Cronin, A. 12, 17, 37, 46, 59, 119, 136, 144
cruel optimism 138; *see also* optimism

de Beauvoir, S. 49, 51
de Landa, M 28, 107–8
Davies, K. 96
Deery, J. 75
dieting 93–112, 133–4; *see also* Weight Watchers
Diken, B. and Laustsen, C.B. 144
Doane, M. 92
Deleuze, G. 18, 32, 84, 144
Department of Health 113, 115, 116–17, 119, 120–2, 128, 130–1
department stores 65–6
docile bodies 96–7

eating 139–40
Elliott, A. and Urry, J. 3, 12–13; *see also* Urry, J
Evans, B. 123, 127, 134; *see also* Evans, B. *et al*
Evans, B. *et al* 114, 127; *see also* Evans, B
experimental individual, the 6–11
expectations 20–2
experiential marketing 30, 120, 129–1; *see also* social marketing
extended present 100–1, 104

false consciousness 96, 98
fear 24
Featherstone, M. 3–4, 5, 12, 38, 47, 50, 65, 75, 124
FiveFaces 62–70; *see also* mirrors
foresight 113, 115, 120–1, 123, 124, 128
Foucault, M. 4, 97–8
Fraser, M. 17, 144, 145–6; *see also* Fraser, M. *et al*

Fraser, M. *et al* 3, 14; *see also* Fraser, M
Fredriksson, C 66
Friedberg, A. 2, 43–4, 55–6
future, the 19–26; *see also* potential; actual, the and virtual, the

Gibbs, A. 31
Giddens, A. 8
Gill, R. 4
Gorton, K. 30, 76, 91–2
Graham, S. 12
Gregg, M. and Seigworth, G. 31; *see also* Seigworth, G. and Gregg, M
Guilt 127

Hall, S. 34–5, 37
hope *see* optimism
Hannam, K. *et al* 11
happiness 22
Haptic visuality 84
Haraway, D. 44
Harvey, D. 5
Heyes, C. 4, 28, 96–9, 107, 108
How to Look Good Naked 72, 74–5, 77–8, 86, 141; *see also* makeover television
Huppatz, D. 53
Hutchinson, T.H. 81

IconNicholson 62–70; *see also* mirrors
IDEO – see Office for Metropolitan Architecture/IDEO
Illouz, E. 30
images: and/as affect 25; and/as experiences 38–9, 48 (*see also* interaction); as future 22; and ideology 34–5, 37–8; and Marxist approach 34–6; and representation 47–8 (*see also* affect and representational thinking); as texts 34–8, 69, 88; as virtual 18; *see also* materialization; actual, the and virtual, the
immanence 79–83, 85–6
immediacy 66–9, 79–83, 85–6; *see also* liveness and television
imperative of health 114, 115
inclination 84–7
indeterminacy 67–8, 70, 139
individualization 6–11
intensity: and screens 48; and time 50, 66–8, 139–40; *see also* power as intensive
interaction 44–5, 59, 95, 102–12, 133–4, 145; *see also* materialization of images; screens and interaction

interaction design 56; *see also* screen as window; screen as transparent
interface 48, 58, 95, 102–12
intra-action 106, 111
invention 15, 16

Jameson, F. 34
Jenkins, H. 76, 91–2
John Lewis 63, 64, 136
Jones, M. 77–9

Kavka, M. 73, 76, 79–80, 82, 89
Keenan, T. 81–2
Knowles, C. *et al* 12
Koolhaas, R *see* Office for Metropolitan Architecture/IDEO
Kuhn, A. 40

Lacan, J. 48
Lash, S. 15–16, 17, 25, 36, 69, 125, 143; *see also* Lash, S. and Lury, C
Lash, S. and Lury, C. 3, 14–15, 37, 38–9, 43, 58, 90, 119, 144; *see also* Lash, S.; Lury, C
Latham, D. and McCormack, D. 39, 124
Latimer, J. and Skeggs, B. 146; *see also* Skeggs, B.; Skeggs, B. and Wood, H
Law, J. and Hetherington, K. 37, 38
Lepore, N. 62, 63; *see also* IconNicholson; mirrors
Lewis, T. 30, 74, 76
Lindsay, G. 53–5
liveness 14; and affect 32–3; and television 82–3, 87
looking 44–5, 55–7, 81, 84, 142, 145; *see also* proximate vision; vision
Lorimer, H. 124
Lorimer, J. 124
Lupton, D. 114
Lury, C. 12, 16, 23, 47, 137; *see also* Lash, S. and Lury, C.; Adkins, L. and Lury, C

Mackenzie, A. 144
McNay, L. 108
McRobbie, A. 4, 9, 75, 137
makeover television 72–92; and affect 30, 72–92; and class 75–6, 80–1, 138
materialization 27, 44–6, 84, 137, 145; of images 35–6, 38, 44–6; *see also* actual, the and virtual, the
Manovich, L. 2, 40–4, 57, 88, 89
Massumi, B. 2, 17, 23–5, 32, 116, 122–3, 125, 134, 135
measure 94, 111–12, 143

mediation 46
Melchoir-Bonnet, S. 49–50
Marks, L. 84–5
Mills, C.W. 145
Mirrors 48–71, 77–9, 136–7
mobility 10, 11–13
Moor, L. 30, 119, 120, 136
Moseley, R. 72

Nava, M. 65–6, 67, 70
neo-liberalism 5–11, 24, 29, 75, 83, 88, 96, 114
non-representational theory 37, 40; *see also* affect and representational thinking
Nowotny, H. 20, 100–1, 109

obesity 113–32, 139–40
Office for Metropolitan Architecture (OMA)/IDEO 53–5, 57–60, 65, 66; *see also* mirrors
optimism 140–4, 146; *see also* cruel optimism
Orbach, S. 93
Orr, J. 136
Ouellette, L. and Hay, J. 73

pilot 136
Portas, M. 136
potential 2, 8, 17–22, 29, 39, 40, 45–6, 47, 86, 90, 103, 110, 116, 120, 124–32, 134, 144–5, 146
power: as intensive 11–17, 25, 68–71, 90, 114, 143; and hegemony/post-hegemony 15, 36; as neo-liberal 5–11
Prada *see* Office for Metropolitan Architecture/IDEO
prediction 122–4
pre-emption 23–5, 116, 122–4, 134, 135
prevention 122, 135
Probyn, E. 31
promises 21–2, 134
proximate viewing 74, 81–3, 134, 142–3, 145; *see also* looking; vision

reflection 51–60, 133
reflexive modernization 6–11
Ringrose, J. and Walkerdine, V. 73, 75
Rose, N. 4, 8
Rose, N. and Miller, P. 5–6, 16
Rozin, D. 51–3, 55, 58; *see also Wooden Mirror*; mirrors

Savage, M. 9
screen theory 40

screens: as barriers 131–2; and interaction 47, 51–71; as surface 30; theories of 39–44, 46; as transparent 40–4, 55–7, 77–8; as window 40–4, 55–7, 77–8, 81–2
Sedwick, E.K. 31, 93, 141
Seigworth, G. and Gregg, M. 31; *see also* Gregg, M. and Seigworth, M
Shields, R. 17, 18
Sheller, M. and Urry, J. 12; *see also* Urry, J
shopping 47, 53, 58, 60–72, 137; online shopping 61–2; *see also* transformation and consumer culture
Skeggs, B. 9, 30, 93, 96; *see also* Skeggs, B. and Latimer, J.; Skeggs, B. and Wood, H
Skeggs, B. and Wood, H. 73, 74, 76, 80–1, 82–4, 85, 89, 90–1, 143; *see also* Skeggs, B.; Skeggs, B. and Latimer, J.; Wood, H
skepticism 141–2
Snediker, M.D. 142–4; *see also* optimism
Sobchack, V. 44, 83, 111
social marketing 113, 116–20, 124, 127–1; *see also* experiential marketing
SocialEyes *see* FiveFaces; mirrors
Spinoza, B. 32
StyleMe™ *see* Cisco; mirrors
suggestibility 48, 70–1, 89, 136
surfaces *see* screens
Swan, E. 7–9
Swan, The 75, 77, 78, 141; *see also* makeover television

Tarde, G. 70
technologies of the self 97–8; *see also* Foucault
Ten Years Younger 75, 86; *see also* makeover television

Ticknell, E. 73
time, as linear 24, 100, 115–16, 134, 135; as non-linear 102–12, 134, 135, 139, 145; *see also* pre-emption; anticipation
Tomkins, S. 31
Topshop 136
transformation: imperative of 1–11; and the body 3–4, 13; and capitalism 5–11, 25, 32; and consumer culture 3–5; and mirrors 48–50; and time 7
threat 24
Trendwatching.com 61, 64–5
Thrift, N. 1, 13, 16, 25, 26, 37, 124, 126, 132, 134, 135
Trinny and Susannah 90–1
Throsby, K. 93, 108–9, 114

uncertainty 123
Urry, J. 3, 12, 20; *see also* Elliott, A. and Urry, J.; Sheller, M. and Urry, J

Van Lente, H. 21, 134, 135
virtual, the *see* actual, the and virtual, the
vision 44
vision and experience 44–5
vitalism 14–15

Walkerdine, V. 73; *see also* Ringrose, J. and Walkerdine, V
Wan, G. – see *How to Look Good Naked*
War on obesity; *see* obesity
Weber, B. 73, 75
Weight 138; *see also* Change4Life; dieting; obesity; Weight Watchers

Weight Watchers 93–112
What Not to Wear 72, 75, 77, 141; *see also* makeover television
windows *see* screen as window 40
Wood, A. 2, 28, 57, 94, 102–8, 112
Wood, H. 81; *see also* Skeggs, B. and Wood, H
Wooden Mirror 5–3, 55, 57–60
Woodward, K. 37